C000107841

.

DYNAMIC DIRECTORS

Dynamic Directors

Aligning Board Structure for Business Success

Allan Blake

MACMILLAN
Business

© Allan Blake 1999

All rights reserved. No reproduction, copy or transmission of this publication may be made without written permission.

No paragraph of this publication may be reproduced, copied or transmitted save with written permission or in accordance with the provisions of the Copyright, Designs and Patents Act 1988, or under the terms of any licence permitting limited copying issued by the Copyright Licensing Agency, 90 Tottenham Court Road, London W1P 0LP.

Any person who does any unauthorised act in relation to this publication may be liable to criminal prosecution and civil claims for damages.

The author has asserted his right to be identified as the author of this work in accordance with the Copyright, Designs and Patents Act 1988.

First published 1999 by
MACMILLAN PRESS LTD
Houndmills, Basingstoke, Hampshire RG21 6XS
and London
Companies and representatives
throughout the world

ISBN 0–333–73902–7

A catalogue record for this book is available from the British Library.

This book is printed on paper suitable for recycling and made from fully managed and sustained forest sources.

10 9 8 7 6 5 4 3 2 1
08 07 06 05 04 03 02 01 00 99

Designed and formatted by
The Ascenders Partnership, Basingstoke
Illustrations by *Ascenders*

Printed in Great Britain by
Creative Print & Design (Wales),
Ebbw Vale

This book is dedicated to Sandra

Contents

Acknowledgements

This book has been written to help boards of directors and the companies that they direct. I owe a great debt of gratitude to all the directors of companies that I have worked with over a ten-year period. They have never ceased to amaze me with their insights and their ability and humility that enable them to step back and reflect on their positions. This is despite the enormous pressures that their jobs involve. They have been the most constructive critics of my approach to board and director development. I have been privileged to be allowed access to their companies and play a small part in their development. Being closely involved helped me to appreciate the wide range of companies that are in existence. Although there are some generic responsibilities and skills required of company directors, there are also important differences which vary according to the type of company. As companies evolve over time, the obligations and responsibilities of directors, and their skills, also need to evolve. Directors, and the boards of which they are members, need to be dynamic.

This book was largely completed whilst I was working at Leeds Business School. I am grateful for the contributions of my colleagues at Leeds, particularly Chris Pierce who encouraged me to write the book and provided some valuable references. When I moved to the PA Consulting Group in March 1997, I continued to pester my colleagues, and am grateful for their tolerance and insights in the final stages. Alan Warr and Lance Lindon have given me great encouragement. One person has straddled my career at Leeds and the PA Consulting Group. David Band's support and comments have been critical to the book's publication.

There are some individuals and companies who have been good enough to allow me to interview them, to use their companies as case studies or reproduce their corporate material. A special thanks to:

Peter Jarrold (Chairman) and Peter Salt (Archivist), at Jarrold & Sons Ltd
Tom Chappell, President, Tom's of Maine
Bob Mahoney, President, Citizens Bank of Massachusetts

Mary Anne Dvonch, Vice President of Strategy and Technology,
  Production Systems Group, Xerox Corporation
Grant Wakelin, CEO, ADC Software Systems.
Leif Edvinsson, Director of Intellectual Capital (and also 'Global
  Knowledge Nomad'), Skandia AFS
Professor Clayton Christensen, Harvard Business School

The greatest burden of writing this book has fallen on my wife, Sandra.
Her patience has been tested to breaking point. Anybody with two
children, Hannah aged seven and David aged ten, will understand the
pressures that a preoccupied partner places on the other. This pressure
is exaggerated when the writing of this book has straddled two jobs
and three houses in a 12-month period.

Using the book

Case Studies

Throughout the book case studies are used as a tool to illustrate key points. Some of the case studies are named, where the company has given permission or all of the information is in the public domain. Where there is a need to preserve confidentiality, I have altered the names and facts to do so, and made it clear in the title of the case study that it is anonymous (i.e. Anon.). In some cases I have taken the facts of a few companies and merged them into one case study compilation. Again, where this has been done I have made it clear in the title of the case study (i.e. Comp.). Some case studies are fictional, although based on the experience of working with many companies. Again, these are clearly marked (i.e. 'Fiction'). There is an index of case studies for ease of reference.

References

All references appear in the Bibliography at the end of the book. There are some references to 'Table A': this is the model constitution that companies can adopt or alter, set out in a UK Statutory Instrument.

Terminology

The terms Chief Executive Officer (CEO), Managing Director and Chief Executive are all used in the book. They all have the same function, the different terminology reflecting the US, legal and UK usage for the term that is used. I have used the actual term used by those being referred to, the default title being Chief Executive.

Where to start

The book flows, hopefully, in the order it should be read. However, Chapters 1 and 2 provide the details of the structure that is used in subsequent chapters. You can dip into Chapters 3 to 8 once Chapters 1 and 2 are completed, without losing too much of the theme.

Case Studies

Figures

1 *Introduction*

all that is human must retrograde if it does not advance
Gibbon, *Decline and Fall of the Roman Empire*

I started to work with boards of companies in 1989, focusing on the role of the company director and the function of board of directors. The input had a legal emphasis. That was my background and the legal rules relating to company boards and their directors were broadly common to all companies, ranging from the listed company to the small family company. However, I soon realized that the need for development was far wider than the legal context. The sheer variety of companies that I came across at different stages of development was daunting. Any set of management tools or materials that I had encountered did not cater for this variety. What assistance there was related to listed companies and had little relevance to the wider range of companies, such as the family or entrepreneur company. This lack of supporting analysis and tools to help the needs of different companies at the top level of management is echoed by Krister Ahlstrom. He was CEO of the Finnish family-owned $3 billion holding company, A. Ahlstrom Corporation. When confronted by a difficult governance issue in his company,

> I turned to the management literature for help. And what a revelation that was! I found miles of shelves with books on management. They all concerned strategy, how to compete in the marketplace, how to organize a company for maximum effectiveness. But there was hardly any literature on how to govern family companies. It was as if all the management experts overlooked the simple fact that every company has owners and a board, and that there are all kinds of pressures on top of the strategic and operating issues. Frankly, I was surprised. I happen to be interested in

history, and most of history is about governance. It's not about the nitty-gritty of running a country; it's about how the country is governed. (Magretta: 116)

Even for listed companies, the literature did not attempt to untangle the complexity of the holding company and subsidiary company relationship, despite the fact that this was of major significance within most listed groups of companies that I worked with, and still is. Therefore, starting from a position similar to Krister Ahlstrom, I started to develop my own analysis and framework to help the boards of directors of this amazing variety of companies. They were needed to help directors plan how they could use and develop this key decision-making body within the company: the board of directors. The objective of the analysis was:

- To ensure that the board is the best decision-making team that the company has to help the company to achieve its goals, and
- To ensure corporate continuity, taking into account the variety of different situations that a company will encounter during its life cycle.

These are now the objectives of this book. I invented and learnt from the experience of working with over 450 directors from a range of companies. I am still going through this process with boards of directors in my role at PA Consulting Group. I will probably never stop if I follow Gibbon's lesson from history.

The analysis, originally designed to improve boards of directors, has started to take on a wider application. Among other things it has been used to assist in account management, sales planning and the assessment of the cultures of companies planning to merge. There is therefore a wider objective: to provide a perspective on the different types of company that can be encountered as clients or prospective clients. Just as you may undertake an analysis of the personality type of the various people that you are dealing with in a client company, why not undertake a personality analysis of the company at board level? Operating at board level is never easy. This book can help to explain why and assist in developing an approach that may be more successful. Chapter 7 provides a range of different perspectives that flow from the analysis of corporate variety and board architecture.

I start from the premise that the board of directors is important to the company. Quite frankly, even if it were not important I fail to see why a company that is required to have a board of directors should not at least realize why it is redundant. Some boards we will observe in the case studies are effectively redundant. If this is identified, then the board or shareholders can at least have the opportunity to alter that state of affairs or save some money. Fortunately, most companies do realize the importance of the board of directors, but have just not had the time to reflect on how the function of the board, and its composition, could be adjusted to gain maximum benefit for the company. This applies to all companies, from the large multinational to the small family company. Indeed, although there are considerable differences between these types of company at board level, there are features of each that the other can benefit from observing and copying.

Apart from a natural desire to reach a wider audience that can benefit from improved board performance, there is another reason for publishing this book now. I have a great concern that the corporate governance debate has deflected management thinking. It has deterred analysis of the board of directors as a key part of a business machine. The debates across the world on corporate governance have raised awareness of the importance of the board of directors. But, they have often also taken a fairly narrow view of 'governance', by focusing on the need to control the perceived vacuum of accountability within companies created by the diffuse and institutional ownership of listed companies. My concern is that the governance debate is leading to a perspective on the board, and in particular the role of non-executive directors, which sees them *only* as a control and monitoring mechanism. This is an important part of the function of the board, but only a part. Another concern is that the basic principles of corporate governance require substantial adaptation to be applicable to the wider range of corporate variety. The principles are relevant to all companies, but are often perceived as being of importance to the narrow range of listed companies only.

Any board can be the epitome of corporate governance narrowly defined: the correct number of independent, scrutinizing non-executive directors, the appropriate subcommittees, and effective disclosure. Has the company looked at its board architecture, assessing whether it has a board of directors that possesses the skills and attributes to take the company forward? Has it looked at the functions that the board performs, or doesn't perform, that will help the company to drive forward? If the top part of the structure isn't analyzed for potential effectiveness against the strategic objectives the company has established and the changes that are being made in the company, how can it legitimately analyze the rest of the corporation? Basically, boards need to continually ask the question as to where they, as a board of directors, can add the most value to the company. This question is asked of others in the company. It needs to be asked of the board of directors, and frequently. Only then will the function of the board and its composition alter with the same dynamism that the board expects the company, and other people and functions within the company, to demonstrate. It would be refreshing to see responses to these types of questions in the Annual Report, as opposed to the fairly anodyne statements on compliance with corporate governance guidelines now required as part of the listing requirements of companies. Any chairman of a company can start this process. Simply start by asking whether the function and composition of the board is a reflection of the position where the company wants to be in five years' time. Or is the board a reflection of where the company has come from, not where it is going? And for fast growth companies in sectors such as telecommunications and software, the timescale needs to be reduced from five years to six months.

Some companies have altered their board structure as a result of strategic analysis of the future of the company. Skandia AFS is a financial services subsidiary of the insurance group, Skandia. The company, based in Sweden, appointed the first group Director of Intellectual Capital, Leif Edvinsson, as part of their strategy to value and capture the intellectual capital within the company. The Skandia CEO, Bjorn Wolrath, identified this requirement as being critical for the future success of any service orientated company. The company stated that:

> The intelligent organization is inquisitive and sensitive to information from its global business environment. But it is also capable of converting this perspective into a business edge, enabling it to advance from its current position to a new life-cycle curve that goes beyond today's. (Skandia: 5)

The changing role of the Chief Information Officer (CIO) and the Chief Financial Officer (CFO) in the US is also a reflection of the need to alter the top structures at board level so that information and knowledge management is related to key decision-making. Coca-Cola's CFO, James Chestnut, has made the connection between knowledge management and what value really means to a company and adjusted his job to include both. One of the missing functions that I have identified on many UK boards is an emphasis on the integration of information technology, information and knowledge management.

The following welcome talk given by the Chairman of a company to a new recruit onto the board of directors summarizes this discussion: the need to review board architecture in light of the business needs of the company. The welcome talk is fictional, but it needn't be.

Chairman's Welcome to Peter, a New Recruit onto the Board of Directors

Peter, we have been watching your progress in the company for some time and it is a great pleasure to welcome you onto the board. Congratulations. You must feel very proud of your achievements, and justifiably so. As you know, the company strategy is to focus our capital resources on the development of our core business and to become the market leader in the sector. You have wide experience in this sector and I was very impressed with your accurate prediction of future trends in the market, some of which are already materializing. The company is a step ahead of the competition as a result. We are looking to you to help us take a further glimpse into the future so that we can gain a further advantage on our competitors. John will be taking charge of the part of the strategy that involves hiving off those businesses that do not fit into our plan. It was a tough decision to move out of some of the sectors where we have a considerable presence and years of tradition. But the board analyzed the market trends, looked at the margins of those sectors and decided that your sector is the most promising for future growth.

You may find that the sense of euphoria that you are experiencing at becoming a board member is mixed with a feeling of trepidation. You will become aware of a growing sense of responsibility. The buck stops with us at board level. We make the decisions that determine whether the company will fail or succeed, and often we have imperfect information upon which to base that decision. There is no referral upwards for approval of the decision. It is quite an awesome responsibility being on the board of a company. There are thousands of employees and their families, our customers and suppliers, and the shareholders who depend on us making the right decision at the right time. As Chairman, I am responsible for collecting around me a group of individuals with the experience and talents that will help the company make those decisions and achieve its strategic objectives. Like any other part of the company's structure or any other member of staff, we will review our performance as a board and as individuals. As the corporate objectives change we will need to review the responsibilities of board members and their ability to contribute towards the revised objectives. I want this board to be the most dynamic structure in the company, and the company to be the most dynamic in its sector. I look forward to working with you to achieve this.

Board architecture, the function and composition of the board of directors, may not be seen as an important factor in delivering the company's strategy. It is only when you reflect with hindsight and consider the options that could have been taken that it becomes clear that the structure and function of the top decision-making forum in the company does have an effect on the decisions that emanate from it. How many boards of directors, having worked to establish the vision, mission and strategy of the company, then turn round and analyze whether they have the appropriate structures and people within the board to achieve that corporate ambition? How many evaluate their performance as a board and as individual directors to assess whether their perception that they are the right group of people doing the right things to take the company forward is a justified one? Some companies are adopting this approach, but are hampered by the lack of a framework to work within. The framework developed in the following chapters can help companies, and chairmen like Peter's, to make informed decisions about board architecture. There is no master plan that applies to all companies. There are a variety of routes that companies can take in planning how board functions and board composition need to change over time in alignment with the company's evolving strategy and stage of development. The objective is to enable a company to build a board of directors that will give the company the best opportunity of achieving its future goals, as opposed to a board that was appropriate to the achievement of past goals.

Listed companies comprise only a very small proportion of companies. In 1998 there were 1.32 million companies registered in England and Wales, but only 12 000 were public limited companies and only 2450 were listed on the London Stock Exchange. There are somewhere in the region of 500 000 to 600 000 companies in England and Wales that have a wide range of ownership and management patterns, including family companies and owner-managed entrepreneur companies. Even within these categories of company there are significant variations in ownership and management. The Department of Trade and Industry in the UK estimates that businesses with less than 100 employees contributed 54 per cent of total employment and 44.3 per cent of total turnover in 1994, the latest year that figures were available. These figures include unincorporated businesses such as partnerships and sole traders, as well as small companies, but they give an indication of the size of the business community outside the narrow band of listed companies. Businesses with less than 100 employees comprised 99.6 per cent in number of the total business population (Bank of England, 1997a: 11). This spread of companies is mirrored in most countries. There are generic functions of the board and generic qualities required of all directors. However, one of the keys to enduring corporate success is in the recognition of the contingent nature of the function of the board of directors, its power, and the skills required of directors on the board. The function of the board is contingent upon the type of company, the stage of development of the company and the direction it wants to move in, or will be forced to move in by the natural dynamism of the company and its markets. Board function is contingent upon this **Corporate Variety**. As Bob Tricker has warned in the context of the development of guidelines for directors of companies:

> ... the fact that boards and directors can be so different ... means that generalizations about how directors operate, or suggestions for change to the legal requirements on how they should operate, may well be useless, and lead to guidelines that are relevant and useful in one situation, yet irrelevant and unhelpful in another. (Tricker: 35)

The function and composition of boards of directors of all companies, **Board Architecture**, needs to be reviewed and altered on a regular basis. I have yet to meet a company that does not want to be forward-looking and innovative for the benefit of its customers and future customers. 'We value people who find new and better ways of doing their job' could be a corporate value in most companies. Yet relatively few companies apply this to the board of directors. Few companies review board architecture regularly, and then improve the board to enhance the chances of achieving the corporate ambition.

As well as analyzing board architecture in the context of achieving corporate goals, there are also predictable events which, if planned for, can influence board architecture so as to promote the likelihood of continued corporate existence. Family companies and entrepreneur companies are confronted with the additional problems of personal and family emotions and relationships that influence the company's ability to alter the board architecture. Any changes in board architecture need to reflect the presence of these additional factors and the stage of the company's development. This is an extra dimension to corporate variety in these companies. Case studies in the following chapters will illustrate how board architecture can best be adapted to reflect corporate variety as well as the business needs of the individual company.

Most adult human beings plan for their future and the stages of life that they and their families will go through. We pay into pension and insurance schemes and choose the education for our children so that they will have the capacity to develop and live without our support. This may involve saving to pay for their fees at a variety of stages of their education. We do this to prepare them for the fact that we will not always be there, and so that they can start to develop lives of their own. In the Western world this is becoming an even more important function for us to perform. The State's role in this planning process is declining and becoming more of a facilitator to the process of personal planning. In some other cultures, planning for the future of your wider family and children is linked into the type of business organization that has developed. The structure of the Chinese family business is predicated on the low level of trust beyond the family boundary, leading to large arrays of connected small businesses run by individual family members. This process is exaggerated by the equal inheritance rules that apply in such cultures.

Just as we plan for future personal developments, accepting the fact that we will not work or live forever, boards of directors of companies can take on the strategic responsibility to plan for the future of their company. The company, unlike the individuals who direct it, does have the capacity to work and live forever. But, in taking on this strategic responsibility, boards of directors need to understand the changing nature of the company over long time-scales and how they can influence the performance of the company in the future. The best-laid plans that we make for our personal lives can be thrown off course by a host of factors. Death, illness, redundancy, birth and promotion are some examples of events which will change the course of not just your life, but also the lives of those around you and who depend upon you. When it comes to the company there is often little discussion about what the future can look like for the structure of the company. Sudden events can take the company by surprise and leave it vulnerable to collapse or unable to take advantage of a market opportunity. Yet there are individuals working for the company and their families, as well as customers and suppliers, who are in some way dependent upon the company just as there are individuals dependent upon you in your personal life. They will be affected by the failure of those in charge of the company to plan for predictable events that could affect the company, just as you and your dependants would be affected by any failure on your part to plan ahead. When is the entrepreneur owner planning to retire from the company and how will succession be managed? Which of the three children will manage the company when father retires? Is the relationship between the holding company and its subsidiaries the right one to break into a new market? There may be three- or five-year business plans that go into great detail about such things as new product development, markets and sales. But, it is unlikely that they will stretch to cover these broader issues of corporate governance that may or may not appear within that time-frame, depending upon natural forces and competition. In many cases the possibilities and options for the company are not understood, and therefore not considered. It may be an unpalatable or very difficult personal decision which individuals wish to defer until the last possible moment.

Companies are treated as a legal person. They can own property, sign contracts, commit offences, give birth to subsidiary companies, be killed (liquidated) and go bankrupt (into receivership or liquidation). However, the company has an attribute that people do not possess: the capacity to live forever. But only if the individuals who control the company have the expertise and skill to enable it to. Peter Senge states, in the foreword to *The Living Company*, that

> Seeing a company as a machine implies that it will run down, unless it is rebuilt by management. Seeing a company as a living being means that it is capable of regenerating itself, of continuity as an identifiable entity beyond its present members'. (de Geus: 4)

Few companies do regenerate successfully. The typical life expectancy of a Fortune 500 company is 40 to 50 years. The life expectancy of family companies declines rapidly as you pass the first generation, falling to 15 per cent in the third generation. Those companies that do survive are so unusual that studies have been undertaken to establish the factors underlying their endurance (Collins and Porras). Part of the reason why companies do not survive is a lack of understanding of the relationship between:

- Corporate Variety – a failure to appreciate a development cycle of companies which varies according to the type of company, and
- Board Architecture – insufficient regard for the need to alter the composition and function of the organ of the company, the board of directors that manages the enterprise as the company moves through its development cycle.

Companies will not regenerate themselves unless the board of directors has a clear vision of the enduring nature of the company as well as a vision for the business. The regeneration seen as necessary by Peter Senge requires timely and appropriate changes at board level, so as to enable the company to have the best top structure and personnel to meet the challenges of corporate continuity.

Children cannot change their parents for each stage of their life as their needs alter: one set for infancy, another for adolescence, perhaps another pair for the first stages of their career, with a pair of caring grandparents for their own child-rearing years. Sometimes this may happen through divorce and natural causes, but hopefully it will not have been planned. There may be exceptional parents who are thoroughly prepared for each of these stages in life and can provide excellent support throughout the development cycle of their children. Even they are natural human beings and cannot live forever. Companies can change their boards of directors, both their function and the personnel. The critical component of the governance of the company can be altered to match the natural development that the company will be exhibiting. It would be surprising if the functions of the board of directors do not change as the company evolves. It would be equally surprising if the personnel on the board exhibit all the necessary qualities and attributes required to direct the company through each stage of development. A director may have performed satisfactorily in an atmosphere where the board was really a puppet for an entrepreneur or dominant chief executive. That director may not be the best person to be a director of the company as the entrepreneur starts to relinquish control of the company as a prelude to retirement. The chief executive of a subsidiary company, which has previously operated fairly autonomously, may find it difficult to cope with a new regime that demands the holding company controls all aspects of strategy. A non-executive director who has been on the board for six years may not be able to provide the independent external view that is now required to take the company forward into its next stage of development: the relationship with other board members may have become too cosy. This may prejudice the non-executive's view on board structure and the skills required from those on the board. The next stage of development of the company over a ten-year period could involve a major drive into one particular international market. Is there anyone on the board to enhance the board's expertise in that area? How do you find someone? These are just some illustrations of the types of situation that do occur within companies. They require a constant evaluation of the functions that are required of the board of directors and the associated skills that are required of the individual directors.

The realization that the board of directors needs to be as agile as the company in order to compete may come too late. Jim Utterback, in his study of companies to ascertain the essential requirements that enable companies to master the dynamics of innovation, makes a powerful case that '... the responsibility of management is nothing less than corporate regeneration in the face of radical innovation' (Utterback: 230).

If that regeneration is not present at the top of the company, at board level, there is little hope for the rest of the company. The company can suffer considerably because of this lack of planning for the top level of corporate direction. In 1998, the German media group Bertelsmann AG, which owns the world's largest book club business, announced an agreement to buy 50 per cent of Barnes & Noble, the US book chain, for $200 million. It has started its own internet bookselling business as a result, but in 1998! Klaus Eirhoff, who runs one of the divisions of the German publisher, admits 'we were too late'. His company missed the start of internet bookselling, pioneered by companies like Amazon, which is now destroying their traditional market. They may catch up, but they have forgone market leadership in internet bookselling. Bertelsmann missed the innovation even though their US subsidiary warned the holding company of the potential threat and the associated opportunity. The group's structure was one of the reasons. The relationship that existed between the subsidiary and the holding company left the subsidiary to its own devices, but an internet strategy cuts across the business (*The Economist*: 1998h). The internet is a destructive technology if you are in retail bookselling (Christensen). With hindsight, the company could have identified that one of the functions of its holding company board should have included the ability to be forward looking for the benefit of the group of companies. Identifying threats and opportunities across the sector that in this case arises from developments in technology. This needed identification of an innovation leadership function at board level. It also required the holding company board to analyze the relationship with its subsidiary boards and the composition of its own board. This could have been achieved years ago. Different decisions would have spun out of the board. It is easy with hindsight to spot the opportunity and the remedy. The important question is why do boards of companies fail to spot these strategic issues? The subsidiary company alerted the Bertelsmann holding company to the potential, but it was ignored. There are other instances of companies missing destructive technologies that are illustrated in Clayton Christensen's book, *The Innovator's Dilemma*. He identifies several reasons why great companies fail to comprehend the potentially destructive impact of technology on their business. One of them is the structure of the company, particularly at the top of the company where the business policies are established and wind their way down the organization, acting as defensive blocks to anything that falls outside of that corporate mindset. Bertelsmann's new chief executive, appointed in the last part of 1998, will need to reassess the relationship between the companies in the group. Of course companies like Amazon may be caught out next time around. There is a natural tendency to promote change from the top, but to leave the top unchanged. Case Study 1.1 illustrates a similar point.

Case Study 1.1

Donby Ltd (Anon.)
The Entrepreneur Company Unprepared for a Business Opportunity

Donby Ltd is an entrepreneur light engineering company. The business was bought out by Donby from a family company ten years ago. Donby owns over two-thirds of the share capital, the remainder being owned by a venture capitalist that has a nominee non-executive director on the board. Donby is the chairman and managing director of the company and the only executive director of the company. There is another non-executive director of the company who has been on the board for ten years. The company has been achieving a regular 10 per cent return on turnover, although this has now started to decline. All the business is based in the UK. Turnover is at £4.0 million. There are 125 employees. All bank loans have been repaid. An opportunity arose for the company to exploit the technology from one of its products in a totally different market. This involves the design and installation of highly efficient factory production systems in the bottling industry. Whereas the average contract price for its traditional markets is in the region of £15000, the average contract price for the design and installation of the factory systems is £175 000 with 25–30 per cent profit margins. The market is based in both the UK and overseas. Donby has been leading the development of the new product. His excellent sales knowledge, commercial acumen and personality have been the driving force behind the whole company. Because the new enterprise is exciting and very profitable, he had been putting a lot of time and energy into it. Orders were coming in. He knew that if he could put more time into the new venture it could accelerate even faster. But, the core business was getting into trouble. People were noticing that he was not around. In an effort to try to stem the problems that were occurring he tried to promote individuals into managerial positions that they were not accustomed to. He was reluctant to bring in new people, and anyway could not find appropriate senior managers. This affected morale in the factories and he had to spend even more time mentoring the new managers and sorting out the difficulties they had got into. He spent some time with recruitment consultants trying to find someone in whom he would have confidence to manage the core business, but failed. All this took six months. In the meantime the new product was not marketed very hard. Rivals had noticed his approach to factory production systems. They adjusted their technology as well and invested heavily in the market. The opportunity to capture a significant share of a market, which he had created, had disappeared. Too much was dependent upon Donby. This did not become apparent until the opportunity arose. Donby was unable to devolve the management of the core business or to find a suitable external candidate in the short time that he had available to make the company dominant as the first entrant into this new market. Time was of the essence. Donby had six months. The board architecture was flawed in that it did not prepare the company for this eventuality. The non-executive directors did not fulfil the role they should have played of forcing Donby to look ahead and plan for his own vulnerability. If there were internal candidates for management they should have been nurtured and brought onto the board long ago. In this case the vulnerability was the inability of the company to respond quickly to a management challenge. It could have arisen through the illness of Donby; it just happened to be the inability to pursue a golden opportunity to its fullest extent. The major commercial opportunity for Donby, his venture capital backers, and the employees and suppliers of Donby Ltd was frustrated by the dependence upon Donby. The company has eventually been able to exploit its technology but this has taken two years and involved lost revenue and market share

Case Study 1.2 (overleaf) illustrates how effective and timely alterations to the board structure can add considerable value.

Case Study 1.2

Adam Ltd (Anon.)
Changing Board Relationships for Profitable Growth in a Holding Company

Adam Ltd is the UK subsidiary of a high technology holding company based in the US. The holding company has subsidiary operations across the world, although the rest of its European business is conducted through distributorship and licensing arrangements. Not all of its subsidiaries are as successful as the UK operation. The UK subsidiary has 25 employees and generates a turnover of £8 million. Adam Ltd, like Donby Ltd, was a family company that was bought out by the US holding company when it got into financial difficulties. One of the former non-family managers, Eric, was asked to lead the company, which he has done very successfully over the past two years. There is no effective board of directors. The US holding company has two directors nominated onto the board and Eric is the managing director. The board doesn't meet formally and Eric runs the company with a small and highly effective management team. The holding company require detailed monthly financial statements from the subsidiary. As long as the company hits or exceeds it financial targets, Eric is left alone. But he doesn't want to be. He realizes that the subsidiary operation in the UK could be the forerunner of similar operations which Adam Ltd could oversee in the rest of Europe. He also sees great potential in developing some of the US products in Europe. Eric wants to be more involved in the development of strategy at holding company level. In order to achieve this he will need to convince the holding company that his strategy is the right approach. This must include reference to a plan that will enable him to be confident that Adam Ltd is being directed properly while he devotes his time to opening up the European market. He also needs to ensure that he is involved at holding company level so hat he can influence future strategy and the allocation of resources. Adam Ltd now has a new board of directors, which includes the promotion of some of the former management team. They are searching for a non-executive director, but are going through a process of ensuring that they know what type of person would best help the company in its current state of development. They expect it will take twelve months to find a suitable candidate. Eric is not on the holding company board yet but he has presented a programme for the strategic development of the business in Europe to the Group board that he is now implementing. He preceded this by identifying and cultivating key individuals on that board. His input into the strategic development of the group has been noted. He was able to help the holding company in dealing with a difficulty in another of the subsidiary companies. He was able to go because he had thought through the vulnerability of the company in its reliance on him and turned that into an opportunity to develop the group.

The above case studies illustrate that whereas companies and their markets are dynamic by nature, board structures, and the skills and qualities of the board's directors, may or may not have changed with the development of the company or the market. The board architecture may be flawed. The following chapters provide practical help to board members like those in Donby Ltd and to those who help to guide companies, like the venture capitalist and their nominee director on the Donby Ltd board. In the rest of the book we will assess and plan board architecture.

Board Function, Structure and Corporate Performance

Does structure affect performance? This is difficult to prove, but it certainly hindered Donby and helped Eric. Following his analysis of four large US companies that had undergone major internal re-structuring, Chandler concluded that 'Unless structure follows strategy, inefficiency results' (Chandler: 389).

Supporting this approach, Professor Arthur Francis put forward a simple but devastatingly profound theme. He argued that the UK isn't uncompetitive, individual UK companies are. Their mode of organiza-tion and operation is outdated; the company's 'organizational archi-tecture' has become ossified:

> [T]here is a major problem about the competitive performance of UK companies. It is individual companies that become uncompetitive, and they do this because over time they get locked into management practices and organizational arrangements that become increasingly outmoded. Other countries industrialize, new firms are set up that compete with old firms elsewhere, these new firms have new forms of organization and management, designed for the present circumstances, and unless the old firms re-engineer they are out-competed … [I]t is the competitiveness of UK firms that needs improving, and not the competitiveness of the UK. Those improvements come from transforming the way firms are organized and managed. It is primarily a management problem and not an investment or a technological problem. (Francis)

This ossification applies equally to the top level of the company's organization, the board of directors. Board restructuring, of the personnel on the board and its function, is often a necessary pre-requisite to successful strategic change in corporate direction.

Restructuring is difficult enough to achieve below board level. It is a major challenge to achieve this 'organizational building' at board level. It requires a clear picture of how the function of the board needs to change and the personnel that are best suited to achieve that aim. Many companies would not hesitate to take this approach with the functional units within the company: the sales department, the production team, the marketing function, or the whole internal structure. So why do so few companies consider 'organizational building' at board level? It is clear that if a company has assets, skills and technology that are rooted in past strategy then competitors and new entrants to the market can take a distinct advantage by investing in future strategy. Improvement and innovation has an obvious contribution to make to international competitiveness in areas such as research and development, learning and training, and modern facilities (Porter: 173). Perhaps it is less obvious what input the board of directors can have on corporate performance? Is this the reason why it is rare for this type of planning, improvement and innovation to be applied to the board of directors as a key functional unit of the company? This book is predicated on the assumption that the function that the board of directors performs and the skills of the individual directors on that board, do make a critical difference to the performance of the company. Whether or not it can be proven that the effective functioning of the board has an impact on the performance of the company, boards of directors and individual directors will still carry the blame if something goes wrong. The shareholder, public and government perception is that boards do have an impact on the performance of the company and they will be blamed if the company performs badly. This is supported by the complex array of legal responsibilities that apply to all boards and their directors, yet which many company directors are unaware of. When things go badly wrong attention focuses on the top management of the company. How has the board of the company allowed the company to get into that particular situation and lose so many people their livelihood? This is not confined to the business performance of the company. Regulators are increasingly targeting directors to make them responsible for actions of the company that have led to death, serious injury or pollution. Although the corporate governance debate in the United Kingdom was mainly prompted by the award of apparently high salaries to senior directors in the newly privatized companies, there had also been a number of corporate disasters. Part of the blame for these were apportioned to the board of directors of the companies involved such as BCCI, Polly Peck, and the Maxwell Group. The board of P&O received a stinging rebuke regarding their ineffectiveness as board and as individual directors following the sinking of the *Herald of Free Enterprise* in March 1987, with the loss of 193 lives. The Sheene inquiry into the disaster reported that:

> The board of directors did not appreciate their responsibility for the safe management of the their ships ... The directors did not appear to have any proper comprehension of what their duties were ... From top to bottom the body corporate was infected with the disease of sloppiness. (Department of Transport: 14)

The reports on corporate governance, from Cadbury through to Hampel have focused on issues such as the financial monitoring of companies, the presence and role of non-executive directors, remuneration policies for the top executives and the length of their service contracts. These issues are important. However, these reports are not intended to provide a framework for all companies to analyze their board architecture and assess their individual corporate needs. The Hampel Report of the Committee on Corporate Governance went a long way to recognizing that there is no single formula that can apply to all companies (Hampel: 7). This is echoed in the report of the Corporate Governance Advisory Group of the OECD, chaired by the New York lawyer Ira Millstein. They rejected a 'one-size-fits-all' approach (OECD: paras. 10, 29), concluding that,

> For dynamic enterprises operating in a rapidly changing world, corporate governance adaptability and flexibility – supported by an enabling regulatory framework – is a prerequisite for better corporate performance. (OECD: para. 16)

The corporate governance focus has been on large listed companies. For example, non-executive directors in listed companies are seen as a key mechanism for overcoming the apparent self-interest of executive directors in determining remuneration packages, filling the vacuum of accountability that exists in these companies with a large diffuse shareholding. There are other roles that non-executive directors can perform in listed companies that we shall examine. The role for non-executive directors in companies that are not listed and small companies is fundamentally different from large companies.

It is the failure of UK small enterprises to grow into large enterprises that may be at the heart of the country's long-term poor economic performance. (Storey: 159)

Any framework for the analysis of the function and structure of boards of directors of these companies needs to include an assessment of how the presence of non-executive directors can help to achieve this objective and other objectives that are more appropriate to them. The concern about companies not growing through their natural development cycle was also echoed by Handy:

Many organizations do not change; they only fade away, and others grow up to take their place. Unable to contemplate a future different from all that they have been used to, they continue to beaver away at what they know best how to do, working harder and more efficiently on a diminishing task. (Handy: 256)

This book attempts to fill a gap by providing a framework whereby all companies can undertake an analysis of the development cycle of their company and implement an appropriate board architecture for their companies that meets their corporate objectives. In Chapter 7 we will see how this framework can also be applied to:

- assessing the strategy for successful mergers by analyzing the differences between the companies the subject of the merger
- the public sector, where there is a need to continually adjust the relationships that operate between the various structures that operate under the responsibility of government departments: Next Steps Agencies, Non-Departmental Public Bodies and the mix of strategy and implementation bodies within the remit of the sponsoring Department
- Assist the sales process within companies by identifying the different corporate and group business needs at the top level of the company or group of companies.

These are interesting spin-offs from the main objective, which is to ensure that board architecture enhances future corporate performance.

Board Architecture and Shareholders

Several authors have applied the architectural analogy to organizational structures. Collins and Porras emphasized the need for leaders of companies to be 'clock builders', developing companies that will last beyond their lives. In order to create institutions like the Walt Disney Company that are bigger than the individuals who help to shape them, there must be an emphasis on the organizational aspects of the company. That starts at the top, at board level. In *Built to Last* Collins and Porras reported on their six-year study into companies that have stood the test of time. They surveyed 18 companies, the youngest of which was created in 1945 and the oldest in 1812, the average age being 92. Companies like 3M, which was formed in 1902 and by 1994, had been through ten generations of Chief Executive Officer. They were looking at these 'visionary companies' to try to understand the factors behind their durability and success. They concluded that:

> all products, services, and great ideas, no matter how visionary, eventually become obsolete. But a visionary company does not necessarily become obsolete, not if it has the organizational ability to continually change and evolve beyond existing product life cycles ... Similarly, all leaders, no matter how charismatic or visionary, eventually die. But a visionary company does not necessarily die, not if it has the organizational strength to transcend any individual leader and remain visionary and vibrant decade after decade through multiple generations. (Collins and Porras: 31)

The presence of 'organizational visionaries' (Collins and Porras: 41) was a key to the success of these companies. They were individuals who built clocks that would survive the generations and keep on ticking. A major part of that corporate clock is the board of directors.

Adopting an architectural approach to ensure the effective future development of the company was also the approach adopted by Tomasko. Applying Tomasko's process to boards of directors, there are three stages:

1. Resizing – what is already in place and how appropriate is it given the direction that the company is likely to develop in?
2. Reshaping – designing the board so to enable the company to develop.

3. Rethinking – continuous assessment of the direction of the development and the appropriate functions of the board and personnel required on the board given that direction (Tomasko: 7–8).

In architecture there are various methods and tools which can be deployed to assess the potential strength of a building. You calculate whether the material to be used will carry the load required of it. The specification for the building, including such things as ducting for cables, lighting, the use of open spaces, will be judged against the function that the building has to perform for the eventual occupant. The function may change over time. For example, a building's use may change from church to radio station, illustrated by the former church now converted and occupied by Red Rose Radio, Preston. In a similar way, the following chapters will provide tools that enable the company to assess whether its board architecture, both current and planned, is appropriate for its stage of development. Corporate variety will lead to different conclusions for different types of company. However, there are two fixed points that enable comparisons to be made between different companies. The relationship between these fixed points will be used as a guide to help boards of directors adjust their architecture in a way that is appropriate for their particular company.

All trading companies have shareholders. This is the first fixed point. Shareholders have devolved responsibility for the management of the company's affairs to a board of directors which they appoint to and remove from. In small companies the shareholder and the directors may be the same people, but the board of directors and the body of shareholders are distinct organs of the company and have different responsibilities, powers and voting rights. These are laid down in the company law of each country and in the constitution of each company. Most companies in the UK, and countries that have adopted the UK model, such as Malaysia, Singapore, New Zealand, Canada and Australia, have an article in their constitution which states that, subject to any statute which preserves the power of the shareholders, '... the business of the company shall be managed by the directors who may exercise all the powers of the company'. (Table A, reg.70)

As illustrated in Figure 1.1, the shareholders have allocated the management responsibility and powers to the directors of the company. The rationale for this allocation stems from the

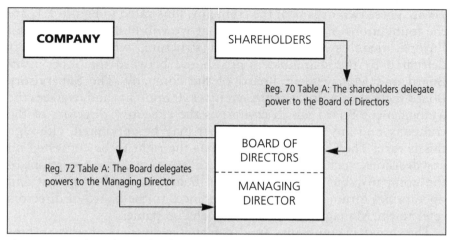

Figure 1.1 The relationship between the shareholders and the Board of Directors

development of the first joint-stock 'companies' in the early 1700s. The company is a very efficient method of bringing capital together from lots of different individuals. This was seen as the main reason for creating 'companies', limited liability not arriving until 1855. The company's constitution creates a standard form contract for the shareholder who invests in the company. The more shareholders there are the more difficult it is to give them an individual say in the management of the company. Therefore, as a matter of necessity there has to be a specialist forum, the board of directors, who are allocated the powers of management under this standard form contract. The shareholders can only withdraw this devolved authority by altering the company's constitution. This requires a special majority of 75 per cent. The board of directors usually has the power to sub-delegate its wide powers to a managing director, other directors or a committee of the board. This power of the board also derives from the company's constitution that normally provides:

> The directors may delegate any of their powers to any committee consisting of one or more directors. They may also delegate to any managing director or any director holding any other executive office such of the powers as they consider desirable to be exercised by him. (Table A, reg.72)

A common feature of companies is the presence of a board of directors appointed by the shareholders of the company. This is the second fixed

point. These two organs of the company, illustrated in Figure 1.1, are
the foundations of the framework that we will build. In continental
Europe, there is a two-tier board structure, where the powers
delegated by the shareholders are shared between the Supervisory
Board and Management Board of the company. The Supervisory
Board includes employee representatives. It appoints and oversees the
Management Board which comprises the executive directors of the
company and any non-executives that may be appointed, although
this is rare. The Supervisory Board has the right to be consulted on
key decisions, such as alterations to the structure of the operations of
the company, but the Management Board is the key policy and
operational forum. In this book, references to the board of directors
refer to the Management Board of such companies.

The variety in companies appears from the diversity of relationships
that exist between the shareholders and the board of directors. For
example, look at the contrast between the following three companies
and the different relationship between the shareholders and the board
of directors.

1. A board comprising one director, Tom – Tom also holds all the shares in the company

Tom is the board and he is also the shareholder, but the functions
remain separate and distinct. Applying the diagram in Figure 1.1, the
shareholder (Tom) confers power on the board of directors (Tom),
which then has the power to appoint a managing director (Tom). Of
course, the reality is that Tom just gets on with running the company.
The structural issues will only become of real relevance if he brings
in another director or more shareholders...and then the board
architecture will need to change. Until these events occur Tom can
have his shareholders' meetings and board meetings in the bath!
However, we are already seeing that the board architecture is unlikely
to stand still. It will need to be adapted as Tom's company moves
through a development cycle.

2. A board of a listed company – shareholding is dispersed in numerous institutional and individual hands

There is very little intervention in the affairs of the company by the
shareholding body. It is the nature of the relationship between boards
of directors and their shareholders in listed companies that has been
a key factor in the debate on corporate governance. The boards of

such companies are often portrayed as having virtual freedom to do as they please without shareholder control or censure. If shareholders are aggrieved they can sell their shares or wait for a hostile bidder to arrive. Turning up to complain at an Annual General Meeting is a mild irritant to the board. Therefore, what legitimizes the decision-making powers of the board of directors? It is the perceived vacuum of accountability between the two main constitutional organs of the company that has led to debates in many countries concerning corporate governance. What regulatory infrastructure should apply at the board level of listed companies? Should governments or self-regulatory bodies step in to fill the vacuum? In reality of course, listed companies put a lot of effort into investor relations at an institutional level in order to ensure that their market capitalization figure is maintained and enhanced, particularly if the board has a lot of share options. In this company's position, the diagram in Figure 1.1 is an accurate reflection of the reality of the relationship between the shareholders and the board of directors. The shareholders devolve their power to the board which then devolves powers to a managing director.

3. A subsidiary company's board of directors – the CEO of the subsidiary company is appointed by the Holding Company

In this situation it will normally be the case that the shareholders of the subsidiary company, the holding company, appoint the managing director of the subsidiary company. The subsidiary company's board is unlikely to make the appointment of its own managing director. The managing director of the subsidiary usually reports to the holding company's managing director, and he can only give his subsidiary company board the authority that he himself is given by the holding company. The position in Figure 1.1 is therefore adjusted to look more like the position in Figure 1.2. The holding company, as shareholder, devolves powers to the managing director of the subsidiary whom they appoint as the executive in charge of the company. The managing director then decides which of those powers will be devolved to the board of the subsidiary company. In the holding company/subsidiary situation the key variables that affect the board architecture of the subsidiary company are the relationship between the managing director of the subsidiary company and the holding company, and the managing director's willingness to devolve authority to the subsidiary board.

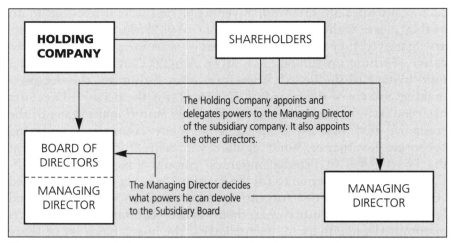

Figure 1.2   The relationship between the shareholders and the Board of
             Directors in a group situation

The shareholders and the board of directors are the two constant constitutional features in all companies. The following chapters will use the inevitable movement in the relationship between these two constitutional organs to assess the development cycle of the variety of companies. This technique draws upon and expands a similar approach that was used by Demb and Neubauer in their analysis of the relationship between holding and subsidiary companies.

The Corporate Development Cycle: the Time Dimension

Each company has a development cycle. It may start as an entrepreneur company, develop into a private company where the entrepreneur starts to play a lesser role in the management and direction of the company, and then obtain a listing on the Stock Exchange. The company could be at any stage of development at a given moment in time. The development will not stop until the company dies. The professional managers, not on the board, could capture the listed company and become the real decision-makers in the company, effectively leaving the board of directors only as a figurehead. That company could then be taken over and become a subsidiary of a larger company. The subsidiary could then be subject to a management buy-out and revert to private company status, and off we go again. The possible cycles of development that companies could go through are endless. When we look at a company we are seeing a snapshot of the company at one moment in time. Case studies in the following chapters will illustrate the cycles that companies tend to adopt. The company will have a greater chance of making a successful transition from one stage of development to the next if it analyzes the board architecture and makes appropriate changes. Indeed, in some cases the transition will not even be possible unless the board architecture is changed in advance. These changes are the catalyst for an effective transition. The transition can be prompted by other factors which are not planned for: a business or financial crisis, the death or illness of the dominant entrepreneur or a family director, a take-over bid, are some common examples. This is the natural dynamism of companies influenced by events that are predictable only in that it is known that they will or may happen at some time in the future.

The format of the book takes the reader through an analysis of how board architecture can alter to reflect and anticipate the various corporate life cycles by

- assessing the company's current position in the development cycle
- assessing the direction the board wants the company to move in
- adjusting the functions of the board and the personnel on the board to ensure that the company moves in the planned direction.

Chapter 2 will develop the framework and tools that will be used for this analysis. Chapters 3 to 6 apply the framework and tools to different types of company, providing practical help to assist different types of company on their development route. Each chapter takes a different type of company and looks at a typical pattern of development, identifying the key issues that will need to be tackled at board level in order to make the route as smooth as possible. This is the creation of an organizational architecture at board level, a form of development and succession planning for companies.

There are some recurring themes that pervade all companies. Chapter 3 will examine the formal relationships between the board of directors, managing director, chairman and the shareholders. Chapter 4 will introduce a process for selecting directors. Chapter 5 will analyze the move towards managing for shareholder value and techniques for assessing the performance of the board and of the individual directors on the board. Chapter 6 will analyze the implications for the board of directors arising from the increasing need to delegate functions and accelerate decision-taking throughout the company and in any subsidiaries within a group. These themes will be applied in the context of the type of company that is under discussion in that chapter, but they have equal application across the whole range of companies. Chapter 7 considers some of the policy implications arising for the need to vary board architecture in accordance with corporate variety.

The main theme running throughout the book is that all companies, no matter how small, need to consider the function of their board of directors and the skills and attributes of the individuals who should be on the board. Board architecture is a key part of running a professional business and ensuring that the business continues to operate.

2 *The Nature of Corporate Variety*

This chapter explores the nature of corporate variety. It will look at the different types of company and their stages of development. The framework used to carry out this exercise has been used with over 250 companies and 450 directors in order to help them to assess the present state of their board architecture and plan for change. To illustrate the power of the technique, the framework will be illustrated through case studies that look at a snapshot of various types of company at one moment in their life. In the following chapters the framework will be applied to observe how these companies will change over time, plotting their progress and assessing how the function of the board and its personnel may need to alter with the company.

Plotting Corporate Variety

The main tool that will be used to chart corporate variety and the impact that the dynamism of companies has on boards of directors is the PAPA Grid (Puppet, Adrift, Partnership, Autonomous). The grid is illustrated in Figure 2.1. Demb and Neubauer used a similar tool to analyze the relationship within one type of corporate structure, national holding companies and their foreign subsidiaries.

In Chapter 1 we saw that there are two fixed points present in all companies: the board of directors and the body of shareholders. The degree of control that is exercised by the board of directors and the shareholders will vary. It is this relationship that is the critical one within a company. The shareholders elect and dismiss the directors. The relationship is an extremely practical one. In companies where the majority shareholder is present on the board of directors, usually as the managing director, the presence of that person will have a

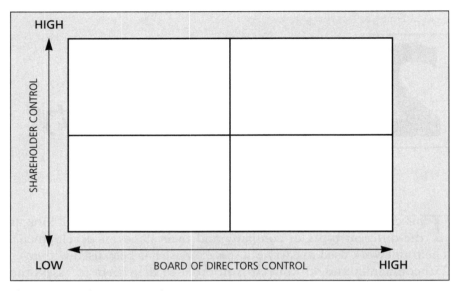

Figure 2.1 The PAPA grid

significant effect on the conduct of the board. In companies where shareholding is dispersed the relationship between the board and the shareholders has been the topic of discussion between two schools of thought: the shareholder and stakeholder schools (Clarke and Clegg: 332-9). The shareholder school focuses on shareholder value as the principal factor that the board should consider in its decision-taking. Other interests, or stakeholders, in the company such as employees and customers, are satisfied if the enhancement of shareholder value is adopted as the motivator behind all corporate decisions:

> This view recognizes that to continue to serve all stakeholders, companies must be competitive if they are to survive. This view further recognizes that a company's long-term destiny depends on a financial relationship with each stakeholder that has an interest in the company. Employees seek competitive wages and benefits. Customers demand high-quality products and services at competitive prices. Suppliers and bond-holders seek payment when their financial claims fall due. To satisfy these claims management must generate cash by operating its business efficiently. This emphasis on long-term cash flow is the essence of the shareholder value approach. (Rappaport: 7)

The shareholder school accepts that the company, through the board of directors, needs to consider a wide range of interests in the company, but that these interests are themselves best served through the enhancement of shareholder value. Shareholder value has the added advantage of being measurable. The stakeholder school of thought requires boards to take into account a far wider range of interests whether or not they add to shareholder value. These interests are less easy to quantify. This school of thought is best illustrated by the report of the Tomorrow's Company Inquiry established by the Royal Society of Arts in 1993. Led by Sir Anthony Cleaver, Chairman of IBM UK, the Inquiry's objective was:

> to stimulate greater competitive performance by encouraging UK business leaders, and those who influence their decision-making, to re-examine the sources of sustainable business success. (RSA: ii)

It concluded that companies needed to adopt an 'inclusive' approach to all key business relationships, as this was the key difference between corporate success and failure. This approach involves:

- Defining and communicating the company's purpose and values that are consistently applied across the range of stakeholders
- Developing and applying a success model appropriate for the individual company, so that it is clear what success means in the company
- Placing a positive value on each of its relationships
- Working in partnership with stakeholders
- Maintaining a strong 'licence to operate', recognizing that inclusion of the community the company operates in as an important feature of good business decisions (RSA).

Whichever school of thought you support there is a golden thread that runs through both of them. The relationship between the board of directors and the shareholders is a key influence on the decision-making of boards. Even the stakeholder school sees the shareholder interest as a key one in the influencing of decision-taking by boards of directors. As we analyze different types of company and their development over time, it will become clear that this relationship is a dynamic one.

The relative control exercised by the shareholders of the company and the board of directors fluctuates. As it does so, the function of the board and the skills required of the personnel on the board will alter.

Take the example of an entrepreneur company, Company X, where Entrepreneur A is one of three directors, as well as owning the overwhelming majority of the shares. Entrepreneur A could exercise the power that this dominant position provides and prevent free discussion at board meetings. In this situation the decisions are those of A alone and the other two directors merely hold the title of director. The board is not operating. Shareholder control is high and board control is low, putting the company in the top left cell of the grid as illustrated in Figure 2.2. There could be gradations of control that influence the exact location within that cell, but the company is located in that cell ... at present. What skills do you need to be an executive director in this position? What is the real function of the board of this type of company?

However, another entrepreneur, B, could have realized that if Company B is to continue and provide an income for B's pension, there is a need to ensure that the company can be managed properly while the attractions of a luxury retirement are enjoyed. In this entrepreneur company the board needs to be given a real role and, although B as the majority shareholder still has a strong input into decisions, the relationship between the board and the dominant shareholder will need to be different. This company is located more towards the top right cell of the grid, as illustrated in Figure 2.2. Again the exact

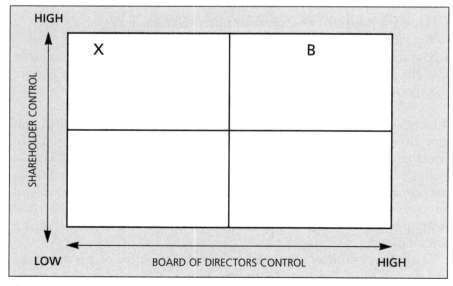

Figure 2.2 Plotting Companies X and B on the PAPA grid

location within that cell will depend upon the relative control exercised by the entrepreneur and the board of directors. It may even fluctuate depending upon the nature of the decision being made with brief movements towards the top left cell. But overall the company is based in the top right cell. The skills required of directors in this company would be different from those in Company X in order to compliment the different function that the board has. These illustrations provide snapshots in time of two companies of the same type, an entrepreneur company. They show how the relationship between the board and the shareholders can vary. We will look at other case studies of various types of company in this chapter using the PAPA grid as the tool to identify the relationship between the board and the shareholders in those companies. In the subsequent chapters we will assess the implications for companies who wish to move from one spot on the grid to another. What does Entrepreneur A's company need to do in order to get to the position of Entrepreneur B's company? This challenge is illustrated in Figure 2.3, where the time variable has been added.

The PAPA grid represents a gradation of the relationship between the board of directors and the shareholders. Companies that occupy the different cells exhibit different characteristics. In groups of companies, the PAPA grid represents the relationship that exists

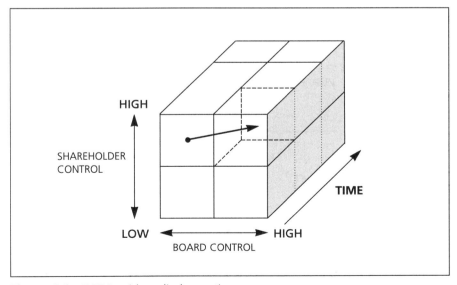

Figure 2.3 PAPA grid applied over time

between the holding company and its subsidiaries, as the holding company is the shareholder. This is illustrated in Figure 2.4. The cells in the PAPA grid are labelled Puppet, Adrift, Partnership, and Autonomous representing the relationship between the shareholders and the board of directors in each cell. In order to provide a quick flavour of what it is like to be on the board of a company occupying one of the cells, the main characteristics of these companies are detailed below.

Puppet Cell

- Shareholder control is high and board control is low. The board is a 'puppet' dancing to the tune of the shareholder(s), who could be an entrepreneur, a family or a holding company
- Formal board meetings may not take place, or if they do it is only on the advice of professional advisers in order to ensure a legal formality is complied with
- Where board meetings do take place, and there are non-shareholder directors on the board, they defer to the shareholder director(s). There is very little open discussion
- The managing director is the main shareholder and the chairman of the board

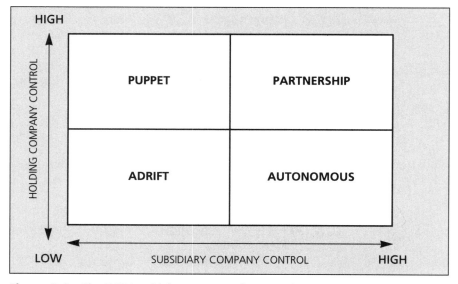

Figure 2.4   The PAPA grid for a group of companies

- The shareholders and the directors may be the same people but there is no understanding of the different roles of shareholder and director of the company
- If you are not the entrepreneur director, you are really a manager not a director of the company although you hold the title...and the responsibility if anything goes wrong
- Any directors who do not own shares or are only minority shareholder have little or no power at board level.

Adrift Cell

- Shareholder control is low and board control is low. The company is adrift
- A strange category, where the board of directors do not control the company and neither do the shareholders. If neither of these two groups have control who does?
- The professional managers of the company below board level may control the company. They were identified and referred to by Galbraith as 'technocrats' (Galbraith: 75–86) and by Chandler as 'professional entrepreneurs' (Chandler: 386–7)
- These companies may have very large boards. In some statutory companies there are very few executive directors on the board (for example Training and Enterprise Councils and some other companies that have a statutory basis, where there is one executive director). Given that the board is comprised almost totally of non-executive directors, the reliance on the 'professional entrepreneurs' is virtually total, particularly in the provision of information
- The managing director is the chief technocrat and there is a puppet chairman who relies heavily on the managing director
- The 'professional entrepreneurs' achieve power in the company through the ambiguous nature of the shareholding body (for example TECs) or its diffuse nature and large central bureaucracy (for example some listed companies)
- Board meetings take place but they act as a 'rubber stamp' on proposals put forward. On occasion, the board may say no or request more information. The board rarely plays a positive pro-active role; it normally reacts to proposals from the 'professional entrepreneurs'. Meetings can turn into lengthy discussions of decisions that have in practice already been made, and in many cases implemented. The exception to this general behaviour of such boards will be when a crisis occurs, usually financial or managerial.

Then it is all non-executive hands to the deck, taking on roles to which they are unaccustomed and unsuited in order to sort out the crisis

- The company is going through a structural change, merger, or searching for a new CEO. It is the corporate equivalent of planning blight when it is difficult to get anybody to make a decision, particularly a strategic decision.

Partnership Cell

- Shareholder control is high and board control is high. There is a partnership
- Shareholders have a clear route through which they can influence the direction of the company, but the direction and decision is clearly seen as a board decision by all parties. There is a partnership between the shareholders and the board of directors each respecting the authority of the other. The board is given the freedom to pursue shareholder values that have been clearly identified
- Shareholders may be present on the board as part of the route to influence decisions of the company, but their presence is not seen as an overriding constraint on discussion. The final decision really is a board decision
- The roles of managing director and chairman are distinct and there may be a tension between the two individuals
- When you attend a board meeting the objective of the company is usually very clear: maximize long-term shareholder value
- There may be a tendency for the financial systems to push the board into a certain decision, when your instinct tells you that another option is the preferable one. You feel free to speak out, but the over-riding ethos of adding shareholder value, which can be interpreted as determined by purely financial parameters on your board, will prevail. The finance director is an even more powerful figure than usual in listed companies that fall into this category
- Subsidiary companies have substantial freedom with the group of companies, but there is 'one company' and the freedom that is granted is conditional upon compliance with:
  - clearly stated values
  - a clear group strategy
  - leverage off the group strengths wherever possible
  - delivery of information to the group corporate as specified and on time
  - constant communication with the CEO of the group holding company.

Autonomous Cell

- Shareholder control is low and board control is high. The board has autonomy. In subsidiary companies that have considerable autonomy the managing director of the subsidiary is acting almost like an entrepreneur.
- The board's autonomy from the shareholders is attained because the shareholding body will usually be large in number, each holding a small proportion of the total share capital: the typical listed company.
- The managing director and the chairman are different individuals in listed companies. There may be a tension between them and the relationship may not be that different from the Partnership cell, or
- The Chairman's role may be titular only as a result of he entrepreneurial role that the managing director adopts
- There will be a limited shareholder influence at annual general meetings, usually during potential take-over situations or at other times when there is publicity concerning the activities of the company. In particular, this reflects the diffuse shareholding of companies that are listed on the US and UK stock exchanges. Every now and then there may be a shareholder rebellion against the actions of the board over the board's pay or a take-over bid. Such rebellions are still relatively rare outside the US and the board's control of the proxy voting machinery will normally be enough to quash any disenchantment. A shareholder lobby group may offset the diffuse nature of the shareholding body
- Shareholder influence on the board will be indirect through contact with shareholders and the market influence that they can assert if it becomes evident that shareholder value is not being maximized by selling their shares, or agreeing to a hostile take-over bid. The more this is recognized by the company the more the company edges towards the partnership cell. The main threat to the autonomy continuing is the threat of take-over by another company. The shareholders' only loyalty to the company is based on annual returns and capital enhancement; the expectation of added shareholder value based on past management performance. If they can be offered a better return by selling their shares to the hostile bidder, shareholder control will become a dominant feature. Autonomy from shareholders and the values they wish to be pursued by the company does not lead to shareholder loyalty in a fight, and why should it?
- Companies occupying this cell have a vacuum of accountability that the corporate governance debate is aimed at. As the corporate

governance movement exhorts institutional investors to play a more active role in the companies that they invest in, companies in this cell will start to drift towards the top right cell.

A visual representation of the PAPA grid can be seen in Figure 2.5. The PAPA grid is only a four-box tool. Its power lies in focusing attention on the relationships that exist within companies and how companies may wish to alter those relationships over time for the benefit of the company. In the end it is up to the various actors to decide in which direction they want the company to develop and whether they are prepared to take action to move in the desired direction.

Types of Company

Later in this chapter we will analyze what different types of company look like when they occupy the four cells of the PAPA grid. However, before we do this, we need to classify the types of company that we will be analyzing using the PAPA grid. Having stressed the corporate variety that exists I am now seeking to pigeon-hole companies! The only reason for this categorization is to provide some structure to the

Figure 2.5   The PAPA grid (visual)

analysis of the different relationships that exist within companies. The categories of companies do overlap. For example, a listed company can be a family company. Ultimately, those companies that do fit into more than one category can look at the various scenarios and solutions for both types of company and select the most appropriate for their company. Most companies can be allocated into one, and occasionally more, of the categories listed in Figure 2.6. Each category of company has different characteristics. This will affect their pattern of behaviour in the different cells of the PAPA grid as well as the tactics that will need to be employed to move from one cell to another.

Company type based on ownership	Private companies	Listed companies
Family	Company owned predominantly by family members who run the family business (most family companies)	Company in which the family holding still predominates (for example, Clark's Shoes, nearly all Chinese family businesses listed on the Hong Kong Stock Exchange and the South Korean *chaebol*)
Quasi-partnership	Company owned by two or more entrepreneurs ('quasi-partners') who are using the corporate form to trade rather than a partnership. The company may have been formed from a pre-existing partnership	Not applicable
Entrepreneur	Company founded or taken over by an owner/manager and still in their control	Company founded or taken over by an individual who holds or controls a dominating proportion of the shares quoted on a stock exchange (for example, Microsoft.
Listed	Not applicable	Companies listed on a stock exchange with a large diffuse shareholding that is usually dominated by a number of institutional shareholders
Subsidiary companies within a group of companies	Entrepreneur, quasi-partnership and family companies that own and operate through subsidiary companies	Most listed companies have a complex web of subsidiary companies, wholly- or partly-owned

Figure 2.6 Classification of companies based on ownership

Family Companies

Family companies must be one of the most common types of company throughout the world and some of the most powerful. There are no studies of the number of family companies, but there is some evidence that the number of family businesses, including partnerships, constitutes the overwhelming majority of commercial organizations. Depending on the broadness of the definition as to what constitutes a family firm the number of family firms operating in the US varies between 4.1 million and 20.3 million (Shanker and Astrachan: 116). This is not just a Western phenomenon. Indeed, there is a marked similarity in the predominance of family business structures across the world.

The Chaebol

In South Korea the economy is dominated by large conglomerates run autocratically by the entrepreneur founder or his family, known as *chaebol*, and developed with state backing. These are companies such as Samsung, Daewoo and LG Groups. The continuing pattern of dependence on the goodwill of the State was fostered by historical insecurity, wars and the military coup in 1961. As Whitley noted, this volatility doesn't encourage the development of trust and mutual inter-dependence between owners and managers who are not related:

> As a result, direct personal control of major resources and choices remains a key characteristic of the modern *chaebol*, and high personal trust between top managers as crucial to their effective operation, typically assured through family membership. (Whitley, p.188)

The group holding company is often used as the vehicle for controlling all of the companies in the conglomerate. The span of control gets larger and larger, the family conglomerates covering everything from prawn farming to underwear retailing, each company run by a different family member. Eventually it is not sustainable, notwith-standing the family connection that binds the conglomerate together. Indeed, the family connection is part of the problem. Subsidiaries are created with the objective of providing companies for relatives to run with only a few financially viable. Clear evidence that this has been the approach adopted by the *chaebol* can be seen in the aftermath of the State's attempt to restructure the debt-heavy *chaebol* as a result of the financial collapse in South Korea in 1997/8. The five largest *chaebol* were fined £34 million in July 1998 by the State Fair Trade Commission, the new *chaebol* watchdog. The fines on Hyundai, SK Group, Samsung, LG, and Daewoo were imposed for giving illegal subsidies to their weaker subsidiaries. *Chaebol* have been characterized by fast rates of growth, and reliance on debt financing as opposed to equity in order to preserve the family control. Readily available debt finance was encouraged by the State and kept the *chaebol* afloat until the Asian equivalent of the South Sea Bubble burst. Some *chaebol* are listed. During a financial crisis they become vulnerable to take-over. *The Economist* reported in February 1998 that since December 1997, the number of South Korean listed companies with a foreign stake of more than 5 per cent had trebled to 26 (*The Economist*: 1998b). Without State support and encouragement they would have failed long ago. When the State finances start to wobble so do the *chaebol*. They have become the whipping-horse for bringing the country to the edge of financial collapse. The companies themselves had developed such a comfortable relationship based on the presumption of continuous State support and guaranteed debt finance that the senior managers found it difficult to react in times when change is required. As *The Economist* reported:

> As for the *chaebol*, although they talk about restructuring, their hearts are clearly not in it. The markets sought an acknowledgement that they had expanded too much, too fast, while taking on too much debt. Samsung, for example, might have abandoned its entry into the car and aircraft markets. Hyundai could have shed its unprofitable semiconductor and petrochemicals businesses. Instead, they offered proposals that were modest to the point of self-delusion ... South Korea will not claw its way back to health until the *chaebol* accept the need to get smaller. (*The Economist*, 1998a)

The basic structure of the *chaebol* is flawed but it is hard to blame them. It has been made difficult for these companies to adapt to change. The combination of family or entrepreneur domination supported by State backing, politically and through the availability of debt finance, distorts the natural life-cycle of the typical family or entrepreneur company. If left alone, they might have moved towards a Partnership approach of running the company, or died. Or, they would split the company up into smaller manageable units as happens in the Chinese family business. The introduction of the State, in an attempt to bolster the State's economy through the creation of large enterprises that can compete in the international market, is a strategy that can only be successful in the short term. The state is now intervening to restucture the *chaebol* through enforced exchanges of lines of business. These are government-enforced 'Big Deals', such as LG's merger of its semiconducter business with Hyundai, and Samsung's divestment of its business to rival Daewoo. It is hard to see how this state-imposed restructuring will help the *chaebol* to reach the agreed target of reducing their average debt to equity ratio from the current 400 per per cent by the end of 1999. The lesson does not seem to have been learnt. If the State does intervene, it must do so to assist companies to develop through the various stages of their life-cycle of a company, and not prevent the evolution that is necessary and inevitable. Government attempts to boost the role of more dynamic small and medium-sized firms, through a new Corporate Restructuring Fund of $1.2 billion, will have to recognize the need for companies to develop and sometimes fail.

The Chinese Family Business

The Chinese family business structure dominates South-East Asia, Hong Kong and Taiwan. They are relatively small and focused and dominated by the head of the family (Whitley, 1992: 53). Professional managers may be hired to operate the companies, but 'entrepreneurial roles ... remain the preserve of the owning family and trusted partners' (Whitley: 54).

This entrepreneurial role is exercised in a personal way and is very responsive to environmental change. If listed, only 20–30 per cent of the capital is made available, in order that control is maintained. Chinese family business (CFB) owners tend not to trust managers. As a result the managers are likely to leave when there is an opportunity: 'Formal status in a managerial hierarchy is less significant ... than success as an independent entrepreneur' (Whitley: 203).

This fear of delegating to non-kin or trusted partners leads to small companies and continual diversification and fragmentation. This is exaggerated by the principle of equal inheritance of the family property. It leads to large arrays of small companies tied into the 'family' group of companies. The Chinese family business can have the characteristics of a 'group' of companies, the size of the group being disguised and thus avoiding State attention, especially in Taiwan (Whitley: 205). However, the decisions are made by the family head, and not by the individual heads of the companies that make up the family business. There may also be partnerships with related businesses through a process of relational contracting where trust has been established. The focus is on flexibility and the ability to move resources quickly because of personal ownership and control. Two consequences of this, according to Whitley, are opportunistic diversification and minimizing risk:

> By establishing separate small firms run by family members for distinct activities the CFB retains control while reducing the risks of concentrating all its resources on one area of business. (Whitley: 204)

Family companies in the Western world do suffer from not having a clear culture that dictates their approach to succession and inheritance. It means that the wheel is constantly reinvented when the time comes to consider how the family company will continue, a pressure that their predecessors did not encounter. Frequently that moment is too late. There is no pattern to refer to for the continuation of the family company in the UK in modern times as there is in East Asian family companies. However, this provides the family companies in the Western world with the opportunity to design their own bespoke approach to long-term structural continuity. That opportunity needs to be taken but it requires a framework that family managers can refer to for help and assistance.

Quasi-Partnership Companies

The judiciary have recognized one aspect of corporate variety. Often individuals trade using the corporate form without considering all the legal niceties that should underpin their informal agreements. There may have been an intention when the company was established that all the promoters of the company should continue to have a say in the management of the company, but this may not be reflected in the formal constitution of the company or through a written shareholder agreement. The individuals may have been trading in a pre-existing partnership and decided to take advantage of the corporate form for a variety of reasons, usually to obtain the advantage of limited liability or to add to the perceived image of the organization (Freeman: 1994). In these situations there may be a 'quasi-partnership' where it can be shown that one or more of the following three factors apply:

1. There is an association between the individuals who established the company, which is based on a personal relationship involving mutual trust.
2. There is an agreement or understanding that all or some of the individuals will participate in the management of the company.
3. There are restrictions on share transfers through the company's constitution (the articles of association) or a shareholders' agreement.

When there is a conflict between the individuals who set up a company, the courts will make decisions that reflect the real relationship that exists between the individuals who own and direct the company and the legitimate expectation that they had on entering the corporate arena. This is as illustrated in Case Study 2.1.

Case Study 2.1

Westbourne Galleries Ltd (1973)

Nazir and Ebrahimi dealt in oriental carpets as partners over a long period. They converted their partnership into a private company, Westbourne Galleries Ltd. They were equal shareholders and the only directors. Later, Nazir's son joined the company as an additional shareholder and director. This tilted the balance of power in both the general meeting of shareholders and on the board of directors. The deadlock built into the company when it was formed had now disappeared. Following a disagreement, Nazir and his son removed Ebrahimi from the board of directors. Ebrahimi's capital was tied up in the company. His fee as a director had disappeared and no dividends were being paid. He applied to have the company wound up, which the court can do if it 'is of the opinion that it is just and equitable' to do so. Ebrahimi thought it was equitable, as it would be the only way that he could get his money out of the company. He had gone into business with Nazir on the understanding that he would always be involved in the business and receive an income from it. He now had no source of income. That understanding had been betrayed, albeit within the boundaries of the law. In this case Ebrahimi was successful, the company was wound up and he recovered his investment.

Companies like Westbourne Galleries Ltd are 'quasi-partnership' companies. The partners have got together to run a business using a company as a vehicle to do so. There is an understanding between them based on mutual trust that they shall all participate in the management of the business. This is often evidenced by a pre-emption clause in the company's articles, restricting the ability of the shareholders to leave the company and pass their shares on to anybody without first offering them to the other 'quasi-partners'. Although the articles of the company cannot prevent the general meeting exercising its power to remove a director by a simple majority the articles can confer weighted voting rights when any such resolution is put before the general meeting. Mr Ebrahimi could have ensured that the articles of the company were altered to give him, and only him, five votes per share on any resolution to remove him as a director and on any resolution to alter this article. He could have also entered into a shareholders' agreement with Mr Nazir restricting the way Mr Nazir could vote on any resolution to remove him. But he didn't.

SOURCE: *Ebrahimi* v. *Westbourne Galleries Ltd*

Quasi-partnerships share many of the characteristics of the family and entrepreneur companies and will not be looked at separately as we apply the PAPA grid.

Entrepreneur Companies

Entrepreneur companies are dominated by a single shareholder who will normally hold more than 75 per cent of the voting rights in the company's shares. This gives them total control, as the company's constitution cannot be altered without their approval. They control the composition of the board of directors where they have a simple majority of the votes (50 per cent +1). If venture capital has been injected into the company this will normally involve an appointment of a director by the venture capitalist onto the board of the entrepreneur company. A shareholder's agreement between the venture capitalist and the entrepreneur will prevent the entrepreneur from removing that director. The entrepreneur's influence may be so powerful that it continues as the company develops and the individual's proportion of the shareholding declines. But, as we shall see, when this occurs the dynamics of the board and the board relationship with their shareholders will normally start to move.

Listed Companies

There are about 2450 companies listed on the London Stock Exchange and 60 per cent of the shares in these companies are held by UK institutions: pension funds, insurance companies, unit and investment trusts. The remaining 40 per cent are held jointly by individual shareholders and overseas shareholders, themselves mainly institutional (Hampel: 40). There are different types of listed company across the world including the Chinese family businesses listed on the Hong Kong exchange, the Japanese *kaisha* and the South Korean *chaebol*.

Groups of Companies

Most listed companies and many family and entrepreneur companies will have established group structures. Listed companies and groups of companies are looked at separately as they involve a different set of relationships. The relationship that the holding company has with its shareholders is not necessarily reflected in the relationship that the holding company will have with its subsidiaries. While the holding company may be in the Autonomous cell, the relationship with its subsidiary companies may oscillate between Puppet, Partnership and Adrift. This is illustrated in Figure 2.7 where the subsidiary has very little freedom to operate, being tightly controlled by the holding company at the centre. In this position there are rules for everything

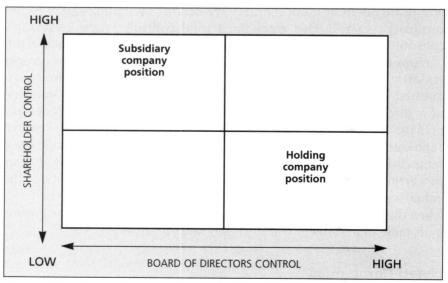

Figure 2.7   The holding company's relationship with its shareholders compared with the subsidiary company's relationship with the holding company

and constant complaints from the senior managers in the subsidiary that if only the centre got off their backs and the central overhead was reduced they could really go places. They are senior managers, not directors, although some of them may carry the title and the office. The listed holding company meanwhile has a lot of freedom and enjoys its autonomy from the shareholders. The central bureaucracy mistrusts the subsidiaries and is constantly seeking new ways to control the little discretion that they have.

The Department of Trade and Industry estimate that only 30 per cent of registered companies in England and Wales are independent and not in a subsidiary relationship to another company. The creation of teams of managers is necessary when decision-making becomes more complex and there is a need to devolve responsibility. Where this involves diversification, or expansion into different regions, this can be undertaken through the creation of subsidiary companies leading to the formation of groups of companies within the listed, family, entrepreneur or quasi-partnership setting.

The relationship of the subsidiary company boards within the group to the board of the holding company will vary from group to group. It is a complex relationship. Each company within the group is a separate legal entity and must have a board of directors. The board of each individual company must act in the best interests of their company, which in most cases will involve acting in accordance with the wishes of the holding company if required to. But no director can sacrifice the interests of the company of which he or she is a director for the interests of another, albeit closely related company. In many cases it will be clear that the interests of both holding company and subsidiary company will coincide, and the directors do not need to give formal and separate consideration as to the respective benefits of all actions (Blake and Bond: 67–8). However, directors cannot just look at the benefit to the group as a whole regarding any particular action, for:

> Each company in the group is a separate legal entity and the directors of a particular company are not entitled to sacrifice the interest of that company. ... The proper test, I think, in the absence of actual separate consideration, must be whether an intelligent and honest man in the position of a director of the company concerned, could, in the whole of the existing circumstances, have reasonably believed that the transactions were for the benefit of the company (*Charterbridge Corporation Ltd* v. *Lloyds Bank*, per Pennycuick J: 74).

This potential for conflict that affects directors of subsidiaries within a group of companies is recognized in the New Zealand Companies Act 1993, where a director of a wholly owned subsidiary may 'act in a manner which he or she believes is in the best interests of that company's holding company even though it may not be in the best interests of the company' (section 131(2)).

In subsidiary companies that are not wholly owned in New Zealand, the subsidiary company directors can act in this manner if permitted by the company's constitution and the independent shareholders. But holding companies pay a price for the ability of their subsidiary directors to act in the best interests of the holding company even though it is not in the interests of the subsidiary. The statutory provision adjusts the duties owed by directors. Therefore, the New Zealand High Court has concluded that the holding company can be made liable for the negligence of its executive directors in respect of the performance of their duties as directors of a subsidiary company (*Dairy Containers Ltd* v. *NZI Bank Ltd*). The courts are struggling with the conflict between the legal autonomy of each individual company and the puppet relationship that may characterize the actual relationship between the subsidiary and holding companies.

The existence of a group environment does have an affect on the board functions of both the holding company and the subsidiary company. Just as with an entrepreneur or a family company, there can be gradation of shareholder and board control. The holding company, as shareholder, may exert a very dominant role over the subsidiary company. Or, it may allow the subsidiary board a considerable degree of freedom to operate. There are different pressures operating in the group environment that are not present in companies that are not part of a group. This affects the functions of the holding and subsidiary boards and the qualities required of the directors who sit on those boards.

Corporate Snapshots in Time

The different types of company, family, entrepreneur, listed and group, can occupy any of the cells on the PAPA grid. This is one aspect of corporate variety. The remaining part of this chapter will take snapshots in time of the different types of company. The analysis, through case studies, will identify what it is like to be in each of the cells on the PAPA grid for each of these companies. The second aspect of corporate variety looked at in the following chapters will add the time dimension. How can the companies move between the cells over time?

Puppet Companies

The Family Company

Case Study 2.2

Precisions Ltd (Anon.)

Precisions Ltd is a family engineering company in its second generation. The board is comprised of six directors. John is the Chairman and Managing Director. He is the founder's only child. He has led the company throughout the last twenty years. He is 60 and is approaching retirement. His two sons, Paul and James, and one daughter, Sarah, are directors. Paul is 22 and has just graduated from university in business studies. There will be a job for Paul in the company, but it is not clear what that job will be. Sarah is 27 and has recently qualified as an accountant. Sarah manages the finances of the company. James is 24 and is a CNC machine tool operator in the company. The Production Director, Ken, is 48 and a qualified engineer. He has worked for the company for ten years and was promoted to the board five years ago to cover a period of one year when John was seriously ill. He acted as a temporary Managing Director and John's wife, also a director, acted as Chairman of the company. John owns 80 per cent of the shares in the company, with the remaining 20 per cent split equally between John's wife and his three children. Until John became ill, board meetings had been a rarity, convened only when there was a legal formality to go through. John, his wife and Sarah took all the decisions. There was little or no consultation with the other directors. The discussions took place around the kitchen table, as Sarah was the only child still living at home. Ken had convened formal board meetings during the year that he took over as Managing Director and they continued to be convened following John's recovery. But gradually it became clear that the three key members of the family had made the decisions outside the boardroom: John, his wife and Sarah. The board meetings were a formality.

Precisions Ltd is a family Puppet company. Control by the board of directors is low, and control is exercised by the dominant family members who are the main shareholders. This is not unusual in family companies. As the shareholding becomes more dispersed family groupings may emerge. The vagaries of operating a business are difficult enough. If you add the complexities of family life and family rivalry, it becomes very difficult to operate. During the period when John was ill there was a brief move towards the Partnership cell, as the board started to gain control and operate as an effective board. Lessons could have been learnt from that trial period in anticipation of the time when John will bow out of the company, but they weren't. Ken is in a very difficult position on the board of directors, confronted with the responsibility of being an experienced professional director yet with little power. He will be thinking about what will happen when John does retire or dies. But, John has not discussed this with him.

The Entrepreneur Company

Case Study 2.3

PR Ltd (Anon.)

PR Ltd is a public relations company operating in the South East of England. It is wholly owned by one individual, Charles, who is the managing director and chairman of the company. Charles started the business on his own and converted into a company several years ago. He eventually appointed Helen and Frank as two other executive directors of the company. This was part of their promotion. Board meetings are infrequent as Charles makes all the decisions without reference to the other directors. He sees their titles as directors as being part of the necessary rewards for the excellent fees they generate. He does not consider that this gives them any say in the management of *his* company.

PR Ltd is an entrepreneur puppet company. The board does not operate at all. One person is taking all the decisions, the entrepreneur Charles. Helen and Frank may disagree with some of the decisions that Charles is taking, but they would find it hard to argue against him, even if the board did meet. The board is not used to operating as a board or making decisions as a board. The board is a Puppet. Helen and Frank are puppet directors. But they are directors. They have the same responsibilities to the company as Charles. If the company were to get into difficulties then they could be as liable as Charles for the actions of the company. They cannot plead that the company was really run by Charles:

> A director is not an ornament, but an essential component of corporate governance. Consequently, a director cannot protect himself behind a paper shield bearing the motto 'dummy director' … dummy figurehead and accommodation directors are anachronisms. (Justice Pollock, *Francis* v. *United Jersey Bank*)

In situations like PR Ltd, puppet directors run the risk of becoming liable for decisions that they have not been involved in. It is difficult for directors like Helen and Frank. If they disagree with Charles then they may lose their position on the board and may even be fired. They owe their position to him and his success as an entrepreneur. Individuals who find it difficult to operate in such a constrained business environment will not fit in with Charles's approach and Charles should not appoint them. Charles wants people who will agree with him and allow him to continue his domination of the company. At least at the moment he does.

Case Study 2.4

Land Travel Ltd

The sorry saga of Land Travel Ltd is a salutary tale for all directors of Puppet companies. Land Travel Ltd was a holiday company. It went into voluntary liquidation owing £12.4 million to creditors, including £6.6 million of lost deposits for holidays. Mr Tjolle was the entrepreneur owner of the company and its sole formally appointed director. He went bankrupt, pleaded guilty to fraudulent trading and was sentenced to nine months imprisonment and disqualified as a director for 15 years. However, Mrs Kenning had been a director of the company. She resigned when she realized that she was powerless and could not influence the running of the company. She had no access to the accounts. She knew Mr Tjolle was in total charge and that she was a puppet director on a puppet board of directors. Mrs Kenning was wise to resign. The Secretary of State started proceedings to disqualify her from being a company director of any company (disqualification proceedings). The fact that she had resigned, in recognition that she could have no real control over the company's affairs, was a major factor that led to her acquittal. Although she carried the title of 'Sales and Marketing Director', it was accepted by the court that the titles were used by Mr Tjolle as a way of motivating his employees, and that,

> 'At all times he ... was really the one pulling the strings ... Mrs Kenning was obviously a very capable manager, but she did not form part of the real corporate governance of the company' (*Justice Jacob, Secretary of State* v. *Tjolle*: 348, 356).

If Mrs Kenning had not resigned the disqualification proceeding would have been successful and it is likely that she would have been made liable to contribute towards the debts of the company, probably leading to her personal bankruptcy. Instead she recognized that she was a puppet director on a puppet board and resigned.

The Listed Company

Case Study 2.5

Mammoth plc (Fictional, but ...)

Mammoth plc is dominated by one person who secured a listing for the company so as to realize some of his wealth. He is the Chairman and Chief Executive. He controls 51 per cent of the shares of the company. The other 49 per cent are owned by a variety of mainly institutional investors. The company is very successful, but the extent of the entrepreneur's power is illustrated by the fact the Chairman has been allowed to use the company assets as if they were his own. For example, he transferred £400 000 of company assets to one of his private companies.

The transactions were not questioned by the other directors who are a mixture of executive and non-executive executives. They do what he tells them to do without question and are fearful of the consequences of disobeying him in terms of his personal anger and their career prospects.

The corporate governance discussions prompted by a number of city scandals have led to proposals that should mean that this type of company, the listed Puppet company, is now a rare creature on the London Stock Exchange. The presence of 'independent' directors and the splitting of the chairman and managing director roles do not guarantee that the position identified in Mammoth plc will not occur. But, it should create an environment at board level where it is less likely. However, on the smaller stock exchanges across the world, there will be listed companies where a dominant personality prevails. They are normally the original founder of a company that has gone public as well as substantial shareholder in the company. The entrepreneur Puppet company has developed into a listed Puppet company.

The Group of Companies

Case Study 2.6

The Armac Group (Fictional)

The Armac Group comprises ten subsidiary companies split into three divisions. Each of the divisions is presided over by a divisional director who sits on the main group board. The subsidiary companies do have boards of directors, but they never meet. The titles of director are given to the executives of the subsidiaries who are formally appointed to the subsidiary boards. This includes the title of managing director. John is Managing Director of one of the subsidiary companies. When asked about the role of his board and his personal position he replied:

All the decisions are made at group level. I implement them. For example, my colleagues and I thought it might be a good idea for our company to look at the possibility of developing a new manufacturing process. My boss Eric, the Divisional Director, told me that it would never get through the group board as they have capital allocation priorities and we are not a priority area. I never see the group CEO. All we get are targets, rulebooks, manuals, and a lot of people chasing us for information from Division and Group. They have a small army of people just to chase us. I think we have a group finance function that has more people in it than the Treasuries of many States. If I were younger I would move on. I know my colleagues are frustrated at our lack of control. After all we know the business and all that expertise is being wasted.

In these groups of companies the holding company, the shareholder, plays a dominant role. The holding company treats the subsidiary as a Puppet. Demb and Neubauer referred to these subsidiaries as 'paper' companies (Demb and Neubauer: 481). Good and Campbell categorized them as 'centralized companies' (Good and Campbell:

146–9). They didn't find any companies in their survey that fully adopted this approach, although BP, Courtaulds, Plessey and United Biscuits had all moved away from the Puppet cell towards the Partnership cell. Satellite companies operated by the expatriate Chinese family business community often fall into this category. In these companies, although the individual family member may have been given apparent control over the subsidiary venture, real authority lies with the family:

> among the expatriate Chinese it is clear that the key decision unit is the family business rather than the often numerous legally defined 'firms' controlled by family heads. (Whitley: 10)

Adrift Companies

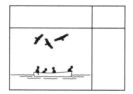

The Family Company

Case Study 2.7

Grocers Ltd (Comp.)

Grocers Ltd is well known regionally, the company trading under the family name in the retail grocery business through a chain of shops. The company employs 100 people, 30 on a full-time basis. The company is in its first generation of family managers. The directors are Mum, Dad and their two children aged 21 and 24. Since the children have returned from their University studies to work in the business all the family now play a specific functional role in managing the day-to-day aspects of the business. Mum and Dad are 15 years off retirement and own all the shares in the company. There are no formal board meetings. Any decisions that the company needs to take are discussed informally over meals or during other family get-togethers. There have been no major decisions to take since the children returned to work in the business.

> One of the children raises concerns about the impact on their business of the opening of a large number of out-of-town supermarkets in the region. The family discusses this, but there is disagreement on the appropriate response, and so nothing happens. When the supermarkets open, the company's takings fall dramatically. The company keeps going for six months but then has to close one store after another. Finally there is not enough cash to pay the wages and the family has no option other than to wind the company up.

This family company is Adrift. Like all companies that fall within this category neither the shareholders nor the board are used to exercising control over the company's affairs. The company is drifting. When an important decision is required, the two organs of the company are so unused to making strategic decisions that they either make a decision not to make a decision, or they agonize at length over their newly found responsibilities before acting. Grocers Ltd does not have an effective board of directors and the shareholders have rarely exercised strategic control of the company.

The Entrepreneur Company

Case Study 2.8

PR Ltd ... the next stage (Comp.)

Charles becomes seriously ill and is hospitalized in a coma. There is nobody in the company who has the experience or skills to run the company. Charles has no immediate family who can step in. Helen and Frank have been dominated by Charles and find it difficult to make decisions. They now start to compete for control of the company, but only at a very low operational level regarding decisions that they feel they have some confidence in making. Other decisions are just not taken. This combination of fighting to make the unimportant decision and not making the important decisions leaves the staff in total confusion. It is also confusing to clients who appreciated the problems for one or two weeks, but who are now getting restless. Contracts are not complied with; staff start to look for other jobs ... the consequences of being adrift build up over time.

The Listed Company

Case Study 2.9

Complexity plc (Fiction)

Complexity plc is a very large listed company. Its shareholding conforms to the norm of listed companies: 80 per cent institutional shareholding with UK or overseas institutions, and 20 per cent individual very small shareholdings. There are ten directors on the board: three are long-standing non-executive directors, one being the Chairman. The remaining directors are executive directors. The executive directors meet prior to the main board meetings that take place every month, excluding August. The executive directors have been briefed on each item by their own staff who have prepared all the papers that have gone to the board members in support of the various items. The Chairman has a briefing with the Managing Director and other relevant executive directors and specialist staff prior to the board meetings. Whether or not additional information is required for the board meeting will depend upon this briefing with the Chairman. Such requests are rare. The board rarely initiates any proposals. It does occasionally ask for more information about proposals that are fronted by the executive directors, and occasionally it will turn such proposals down. The company does have an Audit Committee that is comprised entirely of non-executive directors and is provided with information from the Finance Director, Internal Audit and the auditors. There is also a new Remuneration Committee comprised of non-executive directors that approves the details of the salaries and bonus schemes for the executive directors and other senior staff. The objectives of the schemes were set by the executive directors following consultation with remuneration consultants, but were not discussed at the remuneration committee.

Where does the real power lie? Certainly the shareholders will rarely exercise power. Does it lie with the board of directors? Not according to Chandler, who considered that control was really vested in the 'professional entrepreneurs':

The men who make the critical decisions in any economy can be defined as those who have the actual or real, rather than merely the legal, power to allocate the resources available to them and who, in fact, determine the basic goals and policies for their enterprises. Clearly the general executive is such a man. In the large corporation the stockholders, the legal owners, long abdicated his function. They had neither the time, information, nor (as long as the enterprise was paying dividends) the interest to make the basic policy decision. What little they did know about their company was told them by the managers, who spent all their working time administering its affairs. Unless they were also full-time, career executives of the concern, the members of the board of directors had only a little more knowledge and understanding of the workings of their company than their stockholders…Thus the members of the board, unless they were full-time executives of the concern, were as much captives of the professional entrepreneurs as were the stockholders' (Chandler: 386–7).

This was also the view taken by Galbraith. He considered that although formal control of the company was vested in the board of directors, actual control resided in a group of 'technocrats'. The technocrats expand beyond the executive members of the board. They have access to corporate information and expert knowledge, and can be found in various parts of the corporate network. Some executive members of the board may be heavily dependent upon them and the information and strategic advice that they provide. Galbraith defined the technostructure as:

> all who bring specialised knowledge, talent or experience to group decision-making. This, not the management, is the guiding intelligence – the brain – of the enterprise. (Galbraith: 86)

It is inevitable that in all companies the board of directors will rely on information that is generated by others in the organization. It will and should rely on their expertise to generate ideas and follow them through. This does not mean to say that the company is Adrift. Signs of a company becoming Adrift in a listed company are:

- The Chairman and Managing Director roles are vested in the same person – the Chairman's role is a critical link in the corporate governance chain. It is the Chairman's responsibility to ensure that the board operates effectively. The Chairman must ensure that all the board members contribute towards the effective direction of the company. It is very difficult for an executive director to play this role. The Chairman provides the necessary 'hard look' at proposals that derive from the Managing Director. The 'hard look' will not happen unless there is another non-executive director who adopts this part of the Chairman's role.

- Short board meetings that rubber stamp decisions, preceded or followed by a luxurious evening meal.
- Long board meetings that are made up of presentations from different technical staff from within the company, followed by the rubber stamp and the luxurious evening meal.
- Board members are not encouraged to approach executives within the company who have prepared the papers for the board meeting.
- Agenda items such as company car policy, car parking, expenses policy.
- Non-executive directors who rarely speak at board meetings other than to agree with the management: a 'friend-of-the-management-board'.
- A preponderance of board items which ask for approval of decisions that have in reality already started to be implemented and which it is now impossible to back away from.
- A Managing Director with no written constraints imposed by the board.
- Board members who are surprised to read in the press that the company has launched a major initiative.
- A lagging share price.
- A take-over bid, not necessarily hostile (for example the $13 billion take-over of the Adrift Waste Management, Inc., the world's largest rubbish haulier, by USA Waste Services in 1998). The management realize that the game is up and they rely on well-drafted contracts and share options to ensure that they leave with a degree of affluence.

The corporate governance codes of best practice that have surfaced from the Cadbury and Hampel Committee deliberations are partly intended to ensure that the real authority stays with the board of directors. The principles underpinning these codes recognize two dangers. The first is that companies lose legitimacy if their actions and processes fail to recognize the interests of the shareholders. The second danger is that the boards of companies can themselves become Adrift from exercising real control of the company. By requiring disclosure of corporate compliance with corporate governance principles the intention is to open up the Adrift company to the cleansing effect of sunlight so as to minimize the possibility of these two dangers occurring.

The Group of Companies

Case Study 2.10

Compute Ltd (Anon.)

Tom is the Managing Director of Compute Ltd, a US wholly owned subsidiary company based in the UK. It is a high-technology company, selling specialist computer peripherals and software. A listed US company bought the subsidiary company from an entrepreneur who had acted as one of their distributors under a distribution agreement. They had a disagreement. The US company bought the company from him and promoted Tom, one of the senior managers in the company. Tom has been Managing Director for two years. The company has performed well. The only direction that Tom gets is to produce monthly financial statements that must be at the company's head office in time for the holding company's board meeting. There are three directors on the board of the subsidiary company: Tom and two directors from the US holding company. The board has never met and Tom talks only occasionally to the other two directors. Tom has started to develop a range of software and other products, which enhances the value of the US products. Tom has three senior managers in his company, and they have regular management team meetings to discuss the strategy for the company.

The subsidiary company is Adrift. Tom is frustrated that he doesn't play a greater role in the development of group strategy. He can see that there are other distributorships in Europe that he could manage more effectively through the UK subsidiary. He is also lonely and getting bored because of the lack of challenge. Both Tom and his subsidiary company need a bigger stage to play on. The US holding company is not taking advantage of its potential for competitive advantage through its global network.

Demb and Neubauer identified foreign subsidiaries companies in this cell as 'new venture' companies (Demb and Neubauer: 481), citing examples as a one-off project where the final output, such as a dam, will pass into local hands. This stage of the company's development should therefore be very transitional. Companies cannot last long in the Adrift state. Unless they move, they will collapse or get taken over.

Partnership Companies

The Family Company

Case Study 2.11

Bread Ltd (Anon.)

Bread Ltd is well known regionally and trades under the family name. The business is similar to Grocers Ltd. The company bakes and sells bread and cakes through its own chain of shops. The family is more extensive as this company is in its second generation of family management. The son and daughter of the founders of the company are directors, the daughter being the managing director. Also on the board, on fixed term contracts, are the executive marketing director and a non-executive director with a financial background. Neither of them is a member of the family. The son and daughter own all the shares in the company between them. The board of directors meets monthly, but there are also family discussions taking place at the normal family gatherings. As part of the discussion of strategy to counter the expanding supermarket trade, the board decided to try to sell some of its special branded products to the supermarkets and to expand its lunchtime snack business in those shops close to areas of employment. This was successful but involved modification and expansion of the production facilities and working to tight margins and schedules for the supermarkets. The brand name is now becoming nationally as well as regionally known and there is consideration at board level of the possibility of developing a franchise strategy for the rest of the country. As shops in town centre sites with nearby centres of employment come onto the market, franchise shops would be opened to sell special branded products. The marketing director and non-executive director have been influential in the development of the strategy. The marketing director is concerned about his role in the company in the future as the son and daughter start talking about when they will retire. The son and daughter both have two children, but only one child has expressed any interest in the business, the others being too young or disinterested.

This is a family Partnership company. The family members do see the board as having a proper role to play in the strategic decision taking of the company. They respect the views of the non-family directors. The board makes decisions on most matters, despite the family discussions that inevitably take place outside of the board.

The Entrepreneur Company

Case Study 2.12

Victoriana Ltd (Fiction)

Victoria wholly owns Victoriana Ltd. The company is in the antiques business with six shops. Their reputation for integrity led to the establishment of a consultancy part of the business. At the suggestion of the three staff directors who sit on the board of the company with Victoria, the company now manufactures 'antique' and pine furniture. Having decided at board level that this would be their strategy, the company was prepared to take the opportunity to buy the premises of a small furniture company that was in receivership. They also hired some of the staff who had good technical skills in furniture making. Business is thriving and the board is now considering mail order and internet selling in conjunction with an international distribution company. The board is searching for a non-executive director who has this expertise. They are hesitant to take this extension of their activities forward without some experience on the board. Joe, one of the staff board directors spoke about her experiences on the board:

> I've never been a director before so I can't comment on other boards. All I know is that we are very businesslike. When Victoria asked us to be directors of the company she explained that this was not just a title. She wanted some help. I think she was lonely after her dad left her the business. Board meetings are seen as being very important. We all contribute to the agenda and if we need further information we ask people in the company to come into the meeting. We may ask someone to do some research for us. They help us to understand the whole company and then decide where we want to go. When we are in the boardroom, all comments are taken seriously. We are all equal in the boardroom. We haven't had to vote on anything yet. I'm not sure what would happen if Victoria found herself in the minority. We normally discuss issues and find a way forward that we all agree with. Perhaps that is a problem with the way we operate. Consensus may not be the best way forward on all occasions.

This is an entrepreneur Partnership Company. The board has a clear role to play. Sometimes this is prompted by the presence of a firm non-executive director who can exert influence over the entrepreneur in a way that would have been very difficult for the executive directors. In this case study, Victoria has a personal need to work closely with people and involve them in the decision-taking. This coincides with the needs of the business. It can be very lonely running your own company. It doesn't have to be, although it will involve sacrificing some degree of control.

The Listed Company

> **Case Study 2.13**
>
> **Lloyds TSB**
>
> Lloyds TSB is a banking company that is committed to managing for shareholder value. The focused approach to enhancing the shareholder value has made the bank the largest in the world with a capitalization of more than £47 billion in February 1998. Its pre-tax profits rose 26 per cent in 1997 to £3.16 billion.

It is difficult to see how, in a listed company with a large diffuse shareholding, there could be any other illustration of a more effective partnership than through the total commitment by the board to enhance shareholder value. Listed companies that are in the Partnership cell may also exhibit the following characteristics:

- Good communication and liaison with institutional investors over such issues as the remuneration strategy for the senior executives.
- Clear communications to all shareholders, not just relying on the Annual Report and the Annual General Meeting.
- A total commitment to maximizing shareholder value that is reflected in such issues as allocation of capital, business planning, remuneration policies; the culture is clear and flows through the company.
- Allowing a separate vote at the Annual General Meetings on the remuneration policy for senior executives as recommended by the Remuneration Committee.
- No weighted voting rights attached to shares.

The Group of Companies

Case Study 2.14

Hoechst AG (Aventis)

The realignment of the Hoechst Group, with Hoechst AG as the holding company, was approved by the shareholders in May 1997. Hoechst now has eight independent companies each with global responsibility for steering their operating businesses. It will mean the demise of many of the current subsidiaries as separate entities, including Hoechst UK founded in 1947, as the individual companies are regrouped into the eight global operations. The group strategy is to enable the global businesses to increase their value in a sustainable way. As the 1998 Annual Report states:

> Speed, flexibility, openness, a will to succeed and an ability to learn are the qualities we need to take Hoechst forward.

Implementation of the delegation of responsibility to the eight global companies is well under way. Innovation is fundamental to continued growth of the Group, as is the time-to-market of new products. This is one aspect of the flexibility and the speed that the independent companies will need if they are to enhance value. Hoechst has not always been in the partnership mode. This is a snapshot of the company taking the first steps. We will look at the journey they have undertaken and propose to take when we add the time dimension in later chapters. This includes the Supervisory Board agreement in December 1998 for the company to merge with their French rival Rhône Poulenc under the new name of Aventis.

Partnership groups have devolved key functions to subsidiary board level and have mechanisms for enabling the subsidiaries to influence group strategy:

> The advice and role of the subsidiary board is a robust element in the development of overall corporate strategy...The role of the subsidiary board is to actively balance the objectives of parent, subsidiary and host country partners. (Demb and Neubauer: 482)

The multi-cultural multinational ABB, Asea Brown Boveri, took the partnership model to its extreme through its former chief executive, Percy Barnevik. He stressed that,

... companies need to keep deep roots in local markets, because markets will continue to differ. His answer is a cosmopolitan conglomerate diverse enough to respond to local tastes but united enough to amount to more than the sum of its parts. (*The Economist*: 1996a)

ABB developed a coordinating executive board and an elite team of managers whose purpose was to tie the group together through values which they all share. Under its matrix regional management structure three members of the executive board shared operational responsibilities with the three executives who ran the core businesses: power generation, power transmission and distribution and industrial and building systems. Control operated through 'clan' control, not through formal operational strategic control. The clan members worked globally and at a distance from the small head office and had an appreciation of the common ethic that guides their daily decisions. This huge group enterprise has as many shared values as the board of a small family company, if not more. It has to have them to compete and react quickly. The strategy is to create the benefits of the small company in the large multinational. The individuals to whom decisions have been devolved know instinctively what the right decision is for ABB. Individuals either lacking this awareness of the ideology of the group or who are unable to constrain their decision-making within those boundaries would not have been appointed. Porter disagrees with the Partnership positioning of the ABB group. Porter considers that the ABB subsidiaries are in the Autonomous cell and, as a result, have lost competitive advantage (Porter: 54). He may be right. ABB is now restructuring under a new CEO, Goran Lindahl, who is abandoning the matrix structure. The Partnership philosophy appears to be continuing though, with the eight new core businesses all being represented on the executive board. The matrix regional management structure is to go, removing 100 jobs. Even Goran Lindahl talks about the new structure as an 'evolution' from the former structure aimed at creating greater speed and efficiency. We can argue over the precise location of this group of companies, but the disagreement itself supports the contention that the relationship between the subsidiary companies and the holding company is a key factor in determining long term global competitive advantage. Which cell you occupy, or are heading towards, in the PAPA grid does matter. Collins and Porras also highlighted the nature of this relationship as one of the key attributes of all enduring companies, not just groups. They cited the Nordstrom one-page employee handbook, the company constraining behaviour to be consistent with the Nordstrom ideology, yet at the same time granting extensive operational freedom: '*Ideological* control preserves the core while *operational* autonomy stimulates progress' (Collins and Porras: 138).

In multinational groups of companies, ideological control is a way to coordinate dispersed activities. Porter argues that the coordination, or Partnership, needs to be greater. The operational autonomy of subsidiaries should be curbed where this benefits the Group as a whole:

> In global competition, firms seek to gain much greater competitive advantage from their international presence, through locating activities with a global perspective and coordinating actively among them. (Porter: 55)

We are analyzing gradations within the Partnership cell. But even the gradations will affect the type of people the holding company places onto the subsidiary board in order to make the desired relationship work. The key is for the Group to know what type of relationship they are building and the board architecture required to achieve it.

Autonomous Companies

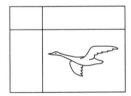

In these Autonomous companies the control of the company and the ownership of the company have been virtually divorced from each other.

The Family Company

The next case study was difficult to find. Family companies will need to have been in existence for a long time before they exhibit any hint of allowing the board to operate independently from family control. If a family company wants to relinquish control, it will normally sell the company or seek an Initial Public Offering (IPO). However, there are two companies that I know that come close to the autonomy category and the following case study is merged from the facts of both of them.

Case Study 2.15

Cereal Foods plc (Comp.)

Cereal Foods is a fifth generation family company producing food and beverages. There are 120 family owners and the numbers grow each generation. The company has 73 000 employees and offices in 66 countries. The CEO is not a family member, although there are some family members working in the company. The family became aware long ago that if they were to realize sufficient cash to support the growth of the family over the generations they needed the best people to run the company. This could be a family member, but it doesn't have to be. The talent is more important than the connection, and this applies to all jobs. The family members operate much like any other body of shareholders of a listed company. They meet once a year for the Annual General Meeting, and have Family Councils with some of the executive directors to receive information about the progress of the company, in the same way that executives would normally meet institutional investors and analysts. There are no places on the board of directors reserved for family members, but given the shareholding it is not surprising that there are a number of family members, although they are outnumbered by the executive and non-executive directors. The chairman is always a family member.

The Entrepreneur Company

Case Study 2.16

Books Ltd (Comp.)

The former CEO and Chairman of Books Ltd was interviewed by a trade magazine following his retirement at the age of 57. The following is an extract from that fictional interview:

Why have I retired? I have been working since I was 14 years of age. I enjoy golf and it is time-consuming. My wife and I would like to go on holiday. I estimate that if I'm lucky I have 15+ years to enjoy the benefits of my business success. I won't miss it. I am absolutely confident that the team I have recruited and nurtured to run the company will be so successful that I will not have the physical capacity to spend what they earn for me over those 15+ years. Of more importance I know the livelihoods of the people the company employs and the values we have built up over the decades will live on. That is why I am not selling the company. Do you want any more reasons?

I have met two people who fall into this category. In each case they spent a vast amount of time selecting the right person to hand over to. One of them found the right person and has now let go of the business in the way described in the above case study. The other is still searching for the right person and the years are rolling by. He is caught between the personal desire to let go and put some balance back into his life, and the understandable concern of ensuring that the people who depend upon the company and the values it has followed under his leadership are not betrayed by any successor.

The Listed Company

Case Study 2.17

Anycompany plc (Comp.)

With just under one million shares the share profile is:

- Private holders – 4.1%
- Banks and nominee companies – 89.9%
- Pension Funds – 1.5%
- Investment and Unit Trusts – 0.6%
- Insurance companies – 1.6%
- Local authorities – 0.3%
- Corporate holders – 2.0%.

Of the 21 655 holders of shares in this company, 219 hold just under 80 per cent of the shares and none of them are private holders.

Returns to shareholders have been just above average for companies operating in this sector. The company is one of the leaders in its sector. The board has changed very little over the last decade, most changes resulting from internal promotion. However, in the last year one additional non-executive director was appointed to meet the recommendations of the Hampel Report. The Remuneration Committee of the Board has also reviewed the remuneration policy for senior staff, including directors, which is now based on a comparator group of 25 companies in the sector and associated sectors. The outline of the scheme has been published in the Annual Report but it is not an agenda item at the Annual General Meeting. There are regular meetings with the major institutional investors in the company, as well as analyst briefings.

This is a listed Autonomous company where the separation of ownership and control is almost complete. No board is ever truly autonomous. There will always be a range of factors that influence and guide their decision-taking, and this includes the shareholders. This is why the Chairman was briefing the institutional shareholders and the analysts who influence the decisions of the institutions. As the individuals who make investment decisions change their rationale for investment, listed companies need to alter their behaviour to match those criteria, hence the recent focus on shareholder value in many listed companies. The corporate governance debate concerns the extent to which the influences on board decision-making should be controlled and managed through the adoption of mandatory and recommended processes, board structures and reporting requirements.

Autonomous listed companies appear across the world. In Japan, *zaibatsu* were large family-owned holding companies that were prohibited when President Harry Truman issued a directive in 1945 that the large industrial and banking combines in Japan should be dissolved. Mitsui Bassan was one of the *zaibatsu*. It dissolved into 170 separate companies (de Geus: 135–6). However, the reunion of these former groups has taken place in a different form. Other groups of companies with autonomy followed the break up of the large *zaibatsu* family companies. These business groups are called *keiretsu*, where they are vertically organized in their market sector. They include Toyota, Nissan, Hitachi, Matsushita, Toshiba-IHI, Tokai Bank and the Industrial Bank of Japan. The *kigyo shudan* or 'firm group' are horizontally organized business groups of large firms in diverse industries (Hoshi: 287). They are the replacements for the *zaibatsu* and include Mitsui and Mitsubishi (two of the former greatest *zaibatsu*) and Sumitomo, Fuyo, Dai-IchiKangyo and Sanwa. Although the separation of ownership and control is virtually complete in these companies, they are 'enmeshed in extensive networks of mutual obligation and trust which both provide support and constrain strategic choices' (Whitley: 25).

These companies are in the Autonomous cell, but exhibit a type of partnership that is not based on property rights. Mutual cross-shareholdings and other links often accompany the relationship. The *kigyo shudan* are linked through the following (Kay: 58–61):

- Bank borrowing through a 'Main Bank'
- Cross-shareholdings
- Board exchanges

- Transactions between the firms
- Joint projects.

For example, Miyaji Iron Works is a firm member of the Mitsubishi *kigyo shudan*. It borrowed 32 per cent of its loans from the Mitsubishi Bank which was its largest shareholder, owning 5 per cent. One of its board members was a former employee of the Bank (Hoshi: 285). The core members of the *kigyo shudan* comprise the Presidents' Council, which in this case did not include Miyaji Iron Works. Abegglen and Stalk raised concerns about the ability of these companies to change quickly enough. This concern can be applied to any company occupying the Autonomous cell. It is a comfortable cell for management to live in. Why move out of it? In Japan this trait of companies operating in an autonomous relationship has enabled the more dynamic and independent *kaisha* companies to succeed in the faster moving technical sectors.

> In sectors that require a good deal of long-term financing, that have long engineering lead times, and that often require good government relations ... the group member companies remain strong. Where the technology changes fast, and where the market changes fast, they do not do well. The trading companies of the groups, with which the manufacturing companies have been so closely associated, are also a troubled group of companies (Abegglen and Stalk: 190)

Fast companies operating in high growth markets need fast and flexible structures. This creates its own pressure of continual change and reorganization but, although there are exceptions, many of the largest and most successful of the Japanese companies are not members of the larger Autonomous groups. In vehicles this includes Toyota, Honda, Hino, Suzuki, and Kubota. In electronics it includes Hitachi, Sharp, Sanyo, Matsushita and Sony. Toshiba is one of the Japanese electronic giants that realizes it needs to change its structure to match these rivals and confront expanding global competition. The company's very survival is at stake. The changes involve altering the product portfolio, board changes (from 34 to 12 members) and cutting the number of subsidiaries from 1 000 to 300. Taizo Nishimuro, Toshiba's chief executive, accepts that, 'We have to make changes not only to the portfolio of companies we own, but also the group's organization and culture' (*Financial Times*: 1998b).

The organizational and cultural change needs to be accompanied by consideration as to where on the PAPA grid Toshiba needs to locate the relationship between the holding company and its reduced number of subsidiaries, and what this means in practical terms. Mitsubishi Motors is confronted with similar difficulties, having relied on the other companies in the Mitsubishi Group to support its huge debt, just as the *chaebol* relied on the state. For both of these companies the directors are confronted with new challenges, including the pursuit of strategic alliances and joint ventures. Are the directors as dynamic as the now want the company to be?

The Group of Companies

Case Study 2.18

Insurit of New York (Anon.)

Insurit is a subsidiary of a German company, acquired in 1993. Tom Curtis is the President of Insurit. There is very little involvement from the holding company as

- Insurit has earned the right to be left alone with rapid growth in annual income, assets and number of policy holders.
- The nature of the business is fundamentally different from the mainstream insurance offered by the holding company.

The cultures and business rationale are completely different. Insurit's strategy is to target the very customers that the holding company would leave alone. Whereas other insurers are closing branches, Insurit is opening them and targeting the relatively poor first generation American communities. These customers want a personal service that is in sympathy with their needs.

35 per cent of their customers do not speak English. Staff are trained to react to their cultural needs, with high service standards adapted according to the locations of the offices and the communities that they serve. The immigrant population has been integrated into the workforce. Branch staff live close to or come from those communities and are encouraged to become an important part of the community. These are the customers that other insurance companies are not interested in. It would be difficult to operate this type of insurance service from within a more traditional insurance environment. The allocation of resources would probably not be forthcoming, and the passion for the strategy would be

subsumed and strangled. Operating virtually autonomously gives Tom Curtis the freedom to pursue and invest in the innovative strategy without interference. Because of the amazing rates of growth in the company there has been significant changes since 1993. But some things have not changed:

● The strategy
● The organizational chart – by recruiting over-qualified people at the beginning they have had a lot of toe room to grow into. They are now only just reaching the point where the businesses they are managing come anywhere near the size of the businesses they were managing when they were recruited.
● The values of the company – they are clear and well-known in the company. They are tweaked every six months but have remained broadly the same.

So while the staff are whirling under the pressure of change brought about by the constant and rapid growth, there are some clear stakes in the ground. As Tom Curtis stated to me, 'people have to know what the deal is; you have to promise something.' Tom Curtis has the freedom to act like an entrepreneur within a large group.

Good and Campbell found no subsidiary companies in their studies that were clearly Autonomous. They observed that anecdotal data from companies that had adopted that approach in the past (for example, BOC, ICI), suggested that they performed less well than companies with other styles (Good and Campbell: 146–7). Demb and Neubauer called this cell the 'devolution' or 'Empire Model'. In these groups of companies, the local foreign subsidiary input into the development of market share is a critical feature as in the confectionery businesses of Cadbury-Schweppes and subsidiaries that are an important feature of the local economy (Demb and Neubauer). However, there is a growing recognition that in order for certain types of innovation to succeed, an independent autonomous company is sometimes needed as an incubator. This was recognized in IBM, Hewlett-Packard and Johnson & Johnson (Christensen: 110, 115–6, 141). We will return to this when we investigate the need for innovation leadership as a necessary board function at some stages of a company's development.

Dynamic Boards for Dynamic Companies

Each of the four cells in the PAPA grid represents a shift of power in the boardroom. As companies move between these cells over time the board architecture will need to change to reflect the change in power. If it does not, tensions will build up within the company. In the following chapters that inject this time dimension we will identify these tensions and identify how they can be alleviated

- by changes in board function and structure, and
- by analyzing the skills and qualities required of individual directors as the company moves between cells.

If the company is to have any chance of creating enduring change, rather than a quick start that soon fizzles out, the mainspring of the corporate clock will need to be altered. This is an important element of the necessary 'clock-building' identified by Collins and Porras:

> If you're involved in building and managing a company, we're asking you to think less in terms of being a brilliant product visionary or seeking the personality characteristics of charismatic leadership, and to think more in terms of being an *organizational* visionary and building the characteristics of a visionary company. (Collins and Porras: 41)

The architectural approach to management, the development of 'clock builders', needs to be applied at board level. The PAPA grid is a tool that helps companies to identify their current stage of development and where they want to be. However, the transition from one stage to another is a difficult management process. It is the point at which many companies fail. Charles Handy recognized this in *Gods of Management*, where he identified that:

> Many organizations do not change; they only fade away, and others grow up to take their place. Unable to contemplate a future different from all that they have been used to, they continue to beaver away at what they know best how to do, working harder and more efficiently on a diminishing task. (Handy: 256)

In Figure 2.3 the dimension of time was added to a situation where a company has identified the need to move from the Puppet stage to the Partnership stage of development. This movement will take place over a period of time. In order for the transition to take place successfully, the company will need to plan changes over that period. For example, directors will need to change or be replaced in order to initiate effective corporate movement. In order for the company to move as indicated in Figure 2.3 there needs to be a process for assessing and adjusting board structures and responsibilities, and the skills and qualities of the current directors. For example, there may be some dinosaurs on the board who will not be able to live in the next stage of the company's development. There may be directors who require development to operate at the next stage. These are difficult decisions for boards to take. In family and entrepreneur companies in particular, emotional ties and family finances will hinder the change. In all companies there may be deeply entrenched mental models which 'determine not only how we make sense of the world, but how we take action' (Senge: 174–5).

Drozdow and Carroll identified this in family companies, referring to: 'The dynamically conservative character of family business, in which change seems to occur but is, in fact, narrowly constrained by the weight of the past ...' (Drozdow and Carroll: 77).

For some boards of directors it will be like asking turkeys to vote for Christmas. A new chief executive may spur the company into action. A crisis brought on by a falling share price or a hostile take over bid may also lead to changes in the positioning of the company. If your company is in the Puppet cell it is unlikely that the board will even take the decision for the company to move. The main share-holder(s) will take the decision, perhaps startled by the realization of their own mortality and the need to ensure that there is an income for them and their family in the twilight of their life. Or, maybe the institutional shareholders can no longer tolerate mediocre perform-ance. We will focus on the following areas that will need to be planned for and changed as a company develops:

Monitoring and assessing the function and structure of the board

- Devolution within the company, corporate vision and strategy
- Monitoring, control and risk assessment functions of the board
- Board subcommittees: role of the Audit Committee, Remuneration Committee and other subcommittees of the board (these governance functions apply across all companies even though they may not be formalized into subcommittee structures)
- Shareholder relationships: for example, keeping key shareholders informed, succession planning for key shareholders
- Assessing the performance of the board of directors as a board.

Monitoring and assessing the function and performance of directors

- Succession planning for directors
- The role of the Chairman and the relationship with the Managing Director and any non-executive directors
- The role of executive directors and non-performance (removing directors from the board)
- The role of non-executive directors and finding them
- Director development and individual performance criteria; assessing the performance of directors
- Terms and conditions for board members, including remuneration strategy

Groups of companies

- Applying all the above criteria in a group context
- Group effectiveness with more than one Board of Directors
- Obtaining the correct relationship between the subsidiary and holding company boards of directors.

Monitoring and Assessing the Function and Structure of the Board

Board architecture depends upon corporate variety. But there are generic functions that apply to all companies and generic skills that apply to all directors. It will be impossible for boards to perform some of these generic functions in certain cells of the PAPA grid. For example, the strategy function of the board will not be undertaken in the Puppet cell. Some other company or individual has control over the strategy. Therefore, it will also be hard, if not impossible, for directors to exhibit the generic skills that are required in some of the cells. As a director on a puppet company, you can try to be as strategic as you wish, but it is likely to end up being a very frustrating experience; one that will probably lead to a number of clashes and your imminent departure.

The five main functions of the board of directors in all companies are:

1. Providing Strategic Direction and Values
2. Approval of Business Planning
3. Monitoring and Control of Performance
4. Ensuring Organizational Capability
5. Awareness of and Compliance with Legal Responsibilities

This list has been informed by the responses of more than 450 directors from a variety of companies. They prioritized the five main functions of the board. Their companies were at various stages of development, although most could be placed on a trajectory somewhere between the Puppet and Partnership or Autonomous and Partnership. There is logic to the list. Unless there is a **strategic direction**, there is nothing to plan for. **Values** accompany the need to devolve authority within the organization. As there is more and more devolution, what are the values that the company wishes to inform the discretionary decision-making that takes place at all levels within the company? One of the values may be the need to add value for the shareholders. If it is not, what are the values that the board is using to underpin its decisions and the criteria for performance (Rappaport: 1–12)? If the board does not ensure that **planning** takes place, the company will not move in the desired strategic direction. There will also be nothing to **monitor performance** against. The board will need to be clear about the detail of monitoring information that it requires. This does not just involve financial information, although it is vital that the board receives regular balance sheet, profit and loss account and cash flow figures, all with forecasts. It also includes the key information that is indicative of performance against the values that the board has established for the company. If the board think that the values are important enough to monitor, then so will the rest of the company. If the company lacks the structural capability to deliver the plans, its plans will not succeed. Although the board cannot do everything it is responsible for ensuring that the right structures and people are in place so that the strategic direction is maintained, the planning is adhered to, the monitoring and control information is available and acted on, and the legal responsibilities are complied with. Therefore, the board has to ensure that the company has **organizational capability**. This includes the extent of devolution within the organization, the development of the right teams for specific tasks, through to personnel development, succession planning and the structure of the board itself. The buck stops with the board when it comes to the company having to comply with its legal responsibilities. Neglect of this function of the board can lead to directors being personally liable, both financially and criminally. Therefore, **awareness of and compliance with legal responsibilities** must be on any list of prioritized functions of the board.

The Institute of Directors has identified four key tasks of the board. These standards were developed from study of good practice involving several hundred UK directors and bear a similarity to the list above (Institute of Directors: 22). They are:

- Establishing vision, mission and values
- Setting strategy and structure
- Delegation to management
- Exercising responsibility to shareholders and other interested parties.

In the USA, the National Association of Corporate Directors established a Blue Ribbon Commission to evaluate the main components of 'Director Professionalism'. Below, their findings are matched to the list of board functions that was identified earlier. Their survey concluded that the main board responsibilities were (NACD: 1–2):

- Approving a corporate philosophy and mission *[Providing Strategic Direction and Values]*
- Selecting, monitoring, evaluating, compensating, replacing the CEO and other senior executives, ensuring management succession *[Ensuring Organizational Capability]*
- Reviewing and approving management's strategic and business plans *[Approval of Planning]*
- Reviewing and approving Financial objectives and material transactions *[Approval of Planning]*
- Monitoring Corporate Performance against strategic and business plans *[Monitoring and Control of Performance]*
- Ensuring ethical behaviour and legal compliance *[Monitoring and Control of Performance]*
- Ensuring that the board is effective *[Ensuring Organizational Capability]*

Bain and Band consider that the most common themes associated with corporate failures include:

- A lack of checks and balances in the system, enabling unfettered power to remain unfettered *[Monitoring and Control of Performance/Ensuring Organizational Capability]*
- Inadequate financial controls and supervision from board level *[Monitoring and Control of Performance]*
- Inappropriate, or, in some cases, no strategic direction allowing management to pursue random interests or at least to pursue opportunistic thrusts

that are not strategically well founded *[Providing Strategic Direction and Values]*

- Management that is not up to the standards required in the modern business world *[Ensuring Organizational Capability]*. (Bain and Band: 36)

There is therefore wide support for the generic list of board functions. We will apply this list as we move through the stages of development of companies in the following chapters, identifying how the functions of the board need to change as the company develops.

Monitoring and Assessing the Function and Performance of Directors

The attributes required to occupy and perform in the top managerial roles must complement the stages of development of the company. But again there are certain skills that are generic. This is an area where disagreement amongst company directors is more common. They disagree most about the skills that were required to be an effective **executive director**. Non-executive directors are different and must be looked at separately. Despite some disagreement amongst the directors that I have worked with, there were some key attributes, which nearly all agreed upon:

1. Integrity
2. Leadership Skills – Team Player/Communicator
3. Analytical
4. Specialist Skills and Knowledge
5. Thinker – Open Minded/ Strategic

These attributes are required of any director. There may be variations in the degree to which those skills are present in each director, but even that caveat cannot apply to **integrity**.

Unless there is integrity, the board will not function properly. Directors will always be looking over their sholder and discussion will be constrained. Integrity also means being true to yourself. Saying what you think is in the best interests of the company even if it means antagonizing a dominant person on the board. This presence of integrity also helps the board to have a good disagreement and manage the conflict that the disagreement may bring about, a feature that is of critical importance in fast growth companies. There is some evidence that conflict within top teams, if managed properly, leads to richer solutions and faster growth (Eisenhardt). The application of real integrity can be very hard. If the decision that is taken by the board is one that the individual director cannot support outside of the meeting, the director will need to inform the board of the seriousness of the concerns, and ultimately resign, rather than compromise the integrity of the collective responsibility of the board. Having left the board, the director should stay quiet. The board has to set the standard for the company as a whole. Running a business is a complicated affair. They have to be able to inspire confidence as well as make tough decisions as part of a package of **complex leadership skills**. This includes innovation leadership and being a **team player** rather than a loner, although directors will not mind working on their own if necessary. They need to be good **communicators**. Otherwise they cannot inspire and lead the staff to accomplish the board's strategy and plans or put views across effectively and timely in the heat of a board meeting. If directors are to play an effective role in the monitoring and control of performance they need to be **analytical**. This does not involve the ability to perform complex statistical analysis, but they need to be competent enough to understand and interpret figures alongside a range of information from a variety of sources. The nature of the job of director has changed, as corporations have become more complex relying more heavily on a wide variety of sources of information in their decision-taking. The growth of Enterprise Resource Planning (ERP) companies is a visible sign of the demands that nearly all companies are facing with regard to their information sources. The management of information is a business critical issue and the source of innovation for future growth. The job of director embraces information management at two levels:

- Corporate strategy on information management
- Personal management of information as a board and as a director, as boards have to make sense of and manage 'a torrid flow of conflicting and ambiguous information' (Sanders: 161).

To both of these they have to add perspective which they bring from their research and experience. The numerical aspect of this analytical skill is a common inadequacy in directors and one that can and has to be rectified with development. However, it is not just financial information that is being analyzed. That information will need to be interpreted in the context of information that is bombarding the director from different sources. The skill is to distil the correct approach for the company from this medley of information. Companies would probably not thrive with a board comprised totally of accountants, engineers or, heaven forbid, lawyers! The board will need to identify the **specialist skills and knowledge** that it needs to complement the other basic skills and the expertise that is already on the board. It could be a functional area like finance, personnel, production, quality control or marketing. Or, it could be wide experience of the industry or a related industry, or European business experience. The question to ask is 'what specialist quality is the director bringing to the boardroom table?'

Finally the director needs to be a **thinker**: an individual who can step back from the chaos of everyday operations and reflect on where the company is going. This includes being a strategic thinker. It involves being able to make good judgements about the future prospects of the sector that the company is operating in so that the company can position itself accordingly. It includes being open-minded. Directors must listen to the views of fellow directors and be willing to contemplate change for the company as difficult but necessary. The willingness to contemplate change is part of leadership:

> Leaders believe in change. They possess an insight into how to alter com-
> petition, and do not accept constraints in carrying it out. Leaders energize
> their organizations to meet competitive challenges, to serve demanding
> needs, and, above all, to keep progressing. They find ways of overcoming
> the filters which limit information and prevent innovation. They harness
> and even create external pressures to motivate … . The concept of leader-
> ship has been lost in many companies. Too many companies and too
> many managers misperceive the true bases for competitive advantage.
> They become preoccupied with improving financial performance,
> soliciting government assistance, and seeking stability through forming
> alliances and merging with competitors. These sorts of steps are not good
> for companies or for nations. Today's competitive realities demand more.
> (Porter: 615)

As we move through the stages of development of companies, we will need to refer to the skills of directors that are appropriate to ensure that the company does move. We have already identified that in a Puppet company, it could be extremely frustrating and cause great friction for an individual who is a strategic thinker and has good leadership skills to be an executive member of the board. However, they may be the skills that are required of a non-executive director appointed to this Puppet board as a catalyst to move the company into the Partnership mode. It is unlikely that all the existing directors in this company will have the necessary skills to operate effectively once the company is in the Partnership stage, but this will need to be tested. What is clear is that the skills of the directors do play a key part in the development of the company and the change in management style that accompanies the development. If there is no analysis of the changing function of the board and the skills required of directors to fulfil that function, it is likely that there will be a dysfunction between where the company wants to be and the top personnel that are required to get it there. But the necessary changes at the top of the company are often hard to bring about, as they are caught up in a web of other relationships and factors such as family, friends, power, wealth and personality:

> ... changes in style (of management) are not easy to bring about, and occur infrequently. Indeed, we have suggested that the personalities and skills of the CEO and his senior team go far to determine the style that is actually adopted by a company – and, without changes in management, these change only slowly, if at all. (Good and Campbell: 241)

The Institute of Directors identifies six groups of personal qualities of directors, which includes 36 subcategories. The six groups are:

- Strategic perception and decision-making *[Thinker – Open Minded/ Strategic]*
- Analytical understanding *[Analytical]*
- Communication *[Leadership Skills – Team Player/Communicator]*
- Interacting with others *[Leadership Skills – Team Player/Communicator]*
- Board management *[Organizational Capability]*
- Achieving results *[Leadership Skills]*.   (Institute of Directors: 44)

The Institute's Good Practice Guide states that,

> It is unlikely that all the personal qualities listed will be required, but at least one director on a board should possess each of these qualities deemed necessary for that board. Ideally there should be a good balance of individuals, whose strengths and weaknesses are complimentary. (Institute of Directors: 45)

The National Association of Corporate Director's Blue Ribbon

Commission on Director Professionalism (NACD: 22) set out five key personal characteristics required of all directors:

- Integrity and accountability *[Integrity]*
- Informed judgement *[Analytical]*
- Financial literacy *[Analytical]*
- Mature confidence *[Leadership Skills – Team Player/Communicator]*
- High performance standards *[Leadership Skills]*.

Collins and Porras concluded from their studies of enduring and successful companies that management development and succession planning are key parts of the ticking clock. The most successful companies they studied had developed strong internal candidates for the most senior position. This led to a 'leadership continuity loop' that reinforced the preservation of the core ideology. Failure to plan long term at the top board level of management can lead to disastrous gaps in leadership. This occurred at Colgate in the late 1920s when it had to resort to a merger with Palmolive-Peet, having traded very successfully since it had been founded in 1806. Whereas, Jack Welch worked at General Electric for 20 years before becoming chief executive in 1981 (Collins and Porras: 170–5). Succession planning at all levels is important, but at board level is critical for all companies and should absorb a lot of board time. In smaller companies the succession issue on the board is intimately connected to the future ownership of the company and often bound up with family politics and sibling rivalry. This is the case across the world, although in some cultures there are clear rules for succession:

> The highly personal nature of authority relations in the Chinese Family Business, the limited separation of the firm from the family and the conditional nature of employee loyalty together restrict the longevity and size of Chinese firms. Succession to the patriarchal role is decided by the founder, but the Chinese principle of equal division of his assets among his inheritors encourages division, conflict and fragmentation…the typical successful CFB goes through four distinct phases – emergent, centralized, segmented, and disintegrative – in three generations. (Whitley: 63)

In most companies the first senior appointments are the architects who will start to fashion the board and the company for future generations of board members (Collins and Porras: 183–4). However, the planning must take into account the direction the company wants to move on the PAPA grid. This may mean that for companies at certain stages in their development, homegrown directors are not appropriate. Indeed, in order for the company to survive, an outsider may need to be brought in. We will see examples of this in some of the case studies. There is a whole range of situations that different companies will be confronted with which impact on succession at the most senior level. For example, at some stage in a company's development it will include a decision as to whether the role of managing director and chairman of the company should be separate and distinct, with a clear understanding behind that decision as to the different nature of their roles. The PAPA grid is a route map which prompts responses to the different practical issues that confront the company as it moves in the planned direction. It will mean making some hard decisions along the way, but at least you are aware of the direction you are headed and making decisions that should take along the desired route. There is a Chinese proverb that states,

If you don't know where you are going you will end up where you are headed.

It is up to those who are directing the affairs of the company to be clear in which direction the company is headed and to ensure that the board of directors, has the capacity and skill to move the company in that direction. For this to happen the board must be clear about its functions both now and in the future, and the medley of skills that are required of directors now and in the future in order to meet those demands on the board.

3 *Board Architecture and Entrepreneur Companies*

This chapter analyzes the development of the entrepreneur company and the affect that this has on board architecture. Some entrepreneur companies may evolve into family companies if succession is handled smoothly. These companies will be analyzed in the next chapter. In this chapter our study of the development of entrepreneur companies will include how board architecture needs to change as the entrepreneur confronts the three crises identified by Mueller:

(1) the crisis of finding the founding owner's successors,
(2) the crisis of reorganization under the new leadership, and
(3) the crisis of the original owners and principals letting go of their dominant hold on the enterprise. (Mueller: 84)

The most important change required will be in the mindset of the entrepreneur owner of the company, for without this the company will not move at all.

Entrepreneur companies possess a speed of decision-taking that large companies are increasingly trying to imitate by turning the heads of divisions or subsidiary companies into 'entrepreneurs', encouraging the individual in charge of the division or subsidiary to react quickly to competitive forces and market situations. Substantial business freedom needs to be conferred to facilitate this desire to create agility within a large corporation. These attempts to create the entrepreneur culture within larger groups of companies will be explored in the chapter on groups of companies. However, there is a major difference between these companies and the entrepreneur companies we are to consider in this chapter. The difference is ownership.

From Puppet to Partnership

It would be unusual if at some stage in their development entrepreneur companies have not been located in the Puppet cell of the PAPA grid, and then considered moving towards the Partnership cell. PR Ltd started in the Puppet cell (Case Studies 2.3 and 2.8), but it isn't there now. We will follow the development of PR Ltd. The previous case studies portrayed PR Ltd as it was nine years ago.

The board of PR Ltd was not operating as a board. Charles was the dominant entrepreneur who controlled everything. The board was a puppet but business was going well. The company was very profitable. This situation is fortunately not uncommon in entrepreneur companies and can continue

- while the entrepreneur remains alive and healthy
- until the entrepreneur decides that he will sell the company and retire
- until the company becomes too large and complex for one person to have oversight of all the company's affairs, or
- while the company is solvent.

Normally it will take an event or a series of events over a period of time to move the mindset of the owner-entrepreneur from Puppet to Partnership. Some of the events that have prompted entrepreneur-owners to explore a different mode of operation for the company include a combination of one or more of the following:

- A desire to explore a life other than work, prompted by a health scare or matrimonial difficulties
- The growing complexity of the market that the company operates dictates that just to survive the entrepreneur has to devolve decisions to others; there is a growing need to bring others in the decision-making as the decisions are getting more and more important for the company's strategic development. Often this is accompanied by increasing competitive forces or the realization that the company has hit a natural growth hurdle which needs to be surmounted by a strategic analysis of the longer-term positioning of the company
- The loss of a key person within the company to a competitor, the loss being caused by the inability of the entrepreneur to let this person operate strategically inside his company
- Attendance at a director development programme where these issues where explored, although the event that led to the entrepreneur

attending the course was the real catalyst: usually advice from a friend
- Because it gets too lonely in charge.

Case Study 3.1

PR Ltd – Puppet to Partnership (Comp.)

Charles knew he had to change the company because of a combination of:

- The increasing complexity of the market – he was losing touch with developments
- The scale of growth of the company – it was getting on top of him
- The company's dependence on Charles illustrated during his illness.

It happened by accident. In order to expand the number of clients for PR Ltd, Charles knew that he had to keep abreast of what was happening in London and the United States. The company needed to expand its regional base as even regional clients expected national and even global awareness. Charles wanted access to high quality advice about current developments in London and the United States, and also someone who could help him with some of the problems of growth that he was confronting. For example, the level of bad debts was rising fast. Charles didn't know where to start. He was good at writing corporate slogans and public relations copy for his clients. He had a friend, John, who had extensive business experience in the industry and had just left a major agency for semi-retirement. He asked John to come onto the board as a non-executive director. After lengthy discussions John agreed. But the appointment was subject to John making the following successful demands from Charles:

- proper board meetings have to be held every month
- monthly financial information has to be presented to the board showing forecasts of the balance sheet, profit and loss account and cash flow
- A business plan is to be developed for the company.

The first business plan was written by Charles. It was excellent prose. John took the plan to pieces in a delicate manner in private meetings and telephone conversations with Charles. Eventually they arrived at a draft, which was acceptable to John and was approved by the whole board. It took a while for the real impact of the appointment of John to be realized by the executive directors and by Charles. Spurred on by the presence of a director, who was challenging Charles in a non-threatening way, the executive directors were now in a position to start to question and develop strategy themselves. They could make proposals affecting the whole range of the company's activities, not just the part of the company that they were involved in on an operational basis. They could act like company directors. Frank could not meet this challenge and, following discussions between John and Charles, he left the board. The board now consider that there is a need for a financial director to join the board. They are also planning for Charles's retirement, which is ten years away.

PR Ltd has now moved into the edges of the Partnership relationship on the PAPA grid and is still moving in that direction. At some stage in the future it could seek a listing and may then move into the Autonomous cell unless the company takes steps to build the wider body of shareholders into a partnership with the board. The movement and projected movement of PR Ltd are illustrated in Figure 3.1. The catalyst for change in this case was the appointment of a very good non-executive director.

The Partnership relationship presents a dilemma or tension between the following:

1. The desire of the owner entrepreneur to have control and influence over the company, and

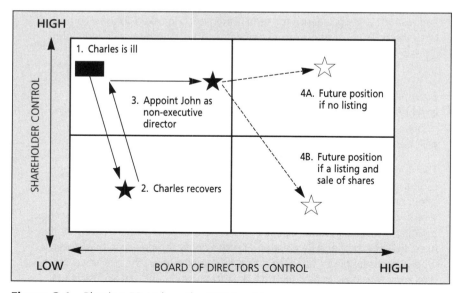

Figure 3.1 Plotting PR Ltd on the PAPA grid

2. The realization that in order for the company to move forward help is needed in the form of an effective board of directors and that the board will not operate properly if the owner-entrepreneur continues to exert dominance.

In order to operate an effective Partnership relationship between the board and the entrepreneur shareholder, changes are required that turn that possibly destructive tension into a creative one. This requires alterations in the board architecture. This is illustrated in Figure 3.2 where the dotted line that bisects the cell illustrates the optimum position for the company. The following is a checklist of the key changes that will need to take place with regard to board architecture in order to locate the entrepreneur company onto that line.

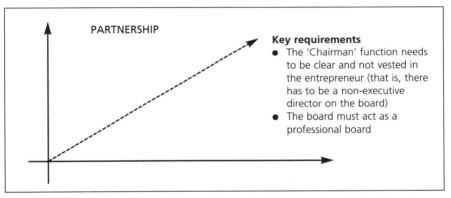

Figure 3.2   Resolving the dilemma of shareholder control and freedom for the board of directors in an Entrepreneur company

The 'Chairman' Function Needs to be Clear and not Vested in the Entrepreneur

The entrepreneur should not fulfil the functions of chairman and managing director of the company. The chairman's role will be explored more when we look at listed companies. In entrepreneur companies the titles are not important. It is the function of a chairman that is critical, and in an entrepreneur company this involves more than just being a non-executive director. Chairman qualities are required to:

- Manage and develop the relationship with the entrepreneur-owner and the other executive directors

- Ensure that the managing director's proposals are given a 'hard look'
- Assess the attributes, qualities and performance of the other directors
- Become a 'friendly and confidential ear' for the rest of the board, including the entrepreneur: listening and advising whilst ensuring that responsibility for the actions and decisions of those individuals remains with them
- Ensure that the board functions properly as a board, performing all the functions cited in Chapter 2
- Gain the total confidence of the entrepreneur over time so that eventually the entrepreneur can be advised to leave the company and let go to a successor that has been groomed or recruited carefully.

This amazing person doesn't have to have the title of chairman if that would bruise egos. It is more important that the functions of a chairman are performed than that the title is conferred. It is easier to describe the desired attributes than locate all of them in any one individual. The company may need more than one non-executive director to fulfil these functions. In exceptional companies comprised of entrepreneurs with real insight into their own failings and prejudices, the transition will be managed without the presence of a 'chairman' role. I have yet to meet an entrepreneur company where this is the case, although Tom's of Maine comes close. Tom's of Maine is a personal care products company in the US producing items such as soap and toothpaste (see Case Study 4.3 in Chapter 4). Tom Chappell is the President and former CEO and the co-owner with his wife, Kate. Tom's insight is that:

> It's hard for entrepreneurs to develop a management team and empower those managers to make their own choices and mistakes. It's difficult because we are such hands-on visionaries. We have trouble making room for the creative ideas and strategies that others envision. And there's no question about the fact that I would sometimes do what's being done here differently. But the point is that the same results are being created that I would have tried to create. And I have to marvel that there was another way of doing it. But that's humility. (Boyers: 198)

Tom did have non-executive directors to help him, even a psychologist who specialized in organizational development. If there is no 'chairman' for the entrepreneur to turn to for help and advice, or just to talk to, the likelihood is that the company will not survive the three crises and make the transition to Partnership. Storey concludes from his study that the nature of the non-owning manager recruitment is a factor associated with successful small-firm growth (Storey: 150). There is also supported by some evidence that the combined efforts of the entrepreneur and the active participation of outside directors positively assists corporate productivity (Daily).

Of course the transition in the company's development may not take place even with an outside non-executive director on the board. It depends upon their ability to perform the 'chairman' role. They may not be able to, particularly if they been 'captured' by the management team because they have been on the board for too long. Have they lost the ability to ask the difficult questions, to question the comfort of the status quo and the way in which the three crises are being approached? The appointment of a non-executive to occupy the 'chairman' role is normally a necessary change in the board architecture of entrepreneur companies if those companies want to move in a different direction. It is therefore disappointing to see the corporate governance debate focusing on the independence of directors and the split between the chairman and managing director function, only in the context of listed companies. The presence of an independent director occupying the 'chairman' role in entrepreneur companies is a major factor in the company's progression to Partnership and to the company's survival long after the demise of the entrepreneur.

The Board Must Operate as a Board

This will require the board at a minimum to comply with the three demands required by John before he came onto the board of PR Ltd:

- monthly board meetings
- monthly financial information has to be presented to the board showing forecasts of the balance sheet, profit and loss account and cash flow
- the board has to approve a business plan; this will be the first step in the board taking a strategic role in the development of the company.

In addition, the Board will need to approve a document detailing the limits of the managing director's powers. This is a list of reserved matters for the board, matters which only the board, as a board, can decide upon. Statements of reserved powers are common in listed companies, but rare in smaller companies. Yet it is vital that the areas of responsibility are carefully delineated. Writing them down and incorporating them into the board minutes is a powerful signal that the board is starting to operate in a different way. The content of matters reserved for the board in an entrepreneur company should at least include the following:

- Corporate procedures for financial limits on commitment to revenue and capital expenditure, and risk management
- Acquisition and disposal of key corporate assets
- Significant press releases
- Hiring and firing of key personnel
- Remuneration strategy for senior personnel
- Corporate restructuring which leads to major changes in the company's management and control structure
- Board appointments and their terms of reference
- Commencement of litigation or receipt of writs and statutory demands
- Health, Safety and Environmental policy and any notifications from staff of major breaches or potential major breaches that could lead to serious injury or death
- Notification of directors' interests in any contract or shares of the company (required under the Companies Act 1985: sections 317, 324; Table A: articles 85–6).

This will be a test for the owner-entrepreneur's commitment to the partnership principle. It is a clear statement that the owner-entrepreneur, who is the managing director of the company, will not do certain things without the prior approval of the board. The other directors will be watching to see if the entrepreneur really means to alter the board architecture and permit the board to operate as a board.

Case Study 3.2

Mitchell & Hobbs (UK) Ltd

Mitchell & Hobbs U.K Ltd was a small private company which at the time of these events was no longer trading. There were two directors, Pearce and Radford. Radford was the managing director and Mill was the company secretary. Radford owned 66 of the shares in the company and Mill and Pearce owned 17 each. They had all fallen out with each other. Mill withdrew £3900 from the company's bank account. He said that he did this to prevent the money being used by Radford in breach of his duties to the company and its creditors. Mill placed the money in a separate account in the name of the company's accountants. Radford initiated a legal action on behalf of the company against Mill to recover the money. Mill argued that Radford did not have the authority to commence the action on the company's behalf, as the board of directors had never conferred that authority on him. The company's articles were in the same form as most articles of UK companies (Table A: articles 70, 72).

The court agreed with Mill. The board had been delegated management powers over the company and this included control over the litigation of the company. There was no evidence that this power had been delegated to the managing director. The managing director requires specific and express delegation of the power of litigation on behalf of the company from the board of directors. The power is not conferred merely because the board allowed Radford to act as managing director on other matters. This case study illustrates that

- majority shareholders who hold the office of managing director cannot ignore the board's authority. The board of directors has a constitutional role within the company and, in this case, the board's power was usurped
- the powers of a managing director do not automatically include the power to control the litigation of the company. They have to be expressly delegated by the board in accordance with the company's constitution (Table A: article 72).

Skills and Attributes required of Directors

As the company starts to move from Puppet mode to Partnership mode, the directors who were content to operate in the Puppet environment may not have the ability to operate effectively in the new environment. They may possess integrity, have some specialist knowledge that is critical to the board and perform well in their functional role. However, there are key attributes that are required of a director in the Partnership environment that will not normally have been tested when the company was in Puppet mode:

- the ability to think strategically about the company

- a clear indication of leadership skills
- the skill of analyzing information from a range of sources before reaching a conclusion that is in the best interests of the company
- even the issue of integrity may not have been fully tested: the board has probably not been put into a position where there is open disagreement; or where there is a need to assert collective responsibility outside the boardroom.

There may be possibilities for development. Directors will need to be appraised in order to assess their capacity for operating in the new environment. This will take time. It can be undertaken formally through the introduction of an appraisal process at director level, identifying their role and performance as a director of the company, *not* their executive function within the company. The technique for undertaking this is examined in Chapter 5. The new environment will mean that the balance of the directors' work will start to move. They will need to step back from their executive function to reflect on corporate strategy and what they can offer in its development. This will have a knock-on effect on the responsibilities of people who work for them. The process of 'adding depth' to jobs across the company has started (Tomasko: 82). As a result the company will start to move faster, encouraging innovation (and forgiving mistakes) at all levels as the puppet strings that started at the top but entangled the whole organization are hacked away. The process of moving to the Partnership cell should send these signals throughout the company and ultimately change every employee's role. For some incumbent directors and other staff in the company it may not be possible to add the necessary depth. The company needs to move on and they cannot. If they remain in post they will hold back the pace of the company's necessary development indicated in Figure 3.1. They will need to be removed from the office of director.

In order for the entrepreneur company to develop, at least one director will need to be a non-executive. This is the director who possesses the 'chairman' skills that are needed to enable the entrepreneur company to move away from the Puppet stage. There are other skills and attributes required of a non-executive director that help the company move along the PAPA line. In particular the non-executive director will also need the following:

- Total respect from the entrepreneur-owner, which will probably mean that they have worked in the same business or a very closely related one at a senior level. The relationship between the 'chairman' non-executive director and the managing director is always a critical one. In entrepreneur companies, the company cannot move to or stay in the Partnership cell unless there is an effective relationship between these two individuals based on mutual respect

- The ability to be firm, which includes the courage to walk away from the company if it starts to slip back down the PAPA line, whilst recognizing that there is a transition period when some slippage will be inevitable
- Mentoring and counselling skills to be applied to all the directors, but particularly the owner-entrepreneur. This will test the integrity of the non-executive who will need to ensure that all directors know that confidentiality of discussions will be maintained.

Finding such an individual is not easy. Finding an individual who can bring these skills and attributes to the company, as well as the 'chairman' skills, is virtually impossible without help. There are professional recruitment agencies that can help, but the key is to take your time and plan the recruitment carefully. A process to help companies achieve this is detailed in the next chapter. There is some research evidence that one of the main reasons for the failure of a non-executive to make a positive contribution in entrepreneur companies is the failure to create a good relationship with the entrepreneur. The matching process is critical and requires considerable thought as to the reasons for wanting a non-executive on the board. Most non-executive directors in entrepreneur companies are found through personal contacts or through the venture capital provider who is insisting that there should be a non-executive. But most venture capital companies will allow the entrepreneur some freedom of choice as to who the non-executive director will be. This allows the entrepreneur the opportunity to match the skills and attributes of the person they would prefer against those of potential candidates. Even if you go to an agency or database service you need to think through the type of individual you are looking for. This applies to all director appointments in all companies.

Puppet to Autonomous ... and Back Again

Some entrepreneurs want to take their companies down the route of Puppet to Autonomous. They draw their PAPA grid as in Figure 3.3. This always involves a listing to ease their path to retirement, usually

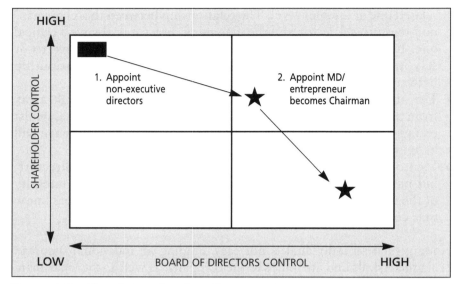

Figure 3.3   Gloss Paints plc – from Puppet to Autonomous

as multi-millionaires. This is illustrated in the case study of a major paint manufacturer, Gloss Paints plc, which is a compilation of such instances.

Case Study 3.3

Gloss Paints plc (Comp.)

Gloss Paints Ltd was started and owned by Hugh Diamond in 1950. The company was very successful. Hugh had a dominating but fair management style. He had gradually come to rely heavily on a range of other directors whom he appointed as the company expanded, whilst retaining overall control. In 1985 the company was converted to a plc in anticipation of Hugh seeking a listing for the company and gradually handing over the senior management. Two non-executive directors were appointed to the board. It was apparent that Hugh's style over more than 35 years meant it was unlikely that the company would find his successor from within. The non-executive directors had reached this conclusion. Hugh hadn't even thought about it as an option. A dynamic managing director was recruited from outside the company. The non-executive directors had agreed with Hugh that he should remain as executive chairman during the period up to and immediately after the flotation. Following the successful flotation Hugh was a very rich man. He stayed as non-executive chairman for one year after the flotation and then left the company completely, although he still has a shareholding in the company. The company has a new chairman. The board is now fairly autonomous, like many listed companies. None of Hugh's fellow executive directors remain on the board. The shareholding is fairly diffuse and exerts little pressure on the board. For Hugh this was a very successful transition from Puppet to Autonomous. The company has expanded and the number of people employed has increased. The company is making above average returns for its shareholders compared to the rest of the sector it is operating in.

This was a fairly carefully planned transition and exit for Hugh and a clear illustration of the planning required to achieve the movement in Figure 3.3. Hugh knew in which structural direction he wanted the company to go, as well as a business direction. The structural vision was a key part of the business vision. There was no danger of Hugh trying to hold onto the reins of power. He had already edged the company towards the Partnership cell before he brought in a new managing director. He had to, because he couldn't carry the increasing complexity of the business himself. Hugh realized that there was

> a need for managerial styles and roles to change as the firm expands. At the heart of this, for the small firm, is that growth leads to increased complexity of decision making for the business owner; it means the individual is required to delegate these functions to others. (Storey: 150)

The non-executive appointments were a great help in clarifying Hugh's thoughts on the three crises identified by Mueller. Hugh had regular discussions concerning the long-term structure of the company with the non-executives outside the formal board meetings, as well as discussions with other senior business colleagues in the region.

Entrepreneurs who take their companies into the public arena as listed companies do not always follow Hugh's example. Robert Maxwell ruled his quoted companies with a rod of iron. The control exercised by him over the companies was extraordinary. His company was firmly situated in the top left hand corner of the Puppet cell ... until he died, when the extent of his dominance over the other directors on the board became clear and the company became Adrift. The directors then suffered the ignominy of having to explain why they allowed themselves to be treated as puppet directors of a listed company. For some, the excuses were insufficient to protect them from legal action for breach of their duties as directors. The Maxwell disaster, for that is what it was for the thousands of pensioners whose funds were plundered, was one of a number of corporate shamings that led to the establishment of the various committees on corporate governance.

Richard Branson's complex group of Virgin companies is almost totally comprised of private companies. In 1998 they had a positive cash flow of about £150 million. A large part of the Branson empire went public in 1986, but was then re-privatized shortly afterwards through the repurchase of shares by Richard Branson. He has stated his dislike of the short-term nature of the pressures that public status exerted, whilst accepting that a Puppet relationship is not a long-term strategy for the group of companies:

> The approach to running a group of private companies is fundamentally different to that of running public companies. Short-term, taxable profits with good dividends are a prerequisite of public life. Avoiding short-term, taxable profits, and seeking long-term capital growth is the best approach to growing private companies ... The major new start-up businesses (or acquisitions) each have their own separate finance and investment, and over time some may become independent (even of me). Others may be floated, but the one thing they will all, I hope, share is a British brand name they can be proud of. (*The Economist*: 1998c)

The great success of the Virgin Group of companies is an illustration that entrepreneur companies can thrive whilst being located in the Puppet cell. It depends on the management approach adopted by the entrepreneur. The Virgin approach appears to be to move the boards of the various companies in the group closer to a Partnership relationship, via franchise-style arrangements and joint shareholdings. This helps to keep the complex business affairs under control. Also, as can be seen in the statement by Richard Branson, it requires an appreciation that being located in the Puppet cell has to be a temporary state of affairs because of our own mortality. Superb as he may be as an individual leader, he is mortal. The companies that he has nurtured are not. Planning for the succession of the company is critical if the company is to survive the entrepreneur. The Virgin empire is well placed in this regard. A significant number of the companies within the group are already joint ventures, with Richard Branson providing the brand name and public relations and others putting up part of the capital, similar to a franchise operation. These are the companies that have already begun to make the move to Partnership status. It requires special skills for the directors of these companies to oversee joint ventures and alliances. This type of planning for the group of companies, and appreciation of the different skills required of these directors, needs to continue if the British brand name that Richard Branson is so proud of is to survive him. The point is reinforced by research undertaken by Collins and Porras:

> From the perspective of building a visionary company, the issue is not only how well the company will be doing during the current generation. The crucial question is, how well will the company perform in the next generation, and the next generation after that, and the next generation after that? All individual leaders eventually die. But a visionary company can tick along for centuries, pursuing its purpose and expressing its core values long beyond the tenure of any individual leader. (Collins and Porras: 184)

Time will tell whether Richard Branson's very special architectural approach to building a group of companies will be an enduring one.

These are just some illustrations of the considerable variety of corporate arrangements that can occur. There is no one set of rules to govern the best approach for companies to evolve. The PAPA grid is only important as a tool to help to understand how the board of directors needs to change as the company changes, and to analyze the options that are available regarding the nature of those changes. Undertaking this analysis will influence the capacity of the company to survive the crises ahead.

Guiding Principles for Entrepreneurs

Although there are no clear rules, there are some guiding principles for entrepreneurs:

1. Have a clear vision for the life of the company beyond your life
2. Ensure that the values you strive for become those of the company; through their endurance you achieve immortality
3. Adopt a professional approach to managing and governing the company
4. Use outside independent help to counterbalance your immersion in the company.

CHAPTER

4 *Board Architecture and Family Companies*

Family businesses account for 66 per cent of all businesses across the world. In the US they generate $1.5 trillion of the gross national product and total 1.7 million businesses (Mueller: viii). In Germany 60 per cent of the mainly family-owned *Mittelstand* companies, like Porsche and Haribo, are among the world's top five in their sector and account for about 20 per cent of Germany's DM900 billion in exports. Others cite even larger numbers of family companies depending on the definition of a family business and whether they have opted for the corporate form (Shanker and Astrachan). The family business and family companies are a very significant business structure. The variety of companies that fall within just this one category is enormous, reflecting the different paths family companies have taken in their survival through the generations of family owners. Some are large listed companies, like Sainsbury's, Fiat, and Ford. In Sweden the major engineering companies are nearly all controlled by ten families. These are companies that have survived the transition through the generations with a large proportion of stock remaining in the family. They have developed so effectively in Sweden because 'Local rivalry, little protection in the home market, and early internationalization have added to the challenges to innovate and upgrade competitive advantage'. (Solvell, Zander and Porter: 139)

The ability to innovate and compete globally is an attribute that most companies would like to mimic. There are many other family companies of different sizes who have yet to undergo the upheaval of development from first generation to third or later generations. Unfortunately not many family companies will survive along that development path. It is estimated that only between 5 and 15 per cent of family companies will make it to the third generation (Neubauer and Lank: 14). All this seems to verify the old Chinese proverb that wealth does not last for more than three generations. The Lancashire equivalent is 'clogs to clogs in three generations'.

Running a business is tough enough without the added potential difficulty of family squabbles and jealousies. The potential for these difficulties to rise up and swamp the company grows as the number of family members with an interest in the business expands. Many authors have highlighted succession as being a major stumbling block for family companies. But, succession itself is not the problem, it is only a symptom. The real problem is the development of a professional board of directors who can ensure that the family values flow through into the company and are transformed into corporate values that endure beyond the life of any one member of the family. In many ways family companies have a great advantage over other companies. They have the capacity to generate a 'clan' atmosphere using family values as corporate values which 'stick' to all who work in the business. We will see in Chapter 6 that the ability to develop such values is critical to the next generation of multinational enterprises. Companies like Ericsson are trying to develop the philosophy of 'small in large' so as to enable foreign subsidiaries the freedom to innovate in their host country without complex methods of governance. Values that are shared by senior executives, on a global basis, assist this approach. Family companies have under-exploited this natural attribute of family businesses which global companies are now pursuing. It requires the clock-building approach that Collins and Porras identified in very large enduring companies like Johnson & Johnson and Hewlett-Packard. Family companies have the potential advantage of kinship bonds and values that can ease the development of a company through periods of succession (Mueller: 87). Of course they also have the disadvantage that those values may be destructive in character. During the stages of development of the company these potentially destructive forces may be kept in check by a strong family member, initially the founder. Another family member may be able to continue this role, particularly if they are supported by family agreement to a set of values which the company and the family members abide by. As the generations pass, that role will eventually need to be undertaken by a powerful independent external force operating on the board as managing director. Unless one person continues to undertake this role there is an inherent danger that the company will become Adrift. Then it is only a matter of time before it collapses or is taken over.

The analysis of family companies in this chapter will enable us to identify some key structural changes that can be made at board level to assist the company through its stages of development. As with the previous chapter I will look at companies moving over time between the cells of the PAPA grid. The family itself will at some point need to assess where its company is on the grid at present and where it wants to be.

From Adrift /Puppet to Partnership

One of the most common features of family companies in the early stages of their development is that the board of directors does not really function at all. There are breakfast discussions about operational matters, family occasions when some company matters may be discussed, and a whole host of informal meetings and decision-making. While only the livelihood of a few members of the family depend upon this style, the pressure for change will be small. The lack of formality is amply compensated for by the ability to innovate fast and make quick decisions based on a shared understanding between the main participants in the business. These decisions are taken by the owners of the business, the family, who in the early stages of development of the company are often involved in an executive role. The board is a Puppet because it doesn't operate as a board. The company is controlled and run by the people who own it, the family in their roles as owners not as directors. This is illustrated in Figure 4.1. Originally developed in 1982 by John Davis and Renato Taiguri, the three-circle model was used by Krister Ahlstrom to identify the reasons for the conflict that he was experiencing in the introduction of change in the family company, The Ahlstrom Corporation (Magretta: 117). In position A all the main members of the family own the company and all occupy board positions within the company. Decisions may be made fairly informally outside of a formal board structure. In position B, some of the family owners of the company are now no longer involved in the running of the company. Decisions may now be made by only some of the family members, there being no consultation with the others, unless a process is designed to facilitate this. These could be major decisions or just minor ones. In many ways the nature of the decision is not relevant. What is important is that the process for making decisions for the business has altered as a result of a change in circumstances. The change could have arisen through a variety of circumstances, such as the death of a family member and subsequent transfer of shares to other family members, or individuals moving to

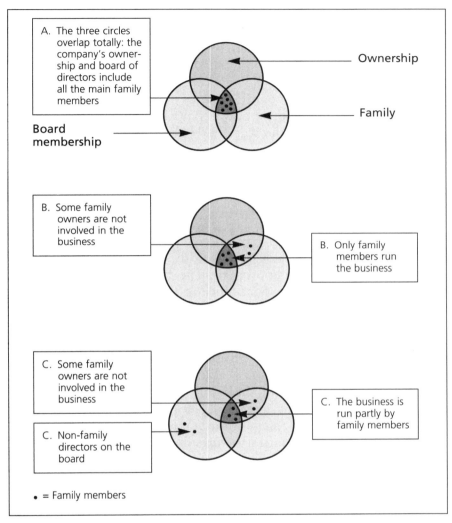

A. The three circles overlap totally: the company's ownership and board of directors include all the main family members

Board membership

Ownership

Family

B. Some family owners are not involved in the business

B. Only family members run the business

C. Some family owners are not involved in the business

C. Non-family directors on the board

C. The business is run partly by family members

• = Family members

Figure 4.1 Identifying the different roles in a family company
SOURCE: Adapted from Gersick, Davis and Hampton

different careers outside of the family business. These events may crystallize who the real decision-makers are, and have been, in the past, but it has happened by accident. The advantage of having a formal board structure with a clear understanding of the proper role of the board is that it can operate regardless of any changes in domestic or personal situations. The two main advantages of running a business through a company as opposed to a partnership are:

1. The company has the capacity to continue regardless of the individual circumstances of its owners, and
2. The owners can appoint a board to run the company who can direct the company regardless of the individual circumstances of, or the number of, owners. Shareholders can die, go bankrupt or insane. The company and the board can carry on regardless, at least until these events lead to control of the company falling into hands that are unsympathetic to the way the board has been managing the company.

Family companies must use these corporate advantages more if they are to progress into future generations. It requires the development of a professional approach to the function of the board of directors. Eventually the family company may get to position C in Figure 4.1 where non-family directors have been appointed to the board. If decisions continue to be made outside of the boardroom by the family the board is not functioning properly. The position of the non-family directors who carry the responsibility of the position of director, is untenable. The board is a Puppet. Some family companies will succeed in the Puppet cell for a couple of generations. But, as the number of family members with an interest in the company grows, their interests will need to be considered. Some form of Partnership structure will be required to mitigate the tension that exists between a board that by now represents only part of the family and the shareholders who represent the wider family interests. The non-executives can play a critical role in this development of the company, as we shall see in the case studies that follow. Board structures that reinforce the Partnership between the shareholders and the board of directors structures will assist in the mitigation of the worst features of family companies – their ability to self-destruct before the third generation.

Figure 4.2 illustrates the key components that are required to help the family company to move into the safer Partnership cell. They are the family version of the criteria that we observed in the earlier chapters embracing family values, a professional board of directors, the presence of independent directors and a communication and participation structure for family non-board members.

Succession

The treatment of succession at board level is a key test of the proper functioning of the board of directors of any company:

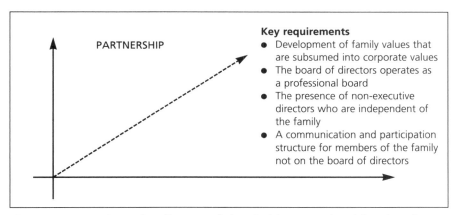

Figure 4.2 Resolving the dilemma of shareholder control and freedom for the board of directors in a family company

> Top-level succession planning both for emergency cover as well as for a longer time horizon, say five years, is a most important part of a board's monitoring role. (Bain and Band: 37)

In a family company many writers have seen it as the overriding challenge for survival (Neubauer and Lank: 17; Mueller: 17). The succession process and decision is an important test as to whether the board and the owners of the company want to operate, and can operate, in a Partnership mode. The approach to the succession decision is an opportunity for family companies to consider, as a preliminary matter, the future direction and management of the company. The company/family can then chart the way they want the organizational structure of the company to develop in order to develop the corporate/family vision. This involves decisions regarding board architecture of the family company.

Several factors combine to make the planning and selection of a successor as managing director the most important process and decision that a family company has to implement and make:

- The loss of this type of director without an heir apparent puts the future ownership and survival of the company in jeopardy – the company slides into the Adrift cell while the family members fight for the top job.
- If there is an immediate appointment, the new managing director has not had the advantage of a period of gradual handover, although

admittedly with some incumbent managing directors this may be in the best interests of the company and of the new appointment.

- Timing of the handover is important and should reflect an appropriate stage in the development of the company or of the individuals concerned:

    '*Father*: My son, I have wonderful news for you. I have decided to retire in four months. You, as I have said so often over the years, are my chosen successor as CEO. Furthermore, you will own 75 per cent of the voting shares and will be totally in charge!
    Son: With respect, dear father, the proposition is ridiculous. You are now 92 and I am 67. My only goal is to retire with my wife and to our country estate in Provence.'
    (paraphrased conversation in a French company – source Neubauer and Lank: 145).

It is clear from the above conversation that the timing of the handover had gone awry. In Germany it is called the 'Kohl syndrome', where the *Mittelstanders* hand over their companies with their last breath. The company has a cycle of development also. Before the new appointment at the top of the company is made there must be careful consideration of the appropriate attributes required of the person who is to lead the company through that development. A managing director must reflect the future needs of the company and not its past.

- Non-family members of the board will feel threatened by the looming and unspoken issue of succession and will start to make plans for their own future that may damage the company. This will particularly be the case if it is not made clear that the succession depends upon merit and not family ties.
- If the family value the views of the full board on business issues, they must take their counsel on the succession issue as they may have some ideas that the family has not considered. If the succession of the company is decided by the wider family only, and the board has no input, this would be a mistake. It would lead to a board that is likely to be disillusioned and ineffective as they are being excluded for a key business decision that affects in a fundamental way the direction the company will take. There needs to be a partnership in this key decision. Similarly, if the views of the wider family are excluded, this could lead to resentment against the new appointment on the part of a large body of owners of the company.

The process of selecting directors is outlined in Figure 4.3. Following the process can overcome some of these difficulties and will help family companies take a structured approach to finding the best person to lead the company. It can be used to select any director of any company. The process itself is part of the development of an enduring family culture within the family company. It is a culture that illustrates that the survival of the company and continued employment for the staff are the paramount considerations.

The stages involved in the decision process are:

1. The Board's Priorities

The board needs to consider its main functions at this moment in the company's development. Board priorities will change over time and so will the attributes required of the individual who is to lead the board and the company into the next stage of development. What are the company's priorities for the next three to five years? If it is difficult to reach a conclusion on this, then the company may well need a new managing director who has the ability to help the company to develop a clear strategy. Some family companies have created governance structures such as a Family Assembly and Family Council where important issues for the company can be debated outside of the boardroom. These debates act as a guide for the board, and also a mechanism for conflict resolution in the wider family outside of the boardroom. (Neubauer and Lank: 77–99). It would be appropriate to raise the succession issue in such a forum if one exists. If there isn't one, this does not stop the board from undertaking wider consultation within the family concerning the future of the company and the attributes required of the next person to lead it. The current chairman or managing director should lead this discussion. If they fail to do so, it is the responsibility of the other directors to ensure that the issue is raised at board level. Directors must act in the best interests of the company and that includes consideration of the current *and* future shareholders of the company. Failure to assess the succession needs at the top of the family company is symptomatic of a board that is not operating properly and not considering the future family shareholder interests. The company is in either the Adrift or Puppet mode. In pushing the issue the directors will start the process of moving the company towards the Partnership cell where survival is more likely. Succession planning can be the start of effective strategy development in some family companies. However, strategic business imperatives for

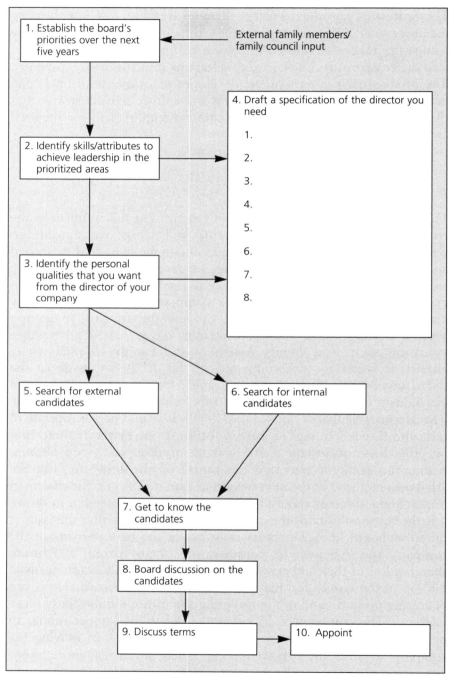

Figure 4.3 Flow chart for selecting a new director

the business do not necessarily align themselves with family life cycles! Early discussion of the succession issue may at least help to bring forward discussion of the development of business strategy in advance of the inevitable human life cycle that may otherwise have triggered the debate. Early discussion of the issue may also help to alter the perception of members of the family regarding the development of the company and their future role in it (Drozdow and Carroll).

2. Identify skills/attributes to achieve leadership in the prioritized areas

This will include the ability to lead a family company and all the family relationships that affect the business, as well as the normal requirement of leading a successful business through its next generation of growth.

3. Qualities of any director

Look at the qualities that are required of any director. There may be some family values that have been agreed by the family. Add these and any others that are high on your list of priorities to the specification. This requirement forces the company to consider the direction it is moving in so as to match the qualities required against the new demands to be placed upon it. One of the key qualities that have already been identified is that the director should bring some specialist skills or knowledge into the boardroom. For example, it might have helped if the family-owned Barings Bank had had some knowledge of derivatives trading on the board. In evidence to the House of Commons Treasury Committee, it became clear that the Board was totally ignorant of the risks associated with the area of trading the Bank had moved into. Protestant immigrants from Holland established the Bank in 1762. On Friday 24 February 1995 at 7.15 a.m., the chairman of the oldest merchant bank in the UK received a phone call informing him that there was a 'hole' in the accounts in Singapore. On the following Monday administrators were appointed (Neubauer and Lank: 209–13).

4. Draft a specification of the director you need

This could include such matters as

- qualifications (academic and professional)
- experience in the sector and with a family company
- experience of leading a company or large subsidiary/division
- personal attributes/values that are matched to the company's

- awareness/perception of the business sector
- languages and international experience
- anticipated current responsibilities of the person being sought.

The process of developing the specification is as important as the content. It will force the company to discuss how it wants to be managed in the future. What will be the relationship between the new managing director and the family? What management values are required, not just of the new appointment, but of all managers in the company? You are not at this stage excluding any potential internal candidate, as the specification should fit the perceived needs of the company in the future. It is not based around the actual attributes of any one individual currently within the company. Indeed, there may be a strong preference to find an internal candidate, but this does not drive the specification. Ericsson went through a rigorous process of identifying the skills required of its senior managers, the results of which are displayed in Figure 4.4. Only after this process had been completed did it become obvious that only one person filled the criteria sufficiently to be appointed Chief Executive Officer of the group. Sven Christen Niellssen was appointed. There was a clear preference for an internal candidate, but nobody would have thought at the beginning that Niellsen would have been appointed. He surfaced from a rank of management below that which would have contained the expected heirs. In some family companies it may be that the clear preference is for an external candidate, at least temporarily, as in Case Study 4.1.

VISIBLE, ACCESSIBLE, INTERNATIONAL

Business Manager
- One company approach
- Customers preferred choice
- Trusted business partner
- Meeting customer needs
- Short- and long-term profitability

Team Builder
- Creates and coaches teams
- Complementary skills
- Creativity
- Open working climate
- One industrial unit

Competence Development
- Short- and long-term needs
- Develops organization and job design
- Demonstrates appropriate behaviour
- Recognition

Operations developer
- Visions, strategy, goals
- Involves employees
- Empowers
- Feedback/follow-up
- Continuous improvement

Figure 4.4 The Ericsson manager
SOURCE: Lars Stalberg, Senior Vice President ,Corporate Communications, Ericsson

Case Study 4.1

Jarrold & Sons Ltd

Jarrold & Sons Ltd has a turnover of £80 million and is a respected family-owned company in Norwich in the East of England. The company is involved in running a department store, and a printing, publishing and stationery business and has been on the same site since 1840, when it had only moved across the road. The company is a thriving independent family business. As for most family businesses, survival involves negotiating some traumas and the emotions of running a business within a family, as well as the business problems that confront every company. Jarrold & Sons Ltd has succeeded in both, reaching the sixth generation, and is now planning the change to the seventh. How much is due to accident and how much to design that it reached the sixth generation? The complexities nowadays of running a successful company mean that to get to the seventh generation much more planning is required. This places considerable responsibility on the family chairman who realizes only too well not only the importance to the family but also that the livelihood of many other people and the community are all affected by making the best succession decisions in the right way.

The first generation
The business was established in 1770 in Woodbridge, Suffolk, by John Jarrold. He opened a drapers shop using £1000 left by his father. He died in 1775 of a raging fever leaving a widow and a two-year-old son, John Jarrold II. The widow and her son moved to Norwich while a friend whom they knew through the chapel ran the shop.

The second generation
John Jarrold II, who became a very competent accountant, discovered that a solicitor had embezzled his father's money. John Jarrold pursued the solicitor and recovered the bulk of the money over a period of time. This helped him to fund the business at the shop in Woodbridge that he ran as a drapers and grocers. He became known by the London wholesalers as 'ready money Jack' because he always paid cash with the order … and received hefty discounts in return. (The Company is still known for the promptness of its payment.) He bought a farm in Suffolk having sold the shop in 1804. In 1810 his sister married a printer, and he bought a property for a printing business for them in Woodbridge, entering into a partnership agreement with his sister's husband under the name of Smith & Jarrold in 1815. In 1823 John Jarrold II moved to Norwich and opened a bookshop and stationery shop in an attempt to revive flagging business. He had four sons, but favoured the first-born

strongly. It was in this move from the second to the third generation that the company first ran into difficulties. John Jarrold II wouldn't let go of power to any of his sons. He continued his entrepreneurial approach to buying and selling, still using cash payments as a method of negotiating deep discounts. He could sell books at better prices than most wholesalers could buy at. He did not consider his other three sons to be good at business. All of them worked in the shop and lived on the premises. By this time they were printing and publishing as well. In 1843 the eldest son died a bachelor. He had been holding the family business together, managing the stormy relationship between his father and brothers. At one stage his brothers thought their father was mistreating them and wanted to realize their share of what they considered to be a partnership. It was the eldest son who convinced them all that the business was an asset large enough to benefit all of them. Within one year of the death of the eldest son, John Jarrold II denied the existence of a partnership with his remaining sons and a considerable conflict ensued. They avoided each other on every possible occasion, and John Jarrold II moved into a house nearby. They stopped talking to each other and communicated by letter. The sons brought in a solicitor to arbitrate, who discovered that their father had been giving partnership money away. The solicitor gave an opinion that there was an equal partnership and that the sons were owed money by their father. With this, John Jarrold II, now getting on in life and profoundly deaf, retired to a house in the country, and died in 1852.

The third generation
The remaining three sons then continued to manage the business success-fully, opening a London office in 1847, shortly after the railway came to Norwich. The clash with their father had probably helped to bring them together. In particular they were known as publishers of temperance and religious material. Only one of the sons, Samuel, had any surviving children, a son by his first marriage, Samuel John James, and a further two sons by his second wife: William Thomas and Thomas Herbert. Samuel John James was the general salaried manager of the business until he died in 1890.

The fourth generation
In 1888 a new partnership agreement was signed which recognized the transfer of the business to the fourth generation. Samuel John James, his stepmother and aunts and William Thomas were the partners. When Samuel John James died in 1890, the other stepbrother, Thomas Herbert, joined the business as a partner. In 1902, the partnership was incorporated at a valu-ation of £90 000 with William Thomas and Thomas Herbert as Chairman and Vice-Chairman of the company respectively. They both died within a year of each other in 1936 and 1937.

The fifth generation

The transfer to the fifth generation was fairly smooth, as Herbert John Jarrold was the only male heir, being the son of Thomas Herbert. Customs relating to the transfer of property upon death backed up by the legal recognition of those customs made succession much easier, if not fair. He chaired the company from 1937 to 1979 and was the first person in England to develop four-colour separation in printing using photographic techniques. He was an knowledgeable technical printer, but quite difficult to work for in a management role, possessing a dominant personality. John had three sons, all of who went to university and then returned to work in the company. Using a practice that is common in family businesses across the world, John separated the company into three divisions and placed one son in charge of each: printing, the store in Norwich, and publishing. Peter Jarrold was the son put in charge of printing and is the current Executive Chairman. He went to Switzerland to learn about printing. When the general manager in charge of printing left, he took over within months of his arrival, at the age of 24. Prior to the sons coming onto the board it had been supplemented with non-executive directors, but they then left, leaving the three sons and their father on the board. According to Peter Jarrold, 'Board meetings were a farce and we never had any budgets'.

The sixth generation

John Jarrold didn't make any decision on his succession between the three brothers. Despite a severe illness he lived until 1976. Peter Jarrold chaired the meetings during his father's period of illness, and in fact, his father returned as Chairman when he recovered somewhat. When his father died Peter Jarrold comments that it 'just happened' that he became Chairman, proposed by a non-executive director. No vote. No family meeting. The burden of getting the succession right is an onerous one for any family chairman. Some don't bother because of the personal difficulty of choosing between close family in a situation where feelings may well be hurt if the right decision is to be made for the business. There is also the problem of coming to grips with the inevitability that someone else will have to run the company at some stage. Like Peter's father, it is easier to ignore the problem and leave it to be settled after their death. However, this can have dire consequences for the company if those left behind cannot agree. Fortunately in this case the succession 'just happened'. John Jarrold's shares were equally divided between the three sons, each of the families now owning about 18 per cent. A charitable trust owns 14 per cent and the rest are owned by more distant family members.

Peter's approach is different from that of his father. It has to be, because there are two brothers who understandably want to have an influence on the direction of the company and, in particular, on decisions relating to the next round of succession, which will take the company into the seventh generation. Peter has three children and his brothers each have two. Of the seven children, four are working full time in the company and another is on the board of a division. The custom that ensured the transfer of property through male heirs no longer applies. Although that is fairer, it adds to the complexity of planning succession, and is one complexity that the board's predecessors did not have. The board has now involved outside directors far more as a valuable external perspective on the continuous discussion and consultation that has to take place within the family on the structure of the company. There had been some non-executive directors in the past, including a shoemaker, a flour miller and a lawyer. But, since 1979, the company has used non-executive directors in a planned way to supplement family expertise and to ease any family tensions on succession planning. There are three non-executives at present with backgrounds in law, finance and business at board level.

> I use the non-executive directors a lot. One suggested that we should introduce the children onto the board at an early stage in their careers. We have done this, rotating them on the board two at a time, each for 18 months. All the children, seven in all, have now been on the board, learning about the board and giving the members of the board an opportunity to see them working in a board environment. (Peter Jarrold)

The family members are proud to own their shares in the company. Under Peter's chairmanship dividends have increased very substantially under a formula that allocates one-third of post-tax earnings to dividend payments, averaged over five years.

Peter Jarrold now wants to retire. Planning to achieve this has absorbed a lot of his time and energy. There is no obvious family successor yet, although there are family members with plenty of potential when they acquire the necessary experience and skills in the future. The company has been fortunate that the somewhat ad hoc succession arrangements have got it through the sixth generation. Most companies fall at the second or third hurdle. In recognition of this the board established an Appointments, Development and Remuneration Committee in 1998. It comprises the chairman, two non-executive directors and the future CEO.

> This is a very important development as it takes the heat out of appointments and remuneration. It defuses the family tensions that do appear over these topics. (Peter Jarrold)

The approach that the board has now agreed upon is to appoint a chief executive from outside the company to bridge and discipline the transition from the sixth to the seventh generation. An important responsibility will be to develop all senior management including the seventh generation. The family members have accepted this. It should enable a more objective approach to be taken with regard to the performance of all family members. A recruitment company placed an advertisement (see Figure 4.5). Whilst there were over 400 applicants for the position, the company is still searching for the right candidate.

The pressure on the chairman of a family company in this position is not to be underestimated. There is an historical legacy the continuance of which relies on the ability of the chairman to take the company into the next generation successfully. Constant consultation with family members means that there are a wide variety of quite strong opinions. The role of the chairman changes significantly in these companies as the change of generation looms. Once appointed there will be a natural tendency to reduce the influence of the family members who are not on the board with regard to the company's direction, conferring more authority on the board. The board will have a significant non-family balance once the chief executive is appointed. This process of a shift in power has already started to happen with the creation of the Appointments, Development and Remuneration sub-committee of the board. The subcommittee was established to create a more objective forum for consideration of the items within its remit. Once the family has started to move down this path towards giving the board more autonomy it will be difficult to turn back, but it should lead to more objectivity and benefit the family as shareholders, which must be in the best interests of the company in the long run. However, the family presence outside the board must not be ignored. The new chief executive at Jarrold & Sons Ltd will have the potential dilemma of running the company and helping the board to make objective decisions regarding the best interests of the company, whilst satisfying the needs of the family and individual family members to continue their involvement in the company.

Jarrold & Sons Ltd is in the transition phase between Puppet and Partnership. Any chief executive in this position will require an exceptional grasp of the political as well as the business position they occupy. What tools can help family companies and their chief executives to make this transition? Neubauer and Lank, in their study of family companies across the world, placed great emphasis on the need to look at the governance structures that can support company

---

CHIEF EXECUTIVE

c. £150,000 package   **EAST ANGLIA**

With a turnover of approximately £80m, our client is a long established and successful private company run as a mini-conglomerate whose activities include printing, publishing and retailing. Due to the future retirement of the current Executive Chairman, the company now wishes to appoint a Chief Executive Officer to lead the strategic development of the group for the next 7–10 years, further develop the divisional management teams and ultimately facilitate the transition of power to the next generation of family members and professional managers.

The Position
● Develop and deliver the vision, strategy and leadership for the group, working closely with divisional heads.
● Manage and develop new management including the next generation of family members engaged in the business, playing a pivotal role in the succession planning process.
● Quickly develop a high profile with customers and staff.

The Requirements
● Successful management track record as either a CEO or General Manager with enhanced finance and IT skills, ideally with some exposure to a family-controlled company.
● The stature and commercial acumen to quickly become accepted by the current management team
● Maturity and sensitivity, with the ability to initiate new ideas and approaches and develop and implement strategies for as successful long-term future.

SOURCE: Peter Jarrold, Executive Chairman, Jarrold & Sons Ltd

---

Figure 4.5 Advertisement for a chief executive at Jarrold & Sons Ltd

boards in the same position as Jarrold & Sons Ltd. They concluded that family meetings, assemblies or councils,

> are vital in the governance of the family *qua* family, but they can also be critical in establishing governance boundaries vis-à-vis the roles of the board of directors and top management of the family enterprise. These latter governance parameters are often made explicit in family statements.. (Neubauer and Lank: 95)

These governance structures outside the board, assisted by statements of family values, can assist boards in clarifying their role, particularly when the company is exploring the potential relationship between the family shareholders and the board of directors. For example, Figure 4.6 illustrates the types of agreement that could be reached in the sensitive area of personnel policy. The relationship between holding companies and subsidiary companies requires a similar identification of the governance boundaries. This sometimes leads to a written statement by the group of companies that identifies where the subsidiary lies on the PAPA grid. Family companies can do the same to clarify the relationship between the board of directors and the family.

Such governance structures also help to minimize the inevitable conflict that occurs within family businesses and ease the burden on the chairman or CEO. Jarrold & Sons Ltd were fortunate to come through the conflicts of the last six generations, but should remember that the Fairfax dynasty, one of Australia's oldest and wealthiest family businesses, took 147 years to build and only one year to destroy (Neubauer and Lank: 78–80).

Bergman's Values and Policies

In a company like Bergman there is no room for compromises when it comes to who is employed by the company. We should try to attract and retain the best competence available.

The basic principle is that family members will not be discriminated against or favoured in regard to terms and conditions of employment. Working with another firm before joining the Holding/Parent Company or any of its subsidiaries may be an advantage and is recommended.

Likewise, there is no assumption that the posts of Chairman or CEO of the Holding/Parent Company or any other management position are reserved for family members. The rules of entry, staying and exit (competence being foremost) shall be the same for all – family or non-family.

SOURCE: Neubauer and Lank: 93

Jarrold & Sons Ltd – Extract from the Mission Statement

To employ, encourage the involvement of members of the family in the business of the company and ensure that those with the appropriate abilities shall have every encouragement to develop and progress in the management of the company whilst at the same time recognizing the aspirations of other able members of the company.

SOURCE: Peter Jarrold, Executive Chairman, Jarrold & Sons Ltd

Figure 4.6 Family company personnel policies

Case Study 4.2

White Furniture Company

In a superb book, *Closing, The Life and Death of an American Factory*, Bill Bamberger and Cathy Davidson tell the sad story, in words and pictures, of the failure of a family company. The White Furniture Company was a family company in Mebane, North Carolina, making high quality reproduction furniture in an area that is still the centre the US furniture industry. It was known as 'the South's oldest maker of fine furniture' (Bamberger and Davidson: 23), dating from 1881 when it was established by two brothers, Dave and Will White. In 1916 when Dave died in a car accident, Will took over as President until he died in 1935. When J. Sam White, a third brother, took over in 1935, having started as a day labourer in 1896, 'The new leadership made barely a ripple in the company's policies or vision'. (Bamberger and Davidson: 30)

The clock builders had done their job. In 1969 'Mr. Sam's' son Stephen became President and his nephew, Steve Millender became Vice-President. They disagreed over the running of the company and it is this disagreement that led to the hostile takeover in 1985 to a conglomerate, the Hickory Manufacturing Corporation (Bamberger and Davidson: 30). There was a great spirit in the company until 1985 when the company was sold by its divided family shareholders. The hostile takeover won by 54 per cent to 46 per cent of the family shareholder votes:

> the shareholders were Steve White's own children, grandchildren, cousins, nephews, and nieces. They accepted a buyout proposal that mandated Steve's resignation because White's was losing money and they feared for the company's future. Afraid that their inheritance, the White stock, would dwindle to nothing, they voted to sell. (Bamberger and Davidson: 19)

Output grew but quality fell under the new owners. In 1993, following some hard years in the furniture industry, White's was closed, laying off 200 people. Of course the White family might not have been able to rescue the company from the inherent problems of the entire furniture industry, but they didn't have the opportunity to because they couldn't resolve their family conflicts.

> What we do know, definitively, is that preserving the old White Furniture Company in Mebane was not the top priority of Hickory-White Corporation. As part of a conglomerate, White Furniture was expendable. (Bamberger and Davidson: 41)

How conflict is managed in family companies is critical, not just for the family, but for all the other people who are dependent upon the company for their livelihood. Neubauer and Lank's study illustrates that healthy family companies have accepted he following six propositions into their family values:

- Conflict is inevitable within the family and between the family and the business
- Conflict can be healthy or unhealthy
- How the conflict is managed is a determinant of the degree to which the family and the business continues to thrive
- There are various methods of handling conflict including avoidance (ignorance, withdrawal, denial), referral (arbitration, triangulation, fate) and confrontation (face-to-face, problem-solving, dialogue). The option chosen will vary according to the circumstances, but the more that you move to confronting the conflict the greater likelihood of effective long-term resolution
- Establishing the 'rules of the game' can prevent conflict as this sets the goals against which the proposed method of resolving the conflict can be assessed
- One of the goals should be to maximize the 'win–win' prospects of all the parties concerned, arriving at the best decision given the family's and the company's mission, goals and objectives (Neubauer and Lank: 74).

The three-circle model in Figure 4.1 is a useful tool for understanding the different sources of conflict within a family company. The model was used by Krister Ahlstrom of the Ahlstrom Corporation when there was opposition from some family members to the selling of a paper-mill to which there was a long emotional attachment (Magretta). It required a person who was separated from the emotional attachment with understanding of the business needs to implement the change, but the successful implementation also required an understanding of the positions occupied by other members of the family. Failure to understand these different perspectives, held by family members who occupy various positions in the three circles, can lead to the closure of the company as happened with the White Furniture Company.

Of course the main item of any specification for a senior appointment to the family board could be that the appointed person is a member of the family. If this is the desire of the owners of the family company, then it is a legitimate part of the specification. The specification can contain anything. However, 'Selecting a new CEO should be an exercise in strategic human-resources planning, not in family dynamics' (Miller: 34).

A similar approach to the one taken in Jarrold & Sons Ltd has been taken in IKEA, the global furniture chain, originating in Sweden and now based in Denmark because of the crippling tax rates in Sweden. Ingvar Kamprad, who founded the company, selected a non-family member, Anders Moberg, to succeed him in 1986. His three sons were too young. There was one condition that Moberg laid down when he took the job: 'He [Kamprad] can go anywhere in the company, speak to anyone, say anything, but he has to tell me what he is doing. And he is very good. He has always respected that' (*Sunday Times*: 1998).

One of the sons may take over, but according to Moberg the most important thing is to find the best successor for the company.

5 & 6. Plan your search

This could be internal to the company and external. There are professional recruitment consultants in this field who will take you through the above process and start to search. You may know someone who fits the specification, but is he or she the best person?

7. Get to know the candidate

Establish if they will fit into the team that you have. This will take time. One of the most common reasons for dissatisfaction with non-executive directors in small companies is that they do not 'fit' and the family or entrepreneur find it hard to develop any sort of relationship. The matching process is important and takes time. This applies to all companies and all director appointments including non-executive appointments. Ivan Seidenberg, Chairman and Chief Executive Officer of the NYNEX Corporation, explained how his board went about finding three directors:

> The board wanted to broaden the skills and perspectives of the entire board. We needed people with international experience and consumer marketing experience. We identified those skills first and didn't settle for anybody who didn't meet those parameters. Also, we wanted to improve significantly the diversity on the board, which we did ... One of the new directors is Richard Carrion, the chairman and CEO of Banco Popular, the largest bank in Puerto Rico. He was not known to anyone on the board. I talked to the head of the nominating committee, and we decided he would be a very good catch.

Since neither of us knew him, we spent over 12 months cultivating a relationship before we made a recommendation to the full board ... But here is the point; it takes time to cultivate good directors. I learned that. You can always take the recommendations of your current directors, and you probably can't go wrong, but if you want to get some fresh opportunities, you've got to work at it. So, in our case, we did both. (*Directorship*, 1996)

8. Board discussion on candidates

The full board should be involved in the decision whether or not the appointment should be made. The individual is about to become a part of the board team and the board must agree to this. It would be very difficult for an individual to sit on the board in the knowledge that nearly all the members did not have a voice in the appointment. Ultimately the shareholders will have the final say as to whether any temporary appointments of directors become permanent at the next AGM. In family or entrepreneur companies where the shareholders are likely to sit on the board, they should still seek the views of the non-shareholder members of the board if there are any.

9. Discuss terms

Salary will be important and should include a performance-related element and possible share options. Share options may be hard for a family company to embrace as it dilutes their ownership. However, it helps to give the outside director some of the same motives for decision-taking that the family may want the director to have. There are other terms to consider that may relate to the individual's family circumstances. Housing and schools are important matters when moving, as is the availability of someone to help the new director and family to settle into the new community. One of the key terms is the length of service contract. The current corporate governance thinking on length of service contracts suggests that they should be kept short. The Greenbury Report recommended contracts with notice periods of one year or less, although recognizing that in some cases two years may be acceptable (Greenbury: Code, D2). The Hampel Committee agreed with this (Hampel: 4.9). This is one instance where the objectives of corporate governance lead to a totally different conclusion depending upon the type of company and the location of the company on the PAPA grid. Any director of an entrepreneur or family company emerging from the Adrift or Puppet cells may need to confront a dominant family or individual presence with some harsh commercial realities. This could require a firm approach to ensure that a dominant family managing director acts in the best interests of the company and not for any personal motivation. Those appointing the director will want to give that individual some protection. Of course, the appointed outside directors may tread on the toes of the family director(s) even if they only have a short notice period, but it is easier to operate in these positions with a long service contract behind you. If the new appointment upsets the family, or the entrepreneur in an entrepreneur company, they will have to pay for the privilege of getting rid of the director and staying in the Puppet or Adrift cells.

The provision of a financial incentive to assist the independence of the new director is not the only reason for opting for longer notice periods in these circumstances. It also forces the board and the family to take the appointment seriously. It should not be an appointment that can be seen to be unravelled very quickly. The cost implications of the long notice period will focus the collective energy on ensuring that the process is a rigorous one and that the right person is found for the company at this stage in its development.

10. Appoint

The board normally has the power to make temporary appointments as long as any maximum number of directors stated in the constitution is not exceeded. Such a director only holds office until the next AGM where the shareholders decide whether to reappoint the individual. Otherwise, it is the shareholders who elect directors by a simple majority. Once the appointment process has been completed, you will need to plan when it will need to be started again, but on this occasion allow more time.

The failure to plan succession is one of the most frequent causes of the demise of family companies. In Germany, by the year 2000, some 300 000 family-owned *Mittelstand* companies, over 10 per cent of all German companies, will have been through succession. From a study in 1994 of 7700 companies with a turnover of more than DM15 million by the Institut für Mittelstands it is estimated that the likely outcome for these companies is that:

- 45 per cent are likely to be continued by family members
- 25 per cent are likely to be taken on by managers from within the company
- 18 per cent are likely to be continued by managers appointed from outside

- 12 per cent are likely to be sold or broken up. (*The Economist*: 1995a)

Some family companies have tried to pre-empt the problem of succession in different ways. In September 1995 E. Merck, a German family-owned pharmaceuticals company, made an initial public offering of shares worth DM2 billion. This will not be the last of such share offerings by family companies in Germany as this is one option available when succession issues are considered. E. Merck is only selling 25 per cent of its capital at present and family members will remain in control. Some of the *Mittelstands* are merging, like Hella, a car headlamp manufacturer, and Behr, a producer of radiators.

In some cultures there is a 'rule' that families have to follow. For example, in the Asian culture the division of family assets equally amongst male children on the father's death often means that the company is split up amongst those children, who are each given a portion of the business to operate. This leads to the phenomenon of the Chinese Family Business with many small businesses trading between each other, but rarely attaining growth greater than is needed to maintain the expanding family. Because there is a reluctance to delegate beyond the family, the ability to grow is restrained:

> [The] emphasis on the moral superiority of the leader in Chinese society means that authority cannot be easily delegated or shared since this would suggest a reduction in moral worth. It also encourages considerable distance between the owner and all employees, including managers ... This leads to strong reliance on family members and close personal friends for senior positions. Thus the dominant coalitions of Chinese firms are usually made up of close kin, and economic issues become fused with family ones ... . (Whitley: 62–3)

In some family companies the founder has made it clear to all the family and the professional managers that the best person will be found to lead the company. Italy's Merloni Elettrodomestici produces white goods under the brands of Ariston and Indesit. It is owned by the Merloni family, and is approaching the transfer from second generation to third generation. Business tutors for the four children, who are the likely successors and a succession committee, are part of the process put in place to ensure a smooth transition. Assurances have been given to the professional managers that the children will not get the top jobs unless they deserve them (*The Economist*, 1996a).

In other family companies the family decides to take a back seat and leave the company to be run by professional managers. In particular this will happen the older the family company is and where there is pressure from other investors. For example, there are family companies like Ford and Sainsbury's, which have managed to overcome the problems of succession and make the transition to becoming public yet the family retain a large shareholding and associated influence. Sainsbury's, the UK listed supermarket chain has just appointed the first non-family managing director. At Ford, Billy Clay, is now the chairman of the world's second-largest car manufacturer, the family still owning 40 per cent of the voting rights in the company 40 years after it went public. We saw in the Jarrold & Sons Ltd case study that the desire to have a family chairman and non-family CEO was going to lead to an interesting relationship between the two individuals. The arrangement at the Ford Motor Company will be the same. It may be one example where it would be better to combine the functions of CEO and chairman as previously happened at Ford when Alex Trotman held the joint position.

The Agnelli family have a complex web of shareholdings in Fiat that enable them to maintain control over the company, although the chairman is now no longer a family member and the family is less involved in the management of the company which is 100 years old in 1999.

Anita Roddick and her husband decided in 1998 to appoint an external managing director to run Body Shop. In part this was an appreciation that the company needs to move into a different stage of development to improve performance. A professional manager from Danone, the French food conglomerate, has been appointed. The company is starting to move from a Puppet relationship to a Partnership relationship in recognition of the need to alter its corporate strategy. It is a business decision.

If you are in a succession situation, or approaching one, you are clearly not alone. There is no one solution. The circumstances surrounding the family, the development of the company, the family's aspirations, the presence of good non-family managers, are just some of the variables that will influence the path that the family company takes. However, although there are different ways of ensuring that the family company does survive, they are all based on the principle that the company plans where its structure is heading. For most family companies approaching or beyond the third generation, this will usually involve moving towards the principles that are to be found in the Partnership cell of the PAPA grid. How the family company gets there is a matter of time and persistence. It will challenge the family's ability to create a secure way for the company to continue. The first step is the development of a professional board of directors who understand the distinction between direction and management. If the board of directors is operating effectively it becomes a powerful tool to resolve the succession issue.

Family Values

If the family has values which are transferred into corporate values, the likelihood of survival as an independent company is greater. Not only do the values act as a source that can be used to mitigate any conflict, they also provide a powerful statement against which proposals for take-over or sale can be judged. The next case study is a good example of this. The first generation family company established by Tom and Kate Chappell, Tom's of Maine, could have been sold to the major personal care product companies and made them extremely wealthy. They haven't sold because they were concerned that the bidding companies would not continue to uphold their corporate values. This has given them the difficulty of planning how the business can continue without them.

Case Study 4.3

Tom's of Maine

Tom and Kate Chappell moved to rural Kennebunk in Maine as part of their goal to 'move back to the land'. They couldn't find personal care products made from natural products so they decided to set up a company to manufacture their own. The company was founded in 1970 and in 1998 had 80 employees, a turnover of $27 million and 45 products, all made from natural ingredients. The products include toothpaste for adults and children, soap, deodorant, anti-perspirant, mouthwash and shampoo. The company is the leading producer of natural personal care products in the US. The company's products are available in over 30 000 shops in the US and there is a big export drive taking place at present, with exports to Canada, Israel, Japan and the UK. Each year 10 per cent of pre-tax profits are donated to non-profit organizations and the company encourages employees to spend 5 per cent of their paid time volunteering in the community, 'the 5 per cent solution'. Tom's of Maine is a business. The values are a key part of the relationship that the company builds with customers. It is the values that are put on the table in front of the customer as well as the products. Tom and Kate know that their beliefs have kept the company on track and are determined that they will do so when it comes to deciding the future management of the company. The staff and customers watch Tom, Kate and the company closely to see if the values will ever be compromised. This has meant long battles to obtain regulatory and professional approval for products without animal testing. It has involved constant searching for the natural product that will enable the company to produce a new line, 'press on until you find a solution that is consistent with your values' (Tom Chappell). Tom and Kate could have sold out to one of the large personal care manufacturers. There have been offers. But, they realize that in a large organization the values of the company would probably be compromised at some stage. Also, there would be no guarantee that the current manufacturing base and workforce would be maintained. So Tom has been searching for a new CEO who shares their beliefs. Their personal values are the company's values at present because they own, direct and manage the company. As Tom and Kate start to separate those functions they need a CEO who will continue the application of those values, really turning them into corporate values that will endure. They have found the right person from Procter & Gamble. Tom told me the story about the handing over ceremony to the new CEO in front of the staff. Tom walked into the hall with a ball and handed it to the new CEO and Tom wouldn't let go. He came in again, handed over the ball, and the new CEO took off and then returned to inform Tom that they were now in the automobile business. On the third attempt, Tom gave the ball to the new CEO who said that he would check back regularly with the board and Tom. Tom's of Maine now has a new CEO who Tom and Kate can trust to uphold the values, yet is accountable to Tom and Kate, the main shareholders, and the board. This has enabled Tom to let go and perform a different chairman function within the company. As Tom himself stated, there is now a partnership in the management of the company, which gives him confidence that the company and its values will endure. He argues that the partnership principle has enabled them to unpack the three dimensions of Owner, Director and Manager so as to enable the company to develop without the constraint of their natural frailty. Tom and Kate have gathered together an impressive range of relevant expert help which comprises the board of directors of the company. There are fourteen members of the board:

- Tom and Kate Chappell
- 3 executive directors
- A professor of management
- A retired Senior Vice-President of Booz-Allen & Hamilton
- A human resources consultant
- 2 attorneys, one with special interests in land trusts (the company has developed 500 acres of farmland for herbs)

- A professor of clinical ethics
- A professor of periodontics (dentistry)
- The Vice-President of PepsiCo who is also on the boards of the National Association of Chain Drug Stores and the National Association of Convenience Stores
- A partner in a banking and investment company

There is a passionate desire to see the company's values continue as well as the business and associated employment in the small own of Kennebunk, Maine. The company's 'statement of beliefs' and 'reason for being' are reproduced in Figure 4.7.

SOURCE: Tom Chappell, President, Tom's of Maine

REASON FOR BEING

The purpose of Tom's of Maine is:

To serve our customers' health needs with imaginative science from plants and minerals;

To inspire all those we serve with a mission of responsibility and goodness;

To empower others by sharing our knowledge, time, talents, and profits, and,

To help create a better world by exchanging with others our faith, experience, and hope.
(Revised October 22nd 1997)

Statement of beliefs

WE BELIEVE that both human beings and nature have inherent worth and deserve our respect.

WE BELIEVE in products that are safe, effective, and made of natural ingredients.

WE BELIEVE that our company and our products are unique and worthwhile, and that we can sustain these genuine qualities with an ongoing commitment to innovation and creativity.

WE BELIEVE that we have a responsibility to cultivate the best relationships possible with our co-workers, owners, agents, suppliers, and our community.

WE BELIEVE that different people bring different gifts and perspectives to the team and that a strong team is founded on a variety of gifts.

WE BELIEVE in providing employees with a safe and fulfilling work environment and an opportunity to grow and learn.

WE BELIEVE that competence is an essential means of sustaining our values in a competitive marketplace.

WE BELIEVE our company can be financially successful while behaving in a socially responsible and environmentally sensitive manner.

Figure 4.7 Tom's of Maine – Reason for Being and Statement of Beliefs

No doubt many companies would argue that they uphold similar types of values to those promoted by Tom's of Maine. In a family company, the benefits of reaching agreement and writing them down are in the process as well as the content. Once they are agreed and in writing the values become a powerful vehicle for avoiding and resolving conflict. They help the family in their decision whether or not to sell to a bidder. The board of directors, whether family members or not, are clear about the context of the decisions that they take. The board can be given substantial freedom to operate within those broad parameters.

Communication

The chairman of most family companies will be a family member. Often the role of chairman and CEO will be combined. In a listed company, the chairman would be a key person in maintaining the relationship with institutional shareholders. The company would put significant resources into ensuring that the information that is provided to the shareholders is conveying the right message in a timely manner. There should be no shocks or surprises, subject to the laws governing the conveyance of insider information that could be price sensitive. Those laws do not apply to unlisted companies. If communication with the main shareholders is seen as being important in listed companies, then it is critical in family companies. It is another method of reducing conflict. This places a considerable burden on the board, and particularly the chairman, to keep the family aware of developments. But, it is part of their function and the function of the board as a whole. It will assist in the smooth running and succession of the business. Various governance structures through which the communication can take place have already been identified (see Neubauer and Lank for more detail). In Tom's of Maine, the communication goes deeper. The company stops production for a whole day to discuss the corporate vision and strategy of the company. This creates enormous motivation for the staff and the company is a small enough unit to achieve this.

Quasi-Partnerships

Quasi-partnership companies are similar to family companies. They exist where entrepreneurs or individuals combine to operate a business venture. They are not members of the same family, but share many of the characteristics of a family company. The potential for disagreement between non-family partners, and their families, trading through the corporate form is just as great. The following case study of Sterling Asset Management Ltd is an interesting example of what can happen when there is such a disagreement and the board is not structured to cope with internal conflict.

Case Study 4.4

Sterling Asset Management Ltd

Mr Wilton-Davies and Mr Kirk were partners in a financial consultant and investment business from 1988. The partnership acquired a company, which they called Sterling Asset Management Ltd. The company had four equal shareholders:

- Mr Wilton-Davies, an executive director
- Mr Kirk, an executive director
- Mr Wilton-Davies's mother, who invested £50 000, a non-executive director
- Mr Vink, who invested £50 000, a non-executive director.

There was therefore equality of shareholding between Mr Wilton Davies and his mother and Messrs Kirk and Vink. The shareholders and the board had created a deadlock structure, which reinforced the Partnership nature of the company. Mr Wilton-Davies and Mr Kirk fell out in 1995. Mr Kirk carried on managing the company with the support of Mr Vink. Mr Wilton-Davies was excluded from the management of the company, although there was an ongoing dispute as to the validity of the board resolution that removed him as a director. The company had now moved towards the Autonomous cell of the PAPA grid. One of the key shareholders was now being excluded from any say in the company's affairs. Mr Wilton-Davies had legitimate grounds for believing that the finances of the company were not being operated properly. A new bank account had been established with a different mandate and he discovered that payments had been made out of this new account to individuals he did not recognize and to Mr Kirk. Both sides in the dispute wanted to buy the other out, but they could not agree who would be the buyer. A legal action had been commenced by Mr Kirk which would probably lead to a resolution as to which of the two would be the purchaser. In the meantime Mr Kirk was concerned that the assets of the company were at risk. The court therefore ordered that a receiver should be appointed to preserve the company's assets until it was decided which of the two parties would be the ultimate purchaser of the other's shares. This clearly placed the company into the Adrift category, as the receiver would take over all the powers of the board. When the court decides which of the two should be the purchaser of the other's shares the company will become an entrepreneur company and probably move into the Puppet cell as the board is unlikely to operate as a proper board. The cycle of movement of the company is tracked in Figure 4.8. Could this have been avoided? Creating a partnership culture within a corporate framework is very difficult. But, in a quasi-partnership company such as this one, the consequences of moving outside of the Partnership cell are severe. The aggrieved shareholder can petition the courts claiming that their legitimate expectation to have a continuing role in the management of the company has been denied. The most likely outcome will be an order requiring one side to buy the other out of the company.

This case study emphasizes the critical importance of adopting a professional approach to the structure and function of the board. In this case the non-executive directors were too close to the parties concerned to assist them in ensuring that their personal disagreement did not prejudice the effective running of the board and the company. Ultimately everyone will suffer as the company is now in an Adrift

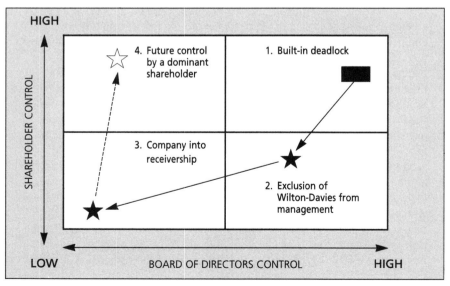

Figure 4.8 Plotting Sterling Asset Management Ltd on the PAPA grid

stage until the courts agree the share purchase. For quasi-partnership companies to survive they must stay in the Partnership cell. If they do not there is always a great risk that one of the shareholders can argue that they have been excluded from a say in the management of the company. This is conduct that is unfairly prejudicial to their interests and therefore a legitimate ground for petitioning the courts for remedial action.

Guiding Principles for Family Companies

The guiding principles for family companies are clear:

- Involve the family in the creation of a clear direction for the organizational structure for the business, including succession: plan for human mortality and corporate immortality.
- Create a set of family values that can become enduring values of the company, shared by all who work for the company
- Communicate throughout the family the successes and failures of the business, the strategic thoughts of the board ... just keep in regular contact and see it as part of the function of the board to do so.

5 *Board Architecture and Listed Companies*

All listed companies will have subsidiaries, but not all subsidiary companies have a listed company as their holding company. The relationship that the listed holding company has with its shareholders will affect the relationship that the holding company can have with its subsidiaries.

Case Study 5.1

Maxwell Communication Corporation

Robert Maxwell's empire was founded on two listed companies, Maxwell Communication Corporation (MCC) and Mirror Group Newspapers (MGN). Maxwell's family together with the Maxwell Foundation of Leichtenstein owned 51 per cent of MGN and 68 per cent of MCC. This market share, plus a considerable personal presence, meant that the boards of the listed companies were puppets in the extreme. They failed to spot or stop the movement of funds between the companies, Coopers and Lybrand Deloitte producing a report in November 1991 showing that a estimated £763 million had been taken from the two listed companies and transferred to the Maxwell private companies.

Maxwell had such command over the running of the company that he pledged MCC's entire stake in Berlitz language schools (£25m) to the banks without anyone knowing. At MGN, Maxwell had similar power. When Laurence Guest, the Finance Director, discovered that the private companies had appropriated £50m of MGN's funds, Maxwell demoted him. Then he bugged his office ... Maxwell's non-executive directors certainly conferred respectability on his public companies. Maxwell appointed many prominent

---

non-executive directors. Two former law officers (Lord Silkin and Lord Havers) accepted invitations to sit on the boards of Maxwell companies in their retirement. Sir Robert Clark, former chairman of Hill Samuel, and Lord Rippon, a Tory politician turned businessman, were also non-executives on Maxwell boards. But they were powerless to stop him. When the non-executives of MCC were told three months before his death that Robert Maxwell had transferred £275m in cash from the public company to his private interests, they failed to tell the shareholders ... The treasury departments of the many companies had to report directly to Robert Maxwell and no one else. (Stiles and Taylor: 42,38)

Even if you could untangle the labyrinthine structures that supported the subsidiary companies, you would be unlikely to discover subsidiaries that exhibited anything other than total obedience to Robert Maxwell. The subsidiary companies were Puppets to such an extent that one of the directors whom I met was not even allowed access to the company's constitutional documents when he asked Head Office, even though they are publicly available.

The Maxwell saga is a graphic illustration of how the relationship between the holding company board and its shareholders can be a determining factor with regard to the relationship that exists between the holding company and its subsidiaries. The holding company was a Puppet and so were the subsidiary companies. The coincidence of relationships in groups of companies is not always present (see Case Study 5.2 in Chapter 5).

The top 350 companies listed on the London Stock Exchange represent 95 per cent of the value of the market. Even within the small number of about 2450 UK listed companies there is a considerable divergence in their ownership structure and therefore the pressures that are exerted upon the board of directors. The distinction between listed companies that fall within that top group and those that do not is considerable. Only those in the top 350 will really feel the pressure of the daily intervention of the institutional shareholder bearing down upon them. According to John Rogers, Director of Investment Services at the National Association of Pension Funds,

If you think in terms of risk and reward, the efforts of most [Fund] managers are going to be concentrated on large cap companies because these are going to be the majority of their portfolios. (*Financial Times* 21 May 1998).

This pressure has increased over the past decade with the frequency of communications between companies and their investors sharply increasing during the end of the 1980s. The number of contacts with investors tripled between 1986 and 1990 (Useem: 134). The reasons for this are:

- Increased awareness of the relationship between the market capitalization of a company and projected **future** cash flows of the company, part of the underlying focus on the enhancement of shareholder value. This requires companies to convince investors of the long-term prospects of the company in order that decisions to sell stock are not made by reference to any short-term dips in corporate performance. Items such as research and development and intellectual capital simply do not appear in any standard historical financial reports. These items will affect future cash flows and shareholder value.
- senior officers of the company having large parts of their remuneration tied up in share options
- the growth of investor power and greater sophistication from institutional shareholders in their investment approach.

Useem concludes that:

> The alignment of company organization with shareholder interests, in response to anticipation of shareholder pressures, had brought a range of changes to the higher circles of management. Whether acceptingly or grudgingly, management could no longer ignore the amassing of investor power. (Useem: 155)

However, prior to this, and still for the majority of listed companies,

> shareholder supremacy has hardly been a conspicuous feature of the British corporate scene in much of the post-war period. Managers have enjoyed a measure of discretion to pursue their own objectives without the need to consider seriously the interests of shareholders. (Dimsdale: 13)

This chapter looks at the development of listed companies as they have come under pressure from two separate but related sources:

1. The world-wide corporate governance movement that has mobilized attempts to fill the vacuum of accountability between the owners of companies, the shareholders, and the board of directors.

This has largely been achieved through attempts to generate structural alterations to the board and reporting arrangements that affect the relationship between the executive and non-executive directors.
2. The developing theme of shareholder value as one of the catalysts that is driving listed companies towards the Partnership cell.

The Maxwell empire became Adrift when Robert Maxwell fell off his boat. Many companies will spend a brief period Adrift, the main causes being:

- rumour of take-over
- actual take-over
- death or illness of the key person in a Puppet company
- slow and badly planned corporate restructuring
- an overwhelming central bureaucracy.

The underlying symptoms of an Adrift listed company are: a weak board of directors, unwilling and unable to take a 'hard look' at management opinions; and a wide shareholding base. Companies only spend a brief time Adrift because they either die, get taken over or escape to Partnership or Autonomous. The company that may spend longer Adrift is the one with an overwhelming central bureaucracy. These are a dying breed. In these companies, there are a few executives at board level and individuals below board level (Galbraith's 'technocrats') who really control the company. The board has no real power. The shareholders have no power. Decisions take a long time. The power base of the individuals who do have control is protected at all costs and hard to dismantle without a fundamental reorganization of which they will attempt to take control. Some centralized industrial conglomerates would recognize this description. Most of them know that they have no future and:

- are changing to gain a focus spurred on by a falling share price and often a new CEO – Hoechst introduced its restructuring and hiving off plans in July 1997
- being taken over – Waste Management, Inc. (WMX) the world's largest rubbish haulier, taken over by USA Waste Services in March 1998
- are declining as their mountain of debt unsupported by free cash flow catches up on them and their countries – the *chaebol* of South Korea.

There are exceptions, particularly in Latin America where the market and political conditions may still favour the conglomerate approach at the moment. The Luksic Group, a Chilean conglomerate, and Globo, a media group in Brazil, are some examples of conglomerates that are performing better than most companies (*The Economist*: 1998h). Most companies will move on from the Adrift stage at some stage in their development, prompted by a combination of a decline in share price and a new CEO.

When the holding company is Adrift, their subsidiaries may well be Autonomous.

Case Study 5.2

Multinational plc (Anon.)

The sector that this group is operating in is fairly slow moving and so is the holding company. The Divisional Director who sits on the main board attends subsidiary board meetings sometimes. He is really only interested in the power struggle that has been going on at Head Office for a few years. It's very political and very frustrating for the CEO of the subsidiary. The holding company has promised more synergy between the different parts of the group, but there is no sign of it. However, there are now some signs of panic. The share price has plunged and investors are calling for the resignation of the CEO. The investors' influence is not likely to reduce until better performance from the company becomes evident. If the CEO is dismissed the pressure for increased performance bearing down on the new CEO could well lead to an attempt to claw back all power to the holding company. It is also anticipated within the subsidiary company that the group synergies, if they exist, will need to be realized quickly. The most likely scenario therefore is that the subsidiary will move into the Puppet cell until a new CEO provides evidence of better performance to the shareholders. If and when this happens, there will be an opportunity for the holding company to develop a Partnership relationship with its shareholders including the adoption of shareholder value as a guiding strategic objective. Alternatively, it could slip back into old habits until the next crisis ... which could well be precipitated by a takeover bid. If the synergies within the different companies within the group do not exist or the subsidiary is seen as not being part of the focus of the newly aligned group, the subsidiary will be sold. The PAPA grid illustrating the holding company position, the options for movement and their impact on the subsidiary company are illustrated in Figures 5.1a and b.

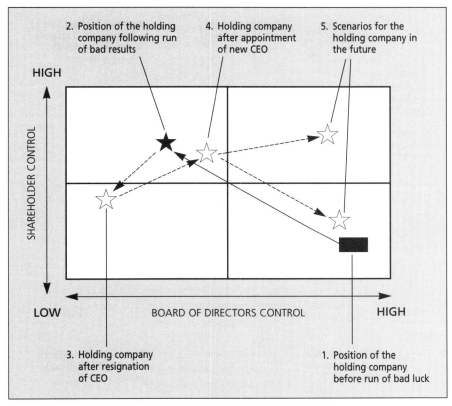

Figure 5.1a   Multinational plc scenarios on the PAPA grid – the holding
company

Autonomous to Partnership: the Driving Force of Shareholder Value

Most listed companies would place themselves in an Autonomous
relationship with their shareholders if they were truthful. The holding
company of Multinational plc would have done so a year ago. It is the
declining share price of Multinational plc that has alerted the
institutional shareholders to place considerable pressure on the
company's senior management. Multinational knows that it now has
to take some drastic action to survive. Ever since the divorce of ownership from control in listed companies was highlighted by Berle and
Means in 1932, there has been a continuous debate concerning the
interests that are relevant for the board of directors to consider when

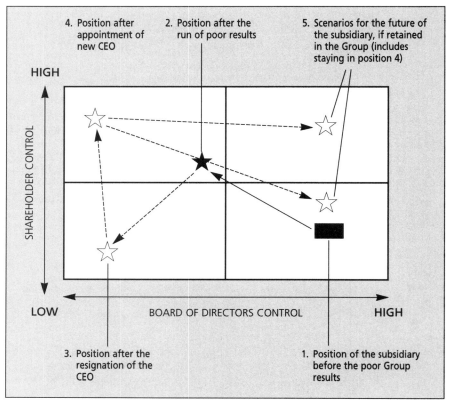

Figure 5.1b Multinational plc scenarios on the PAPA grid – the effect of the
holding company's changing relationship with its shareholders
on the subsidiary company's relationship with the holding
company

making decisions. The 'stakeholder' approach requires directors to
consider a wide range of interests, from employees through to the local
community. This could allow boards substantial freedom to justify their
decisions by reference to whatever stakeholder interest is the most
appropriate. In practice, a wide range of factors will influence decisions
at different stages in the decision process. There is never total
autonomy. The pressures exerted by shareholders start to bite as the
company share price or dividends fall. The shareholder pressures even
gnaw away if the company does not produce over and above the
expected rate of return on capital employed. It is therefore not
surprising that the research shows a greater willingness, indeed desire,
for companies to woo their institutional shareholders (Useem). The

numbers matter in such conversations, leading to an enhanced role for the financial directors of listed companies. However, few companies have developed an approach that enables them to provide an accurate projection of the real value that they are earning for the shareholders. Without these figures the discussions between companies and their institutional shareholders are partly based on conjecture or figures that do not represent the real value that is being added for the shareholder. This has led to a trend in listed companies across the world of looking at a management approach linked to 'shareholder value'.

It is hard to find an Annual Report of a listed company that does not proclaim as the board's objective the desire to enhance shareholder value. It is rarer to find an Annual Report that provides evidence to support this assertion. In order to satisfy the market, evidence will be needed – and quickly, as we see in Case Study 5.3.

Case Study 5.3

BTR plc (now merged with Siebe as BTR Siebe)

BTR's Annual Report for 1996 stated that: 'The Board is responsible for adopting and implementing a strategy for the Group that is designed to deliver increasing value to shareholders.'

The strategy for this sprawling industrial manufacturing and engineering conglomerate did match the stated objective on shareholder value. It was focusing resources within BTR in those areas that had the greatest potential for growth in value and divesting those that were a drag on performance against that shareholder value objective. The company had also abandoned its former policy of recruiting all directors from within BTR and had appointed independent non-executive directors to supply a wider perspective. The new board with a new CEO, Ian Strachan, appointed in April 1995, was driving all this. After three decades of Sir Owen Green's driving force, the board structure was changing to take the company into a new stage of development towards the Partnership cell and away from Autonomy. I was editing this case study in November 1998. The original text asserted that the figures that support the BTR transition to a shareholder value culture would need to come quickly as their shares were at a 14-year low. Three years is a long time for the market to leave a chief executive to prove the strategy is working. It was too long, and BTR's effective takeover by Siebe was announced in November 1998 in an £8.5 billion 'merger' approved by BTR shareholders in January 1999. Ian Strachan will take the new position of 'Executive Deputy Vice-Chairman' in the new company.

Case Study 5.4

The Phillip Morris Companies Inc.

In its Annual Report for 1997, the company was pleased to report that:

'in 1997 we continued to achieve our twin goals: to increase earnings by growing our businesses and to increase shareholder value'.

Phillip Morris is the world's largest manufacturer and marketer of consumer packaged goods, comprising the largest tobacco company, the second largest food company and the third largest brewing company. However, as a shareholder reading this Report, where is the hard evidence that shareholder value has been enhanced? Maybe it has. Earnings per share have increased, but that does not necessarily mean that shareholder value has been added.

Case Study 5.5

Mayr-Melnhof Karton AG

Mayr-Melnhof Karton AG is the European market leader in packaging and recycling of waste paper. Its 1997 Annual Report states that,

'The Mayr-Melnhof Group's strategy is centred around the concept of Shareholder Value. Our goal is to achieve increase in the value of your company.'

In order to achieve this increase in shareholder value the company adheres to the following principles:

● Focus on core business areas
● Be a market leader in the areas it operates – in order to achieve this:

'Each division pursues this objective as an independent organizational unit with separate responsibility for its results'

● Expand in growth markets
● Profit orientation – enhanced through controlling the entire value-added chain, intensive benchmarking or internal markets, economies of scale as a result of the size of the Group, and:

'Great importance is attached to return on equity and return on capital employed as strategic parameters for the individual divisions, ensuring optimal use of the capital'

- Our shareholders –

    'Up-to-the-minute reporting and ongoing communication ensure that the development of the Group is as transparent as possible. The MM-Website provides information using the latest technological standards. The financial community is kept informed by means of regular road shows, and presentations to international investors and analysts, as well as events for private investors.'

- Staff –

    'The continual development of one's knowledge and an ongoing willingness to improve create opportunities for both company and staff in the future'.

This is a clear and unambiguous statement to shareholders on the strategy supporting the enhancement of shareholder value and is supported by figures that relate to and prove the enhancement of shareholder value.

As Clarke and Clegg have pointed out, the focus on shareholder value, illustrated by the German company Mayr-Melnhof Karton, sits uneasily with German corporate traditions that have emphasized, with legal backing, the obligation of companies to contribute to the social well-being of the community (Clarke and Clegg: 350). This has facilitated the Autonomy of many German companies. The need to move towards more of a Partnership relationship with shareholders, evidenced by refocusing performance measures onto shareholder value, is prompted by the move into the international capital markets and the greater visibility that this brings.

The emphasis on shareholder value is pushing companies towards the Partnership cell of the PAPA grid. The attributes of listed companies occupying this cell are well illustrated by the Mayr-Melnhof case study and are summarized in Figure 5.2. They are:

- A clear and shared vision which leads to the objective of enhancing shareholder value
- Delegation of responsibility to divisions, subsidiaries and individuals who share the vision and the objective – the subsidiaries or divisions will need to see themselves as also sharing a Partnership relationship with the holding company. If the subsidiaries have been enjoying a period of autonomy, they are likely to interpret any move towards mandatory information systems and a shared vision as a move in the

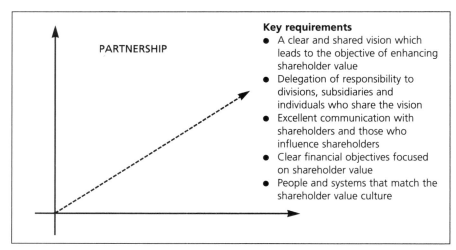

Figure 5.2 Resolving the dilemma of shareholder control and freedom for the board of directors in a listed company

Puppet direction. They may attempt to resist, rubbish, sabotage and destroy it. They need to be reassured and, if this fails, stamped upon.
- Excellent communication with shareholders and those who influence shareholders
- Clear financial objectives focused on shareholder value
- People and systems that fit the shareholder value culture

Why Manage for Shareholder Value?

Rappaport published his book *Creating Shareholder Value* in 1986, identifying that the focus on earnings as a measure of performance failed to capture the real changes in the economic value of a company for three reasons:

1. Accounting methods vary in their application and calculation of 'profit', leading to the classic quotation which can always be used when a chief executive informs you how profitable their company is:

   'Remember, cash is a fact, profit is an opinion.' (Rappaport: 14)

2. Investment requirements are excluded from the calculation of earnings. This is the fundamental difference between an earnings measurement and a cash flow measurement of performance. The cost of equity and

debt is included in the cash flow measurement. For example, the area of high revenue and profit growth in a company may be in the commercial and consumer divisions. Yet when the costs of capital used in that division is inserted into the equation and the returns are compared to the average cost of capital for that sector, other divisions may be seen to be adding greater value, although their revenue and profit growth is less

3. The time value of money is ignored when earnings are the focus of measurement:

'Shareholder value will increase only if the company earns at a rate of return on new investment greater than the rate investors can expect to earn by investing in alternative, equally risky, securities'. (Rappaport: 18)

Rappaport developed a model called 'Shareholder Value Added' (SVA) which included illustrations showing how companies could measure corporate value added, the disaggregation of the enhanced value within different sectors of the company, the benefits of returning capital to shareholders, and the added value of potential mergers and acquisitions. Aided by the promotion of the concept by consultants Stern Stewart & Co. of New York under the banner of 'Economic Value Added' (EVA) and 'Market Value Added' (MVA), companies such as Coca-Cola, CSX, Briggs and Stratton, Quaker Oats, AT & T, Wal-Mart, IBM and TSB embraced the methodology. The PA Consulting Group has a wider model that they use to help companies, 'Managing for Shareholder Value' (MSV). In late 1996 the PA Consulting Group conducted a survey of Chairmen, Chief Executives and Finance Directors of the FTSE 500 and ISEQ Top 40, asking for their opinions. Of the 132 responses, 96 per cent agreed or strongly agreed that the key objective of senior management is to manage for shareholder value (PA: 4). However, there is a gap between those respondents who agree in the principles that support an MSV approach and implementation of those principles. The statements in the Annual Reports are not supported by the application of the principles that underpin the implementation of a commitment to shareholder value, which include:

● Measuring results on cash flows rather than earnings per share:

'Frequently, a company states it is oriented to Shareholder Value Principles, yet when it comes to reporting performance, company-wide

or in individual units, the reports that managers look at each month relate to revenues or profits, rather than cash flow returns. Of course, if management information reports focus on one set of measures, then whatever rhetoric may exist within the company, managers will automatically seek to do well by those measures' (PA: 29)
- Allocating capital to divisions
- Measuring and compensating top managers and other staff on the basis of their contribution to shareholder value.

The PA survey highlighted two areas of implementation that seem to make a larger contribution towards the enhancement of shareholder value: remuneration and business planning, with remuneration having the greatest impact (PA: 17).

The shareholder value ball is rolling at a pace. Ericsson are starting to implement the Price Waterhouse version of shareholder value, 'Value Reporting'. In 1997 the *Sunday Times* started a league table of companies based on MVA and EVA (*Sunday Times*: 1997; 1998b). One of the reasons that companies are adopting the approach is that: '... those who say they have succeeded in implementing an MSV approach enjoy significantly higher returns to their shareholders than those who have not' (PA Consulting Group: 1997).

Case Study 5.6

CSX Inc.

Fortune reported on CSX, a capital-intensive freight group, in 1993. The group had fleets of locomotives, containers, and railcars. One of the divisions had a negative EVA of $70 million in 1988. Using EVA as the performance measurement the local management were ordered to improve the position to breakeven by 1993 or be sold. The volume of traffic improved in that business but the amount of capital employed fell dramatically from 18,000 containers and trailers to 14,000. Previously idle capital suddenly appeared as a cost and was reduced. The locomotive fleet was also reduced by one-third through better scheduling. This led to a positive EVA for the division of $10 million in 1992. (Fortune: 1993)

Lloyds TSB is the world's largest bank in terms of market capitalization, yet back in 1983 it used to be known as 'That Sorry

Bank'. It adopted the EVA approach in 1983 and set a target of doubling its share price every three years, a target that it achieved in 1998 when its shares were worth seven times their book value. The sector average is twice the value (*The Economist*: 1998e).

This increasing gap between book value and market value is a trend that will continue as knowledge-based companies dominate the economic environment. Intellectual capital, and the opportunities that derive from the exploitation of that intangible asset, will be factors that affect the market's determination of the price of a company's stock. The difficulty, identified by Leif Edvinsson, Director of Intellectual Capital at Skandia AFS, is that the information provided to the markets about the growth or decline of this new asset is negligible. Of course markets are used to taking risks. However, we are fast approaching a position where the book value of a company is becoming an irrelevance and the market value is an uninformed guess as to the prospects of future cash flow. This is derived from an assessment, amongst other things, of the potential of the intellectual capital residing within the organization. The dangers of misinformation affecting stock prices are become greater. The shareholder value approach has gained impetus because investors are demanding 'future oriented business information' about cash flow. They see this a key factor in decisions concerning the allocation of economic resources to companies (Coleman and Eccles: 8–9). Institutional shareholders will seek out and react to any information that can be illustrated to have a potential impact of the prospects of future growth in value of their investment.

Shareholder value techniques ignore intellectual capital and the cost of capital calculation ignores the cost of using, losing, utilizing and renewing the most important capital assets that the high growth companies possess – their intellectual capital. How many companies inform shareholders of their intellectual refurbishment plans in the same way as their factory refurbishments, so that a better-informed economic judgement about the allocation of economic resources can be made? This is one of the reasons why many chief executives of knowledge based companies find the market valuation of their companies an absurdity. Companies like Skandia in Sweden and Mayr-Melnhof Karton in Germany are justified in seeing the renewal and development of the intellectual capital of their companies as an integral part of the equation that enhances shareholder value. The US Securities and Exchange Commission (SEC) is rightly concerned that what they are measuring and requiring disclosure of to maintain a fair market, reflects a former economic paradigm and not that of the present or the future. Sometimes ignorance of intellectual capital movements blows up in the face of the company, the stockholders, the regulators or a purchasing company. Key staff members can leave, taking their knowledge with them, leaving the purchaser with an empty shell of a company. The company failed to mine that knowledge and capture it.

The shareholder value approach is one way for companies to illustrate their partnership approach to operating the company. The interests of shareholders, in respect of their future earnings and asset value, are pushed to the front of factors that affect all decision-making within the company. It can be a powerful tool if:

- It is fully implemented across the company and group and becomes one of the values which people within the company associate within their daily decisions
- It is explained in simple terms and not shrouded in accounting terminology.

The adoption of shareholder value, and in particular the strict EVA version can cause problems for companies if pursued relentlessly without regard for other perspectives. The two key perspectives that can get ignored are:

- The important 'capital' values which have a cost if they are *not* invested in or refurbished. This applies particularly to the people who work for the company and the corporate knowledge that they carry in their heads and take home every night, the intellectual capital of the company. When information becomes available about the enhancement, or destruction, of intellectual capital in companies shareholders will then be able to make better judgements about the market value of the company using that new information
- The danger of destructive technologies that can seem to be irrelevant if scrutinized through a narrow short-term EVA logic, but which can creep up on a company and destroy it. This is the innovator's dilemma identified by Professor Clayton Christensen.

We will look further at these two perspectives in the concluding chapter.

Shareholder Value Aligned to 'the Interests of the Company' Test

A shareholder value emphasis in the boardroom has another purpose. It aligns the commercial behaviour of boards and directors with the fundamental principle that has underpinned the legal requirements of boards of directors. It has always been a principle of company law that directors, acting as a board, must exercise their powers 'bona fide in what they consider – not what a court may consider – is in the interests of the company' (*Re Smith & Fawcett Ltd*).

This has been interpreted as requiring directors to have regard to the interests of the company's shareholders, both present and future. Companies have a long tradition of proclaiming that they owe duties to the community, employees and even the nation. This was only ever recognized at law in the UK if those interests coincided with the long-term interests of the shareholders. The coincidence of interests has never been hard to justify. Such links have allowed companies to make political and charitable donations. It enabled ICI to give money for scientific education despite a legal challenge (*Evans* v. *Brunner Mond & Co, 1921*). In the USA it allowed the Theodore Holding Company to provide homes for destitute children on the ground that if their needs were not satisfied they would grow up intolerant of capitalist society and thus harm the company's long-term interests (*Theodore Holding Co.* v. *Henderson, 1969*)! This same coincidence of interests between managing for profit and the stakeholder approach was echoed by Thomas A. Murphy, past Chairman and CEO of General Motors Corporation:

> To those who carry the responsibilities of management, to those who every day seek the balance among the obligations we owe to our stockholders, our employees, our customers, and to society as a whole, to those I point out that there need not be a conflict between seeking profit and meeting the social and environmental demands of our people. It may even be, I suggest, that upon our ability to respond to these demands depends the preservation of free enterprise itself. (Thomas A. Murphy).

The coincidence has not been left to chance as regards employees of companies in the UK. The Companies Act 1985 contains a provision first introduced in 1980, which states:

The matters to which the directors of a company are to have regard in the performance of their functions include the interests of the company's employees in general as well as the interests of its members. (Companies Act 1985, section 309(1))

The shareholder value approach asserts that stakeholders' interests can only be maximized if the company maximizes shareholder value. The coincidence is total.

Shareholder Value and Governance

Alfred Rappaport, the guru of shareholder value, claims that, 'Over the next ten years shareholder value will more than likely become the global standard for measuring business performance' (Rappaport: 1).

The take-up of shareholder value is a reflection on the results that have been achieved by the companies that have adopted the approach. It is also partly a corporate response to the claims of unfettered management, which have in turn fuelled the debates on corporate governance. Corporate claims to be adopting a shareholder value approach to business performance measures can be seen as an attempt to overcome hostility towards some of the perceived corporate excesses: scandals such as BCCI and the Maxwell Group, or large pay awards to directors of listed companies. The shareholder value approach in companies is part of the self-regulatory response to this pressure. It appears to provide a clear indication, boosted by the constant references in Annual Reports, that the listed company board of directors is moving from the relationship with its shareholders of Autonomy or Adrift towards a Partnership. Better to have this response than institutional shareholders and governments being prompted to take greater action than has occurred so far as a result of the various reports on corporate governance.

Shareholder Value and the Role of the Centre

The shareholder value approach also has an impact on the role of the centre within large companies.

Research conducted by the PA Consultancy Group has shown concern amongst companies and public sector organizations about the position of the corporate centre and the extent to which its function, structure and even its existence links into the overall corporate strategy.

One High Street bank is quoted as saying in the research that, 'Slimming down your corporate centre is a bit like getting rid of rucks in the carpet – as much as you try to get rid of them, they'll always turn up somewhere else' (PA, 1998: 1–1).

As companies move through stages of development, the rationale for the corporate centre does change. This is a design issue:

> Our research confirms the need for design, and confirms the need for a continuous process of development and change at the corporate centre. The corporate centre must be designed to fit the organization's strategic goals. There is no standard 'ideal centre', and we offer no 'correct' model. The ... design model is fitness for purpose depending on the needs of the organization at that time. (PA 1998: 3-1)

Technology has an important part to play in this design. The growth of ERP systems in companies, and a growing realization that information that a company retains is one of its greatest assets, enables a different perspective to be taken of the role of the corporate centre. This is particularly the case for those companies moving towards, or already in, a Partnership relationship with shareholders. Then the question to be asked of the corporate centre is: 'What needs to be at the centre to add value to the company, the group and the shareholders?'. The emphasis on shareholder value, combined with the growth of the knowledge economy, will lead to a different role for the corporate centre and for directors that are based there. James Chestnut, the CFO at Coca-Cola, is developing that new capability, and changing his directors' role as a result:

> For our people to make the best decisions, they need to have the facts. There's no point in having a hunch and making decisions purely based on that hunch. We want people to use their hunches and their good judgement, but on a foundation of facts. [That creates] the need for a greater information capability. We've been doing a fair bit on that in our 'project infinity' ... We think we're pretty much ahead of anybody else in pulling information from a worldwide system and using information on a structured, disciplined, and routine basis. But we need to make sure that in a couple of years, we'll have even better information capabilities. (CFO: 38)

The emphasis in Coca-Cola is on the centre providing managers, on a global basis, with the information that helps them to make better decisions. Sharing the information, and providing the managerial ability to leverage off that information on a global basis releases the value locked up in the corporate information. Knowledge, to be of any value to the company, has to be applied. The design and structure of the corporate centre in Partnership companies needs to reflect the emphasis on how this part of the value locked up in the company can be released to generate shareholder value. The centre's role is to provide the information and the corporate infrastructure that enhances the freedom for managers throughout the company to apply that information. As a contrast, the role of the centre in Maxwell's Puppet MCC was totally different. It was designed to facilitate absolute control and absolute power. The design was intended to ensure that information was *not* shared, as the information was the source of power.

In a group of companies, the central financial monitoring function will always be present, again aided by new technology that allows for real-time reporting. How the group develops corporate policy and strategy, where those decisions are made, and the input that is made by the subsidiary directors, is a major factor in determining the dynamism required of those directors. This is analyzed in the next chapter that looks at the group of companies. The wisdom generated from the application of the corporate knowledge base will itself add value to the company in the development of its strategy. This value will only be captured if those involved in the operational side of the business have a clear route to influence strategy development. For example, the Next Steps programme that was implemented across much of central government created Agencies and Non-Departmental Public Bodies (NDPBs) that undertake the operational aspects of government. This is part of 'Reinventing Government' seeing government's role as being responsible for the provision for a service, but not necessarily involved too much in the operational aspects of the delivery (Osborne and Gaebler). Social security benefits are administered by a Benefits Agency, legal aid is administered by the Legal Aid Board. The next stage of development for government will be to ensure that the knowledge that resides in these operations is utilized to develop even better solutions and strategies. The role of the government department as the 'centre', and of government, will need to change for this to occur, just as it changes in companies when you move from a Maxwell Puppet relationship to a Hoechst Partnership (Case Study 6.1, Chapter 6).

Adopting the shareholder value approach can be a useful tool to move a company towards a Partnership relationship between the shareholders and the board of directors. But its power and scope is as yet not fully understood. It will affect the role of the centre and the jobs of everyone in the company. Inevitably, because part of the emphasis is on the market value of shares, it only appears to apply to listed companies where there is an easy mechanism of judging the market value. Yet every company, and government, can benefit from this approach.

Evaluation of the Board of Directors

I have argued that the location of the relationship between the board and the shareholders is fundamental to an accurate assessment of the desired function of the board of directors. The next step is to ensure that the necessary skills and attributes to achieve those functions are present on the board of directors. This is the skill of board architecture. Yet it is still fairly unusual for boards to undertake an evaluation of their performance both as a board and as individuals. A survey by Korn/Ferry in 1996 showed that only 10 per cent of Fortune 1000 companies evaluated the CEO, the whole board and individual directors (see Figure 5.3). Having undertaken the process of director selection and appointment as outlined in the last chapter, performance should then be evaluated. There is some evidence that institutional shareholders want to be asked for their view on board performance (Conger, Finegold and Lawler). But tools are needed that enable at least the board to evaluate itself. The starting point is agreeing the desired function of the board and the skills required of directors. It is against these objectives that performance is evaluated. As we have seen throughout this book, we cannot assume that evaluation of performance takes place against a static situation. The role of the board and of the directors is a dynamic one. As the function of the board and of the individual directors changes, so must the criteria against which they are evaluated. For example, a company may have embraced the strategic issues that are identified in Chapter 7 as being of critical importance to the future development of the company. Innovation leadership and the development of intellectual capital within the company could then become criteria against which the board's performance is tested, directors are selected and their performance evaluated. The German media and publishing company, Bertelsmann AG, is seeking to overcome its late entrance into the online book-sales market by creating joint ventures and alliances in

Type of evaluation practice	%
CEO	69
Whole board	25
Individual directors	16
CO and whole board	23
CEO and individual directors	14
CEO, the whole board and individual directors	10

SOURCE: 1996 Korn/Ferry Survey (Conger, Finegold and Lawler: 138)

Figure 5.3 Percentage of Fortune 1000 companies with evaluation practices

Europe and Asia as well as launching its own online bookstore. Having admitted that it was late in getting into the online market, partly because its Autonomous subsidiary structure inhibited innovation leadership, Bertelsmann will now need to ensure that the skills of its board and directors include the ability to implement and monitor a joint venture strategy. This strategy requires different skills and attributes of directors and of the board. The evaluation of the board and of the directors would need to assess their effectiveness in developing and implementing this strategy. It is a good example of dynamic directors needing dynamic tools for evaluation.

In Chapter 2 we identified the generic functions of the board and the attributes required of directors as contained in Figure 5.4.

The five main functions of the board of directors

1 Providing strategic direction and values
2 Approval of planning
3 Monitoring and control of performance
4 Ensuring organizational capability
5 Awareness and compliance with legal responsibility

The five main attributes of executive directors

1 Integrity
2 Leadership skills – team player/communicator
3 Analytical
4 Specialist skills and knowledge
5 Thinker – open-minded/strategic

Figure 5.4 The five functions of the board and the five attributes of directors

It is against these functions and attributes that companies need to evaluate the performance of the board and of individual directors. This includes all members of the board, not just the executive directors. The questionnaires in the Appendix are examples of one method of undertaking this evaluation. In designing the questionnaires I have drawn heavily on a range of questionnaires from other companies, mainly in the US where evaluation is a more common feature at board level (NACD: 41–52). Sample questionnaires are provided in an Appendix at the end of the book. They include:

- A questionnaire to be completed by all directors on how the board is functioning (the questionnaire can be adapted to 360 degrees by asking those connected with the work of the board both below board level and outside the company, for example, major shareholders, banker)
- A 180-degree questionnaire to be completed by each director about their own performance, and by each director about their colleagues' performance as individual directors (the questionnaires can be adapted to 360 degrees by asking those connected with the work of individual directors both below board level and outside the company, for example, major shareholders, banker)
- A 180-degree questionnaire to be completed by the Chief Executive about their performance as a Chief Executive, and completed by each director also
- A 180-degree questionnaire to be completed by the Chairman regarding their performance as a Chairman, and completed by each director also.

The responses to the questionnaires can also be used to assess the company's current position as regarding the board relationship with the shareholders, and the desired position. When completed across a range of companies in a group, the relationships between the holding company and the subsidiaries can be analyzed. The questions need to be customized to accommodate the current and future requirements of particular companies.

The results from the questionnaires need to be handled carefully. It is recommended that the questionnaires should be administered in the context of a board and director development programme facilitated by external consultants, but then again I would suggest that! Individual members of the board of directors would normally agree that the Chairman should meet with each of them to assess their individual results and development needs. The Chairman would meet a senior non-executive director for feedback. The power of board evaluation, particularly during periods of change, is that it reinforces:

- to executive directors – that they have two responsibilities that are different and need to be evaluated differently: functional and board responsibilities
- to non-executive directors – that there is an important job of work to be undertaken
- to all staff – that the board is not immune from evaluation
- to all – that the board is not perfect and needs to continue learning like everybody else in the company.

The evaluation should be undertaken each year so that progress can be monitored.

Guiding Principles for Listed Companies

The guiding principles for listed companies are:

- Create a vision and a strategy that meets the benefit of enhancing shareholder value, and prove it
- Reflect the Partnership approach throughout the organizational structure, particularly at subsidiary company level: let people know where the company is going on the PAPA grid and why. Their perception of the direction may be different
- Communicate effectively with shareholders and the individuals who influence them
- Understand where the real decisions are being made in the company and ensure that this is where you want them to be made
- Evaluate the performance of the board and individuals on the board: develop, refresh, remove and rethink as a result.

6 Board Architecture and Groups of Companies

An organization is like a pendulum. It swings from too much centralization to too much decentralization; and comes to rest only when the mainspring is dead

(Chris Hogg, former Chairman of Courtaulds)

The relationship between companies in a group is a key factor in the success and survival of the group. As we have already observed in the previous chapters the relationship will usually be a dynamic one. The best positioning of the holding and the subsidiary company will vary according to the needs of the group and the rationale for the creation and continuation of separate subsidiary companies. However, the analysis of the reasons for the establishment and continuation of operating through separate companies within a group is not undertaken that frequently. Most of the research into holding and subsidiary company relationships has involved large multinational groups of companies. However, the lessons are the same for any group relationship. Indeed, they even apply to a situation where responsibility is devolved within an organization to operating units rather than to separate companies.

Where the group wishes to position the relationship will vary. Most companies, both holding company and subsidiary, usually express a desire to be in the cells on the right of the PAPA grid. However, there is often disagreement as to where they are starting. One technique is to try to get the members of the boards of the holding company and the subsidiaries to separately indicate where they think the relationship is between them, and what they would like the relationship to be. There will be a difference of view. The subsidiary directors will often consider that they are more towards the left of the PAPA grid than the holding company directors. It is then a matter of exploring the areas of difference, achieving a consensus and focusing on the action that is required to move the behaviour of the two boards in the desired direction. This approach can be used with just one of the company boards, the holding company or the subsidiary. The output is a plan to manage upwards or downwards to seek the alteration of the relationship. For example, Figure 6.1 is the typical output from this process from two separate subsidiary companies in different groups. We will analyze later on in this chapter the action that is necessary to make the movement possible for these companies. However, before we do this we need to assess why groups want to move to make the relationship usually one of either Autonomy or Partnership and some of the barriers that will stand in their way.

There are three structural impediments that often prevent the group from moving to a relationship between its constituent companies of greater Autonomy or Partnership:

1. A failure to clarify the original reason for the creation of subsidiaries, to denounce or verify that rationale, and if denounced to replace it with a different rationale.
2. A failure to appreciate the relationship that exists between the managing director of the subsidiary, the holding company, and the board of the subsidiary. In Chapter 1 we saw that this is a special relationship which the board of a subsidiary company, the managing director and the holding company needs to appreciate (see Figure 1.2).
3. The power of the holding company's central bureaucracy, the technocrats at Head Office, to frustrate changes that may affect their power base.

Identifying the Original Reason for Establishing the Subsidiary Company

Frequently the original rationale for the establishment of a subsidiary company has not been identified, but still lingers on, unnoticed within the companies, affecting the development of a new relationship. What is the attraction of creating subsidiary companies? If you know the reasons for their creation, you can understand the role the board of directors of the subsidiary is expected to play and their relationship with the holding company board. The reasons for creating a subsidiary company include the following:

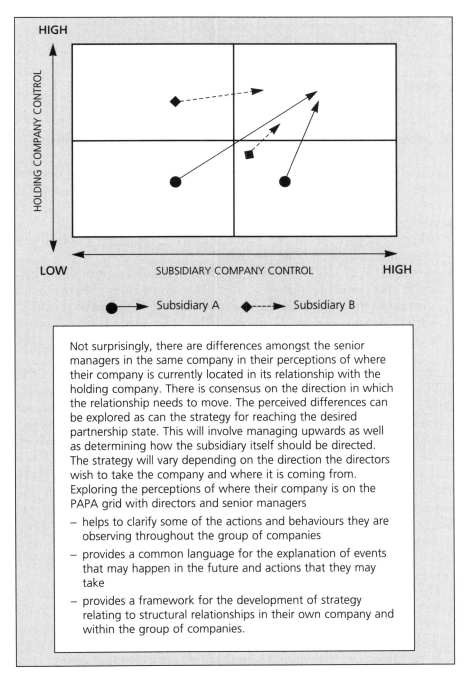

Figure 6.1 PAPA grids – two UK subsidiaries both with overseas holding companies

- To provide greater autonomy for a part of the business
- To resolve a succession problem within a family company
- To operate in a different country
- Historical accident
- Protection of a trade name.

To provide greater autonomy for a part of the business

Business operations can be structured to assist the vertical or horizontal nature of the group activities:

- vertical – separating the bread and cake production facility of a bakery company from the retail side by creating two subsidiary companies, one supplying the other
- horizontal – in 1997 Hoechst, Europe's largest chemical company, broke the company into six subsidiary companies that have no substantial links between them, each focusing on different products – drugs, organic chemicals, plastics. The businesses identified as not being core to the new group, such as paints, were identified for sale.

Subsidiary companies may have operational independence from the holding company and/or be joint ventures with other companies, rather than wholly owned subsidiaries. Most of the Virgin group of companies has been joint ventures, with only one wholly owned subsidiary company, Virgin Atlantic Airways. Virgin Retail UK which owns the music shops known as Virgin Megastores was only 25 per cent owned by Virgin, the other 75 per cent being owned by WH Smith, until Richard Branson exercised the right to buy back the shares. One of the advantages of both horizontal and vertical separation of the business into subsidiaries is that managers of those subsidiaries have the ability to control more of their own costs and focus on their market needs. It also provides board of director experience for managers.

The rationale of greater autonomy can sometimes be taken to extremes quite deliberately and very successfully. Clayton Christensen has identified that one of the structural ways of overcoming the threat of technologies that may kill the company – destructive technologies – is to allow the potential technology to develop and thrive in a completely autonomous company. IBM created an autonomous company in Florida to develop the personal computer market

(Christensen: 110). Hewlett-Packard created a separate division for exploitation of the ink-jet printer market, established to compete with its own laser printer division and ultimately to dominate the desktop printer market, capturing markets that had been the domain of the laser printer (Christensen: 115–7). In both of these cases IBM and HP are accepting that the spin-off companies needed to be autonomous in order to break away from the prevailing corporate commercial metrics. These groups of companies identified that there may be some benefits to be gained for one subsidiary company occupying a different cell on the PAPA grid so that it has more freedom to break the mould and innovate. This is innovation leadership at board level. Johnson & Johnson's total revenues of more than $20 billion are generated through 160 subsidiaries. The group uses the power of the small company to generate innovation untrammelled by the financial requirements and metrics of the large organization ... except for the statement of values that pulls the group together and creates a brand which is unrivalled in its field (Christensen: 141). Some groups of companies adopt the approach of seeking to obtain a 'local' advantage in overseas subsidiaries by encouraging the subsidiary to develop its own set of values to match the cultural and strategic environments in which they are operating. This can be observed in the Citizens Bank of Massachusetts, a subsidiary of the Royal Bank of Scotland. The Citizens Bank has six 'Areas For Excellence'. They are clear statements of how the Bank conducts business and what it stands for. Echoing the 'Areas of Excellence', Bob Mahoney, the President of the Bank, declares that 'Nothing stands between us and success other than our own wills and skills'.

The six 'Areas For Excellence' are listed in Figure 6.2. There are rituals associated with the values, with six awards every quarter for achievement by staff in the six areas. This reinforces the values, which are also a key and substantial part of a simple performance management system. Bob Mahoney and the management at Citizens are intolerant of behaviour that conflicts with the six areas.

Gradually more groups of companies are realizing that, in order to succeed in a rapidly changing market place they cannot put in place numerous controls emanating from the centre and, at the same time, expect individual managers to operate innovatively. Onerous controls deter flexible responses to market pressures. At the same time, if synergies can be realized from the group as a whole which add value to the group, they need to be harnessed. Groups of companies where the subsidiaries occupy the puppet cell or autonomous cell on the PAPA

AREAS FOR EXCELLENCE

OUR PEOPLE

We share a common challenge to serve customers, sell, and manage risk. We will succeed by approaching these responsibilities in a creative and ethical manner with a commitment to the communities we serve. We value team work and seek the true success that comes from collaboration.

CUSTOMER SERVICE

We strive to provide a unique Citizens Service Experience every time we interact with a customer or colleague to set ourselves apart from our competitors and create value for our customers. We will exceed our customer's expectations by providing prompt, consistent and knowledgeable service in a friendly, caring and neighbourly fashion. The Citizens Service Experience is most important when we have the opportunity to resolve a customer's problem. We will treat our customers and colleagues as we would like to be treated with courtesy and enthusiasm.

SALES SUCCESS

We know that financial success at Citizens will be determined by the sales effort of every one of us. Sales is not a passive exchange but an aggressive pursuit of a solution to a customer's needs and problems that we identify. Our sales approach will be creative, professional and informed while we build a reputation for predictability and integrity in all of our dealings with customers.

RISK MANAGEMENT

We recognize that virtually every aspect of our business involves a degree of risk. Our mission is to manage risk and prevent losses so that we can achieve our objectives. We are all responsible for identifying and evaluating risk as well as knowing and appropriately exercising the policies that apply to our area.

PEOPLE MANAGEMENT

We commit to provide the tools necessary to succeed at Citizens while consistently adding to the opportunities for our high achievers. Key to this commitment is an evolving Performance Management System which communicates high standards, provides frequent feedback and rewards achievement fairly. We take great pride in our diversity and intend that nothing stands between us and success other than our own wills and skills.

COMMUNITY INVOLVEMENT

We seek to distinguish ourselves within banking and industry by our extraordinary commitment to community involvement and public service. Our financial contributions will be augmented by a spirit of volunteerism for each of us has a special responsibility for community service. Through our collective efforts we will improve the communities we are privileged to serve.

Figure 6.2   Citizens Bank of Massachusetts – Areas For Excellence
Reproduced with permission of the Citizens Bank of Massachusetts

grid are identifying the need to move towards the partnership cell. The need to move arises for good business reasons. For example, the Ericsson corporate culture is characterized by an 'increased sense of urgency' requiring 'competencies and resources close to the market'. This has led to the adoption of a policy of 'small in large' for its subsidiary companies. This harnesses the power of corporate strategy, research and development and the brand name ('one company'), with local knowledge and expertise. This is an attempt to create the advantages of having a national home base whilst retaining the advantages of being a large multinational player (Porter: 606). One of the Ericsson senior managers working in an Ericsson subsidiary likened their freedom to being given dough, tomato and cheese. These are the raw ingredients, but one subsidiary could make a sandwich, another a pizza. One of the new Ericsson ingredients that is being introduced is a commitment to shareholder value across the group with management systems to support the move. A group CEO may want to free up the ability of the operating companies to respond quickly, but will also want to know what is going on: are you making a sandwich or a pizza? The operating freedom of subsidiary companies in this type of group may be matched with a responsibility to adhere to the detailed reporting framework that is in place, which has embedded within it the underlying emphasis on enhancing shareholder value. In this case the reporting framework is one of the methods that can be used to resolve the dilemma between holding company control and subsidiary freedom, and to reinforce the values that the group adheres to.

The dilemma of giving freedom yet retaining control is not confined to groups of companies. Individual managers may wish to give as much freedom as they can to their staff. This enables them to use their discretion and knowledge of their work, and the customer's needs, to achieve better results for the company. The technology base that is being created in many organizations allows individuals more access to information and tools. How the people in the business use that information and the various tools is the source of added wealth for the company and benefit to their customers. A line manager, may want staff to be innovative and exercise discretion, but will expect that freedom to carry responsibility.

The partnership relationship can flow through the group to the subsidiaries, units, and the individual line managers as illustrated in Figure 6.3. There are five approaches that assist in the resolution of the dilemma between management control and subsidiary/unit/

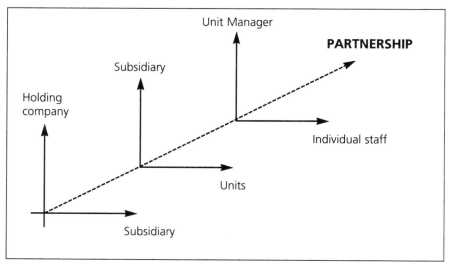

Figure 6.3   The partnership relationship flowing through the organization

individual freedom. In the language of Collins and Porras, once this core is in place you release enormous energy into the organization to stimulate progress (Collins and Porras: 88). The five approaches are identified in Figure 6.4 and are summarized by a speech that a new Group Chief Executive could be giving to the subsidiary Chief Executives when first taking up office.

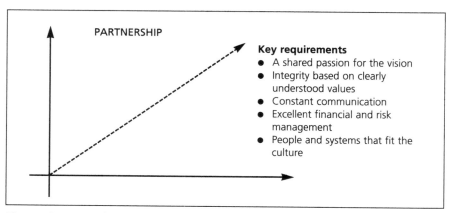

Figure 6.4   Resolving the dilemma of shareholder control and subsidiary/ unit/individual freedom

Group Chief Executive Speech

'I have a dilemma. I want to share with you an approach to resolving that dilemma that I have been considering since I joined the Group. The dilemma stems from conversations that I have been having with people in our company, our customers and through observation of the external factors affecting the sectors we are operating in. We are an industrial conglomerate. The era of the industrial conglomerate has passed. None of the top companies in our industrial sectors are conglomerates. Some of the industry leaders were not even in existence three years ago. Only a few companies will be able to keep up with the leaders as regards their technology and market positions. We cannot be leaders in all of the sectors we are currently operating in. I don't want us to be in any sector where we are not one of the leaders. It is a dynamic market and we need a dynamic structure to compete in it; a structure that will enable **you** to compete.

Some of you have been complaining that the central control on your decision-making powers is too strong and that this inhibits the flexibility you have in dealing with your customers and local markets. Others have told me that they would like to have a greater say in the group strategy. They feel independent of the main group and isolated. They might as well be a separate company altogether. Perhaps some of them should be. They particularly dislike having to pay a central overhead when they feel that they have no control over the costs or functions that reside at Head Office. Certainly, there is no overall strategy or vision that they can associate with. There is a connection between these two separate views that have been expressed to me quite openly.

Unless there is a shared passion for a common corporate vision, freedom cannot be shared. We do not have that vision at present so freedom is not shared. Unless there are common values based on integrity, freedom cannot be shared. We have a statement of corporate values, which is displayed on office walls across the Group. But it hasn't moved off the walls and into the minds and behaviour of the people who work for the Group. How many of you know what they are and behave accordingly? How many of you take action against those whom you observe breaching these values? Is the approach in this company: "hang it on the wall and it's in place; tick that box in the management manual"? If we don't have shared values and behave in accordance with them we will have more and more head office rule books governing decisions, and less freedom to make decisions based on our individual and subsidiary knowledge of the local market place. This is the essence of the dilemma: Group control versus subsidiary freedom.

There are two key commercial imperatives that are driving us which require a fast resolution of the dilemma. The imperatives are:

- understanding better the needs of our customers, anticipating their future needs and stimulating curiosity and demand from them for our innovations and solutions
- adding value to our capital base, for without that our investors will desert us or support a hostile bidding company that will promise it *can* add that value ... without you!

In order to satisfy these commercial imperatives the Group has to be innovative and flexible, whilst illustrating that there is added value to operating as Group as opposed to separate companies. I want to take the Group to a position where we have a lean holding company. Operating companies will be leaders in their sector, with the freedom to take decisions quickly to achieve that position. Central overheads on operating companies will be slashed. The added value of our company, compared to companies that are not part of a Group is dependent on our taking advantage of every possibility to harness the power of synergies that will reinforce our leading position whilst promoting local innovation and freedom. No synergy, no overhead. No added value, no overhead. One company, but small in large.

You might be rubbing your hands at the prospect of the influence that this will give you. But, there is always a trade-off when freedom is granted. With freedom comes responsibility and accountability. Here come the responsibility and accountability that I will require in exchange for the freedom it confers on the subsidiary companies within the Group. I will trust you, but trust only goes so far. You must keep me informed. I want to talk to each subsidiary CEO at least every other day, if only for a few minutes. I want real-time communication with you. Voice mail and e-mail will also occur, but I want to really talk to you. I will soon be installing technology in your offices that enables us to see each other when we talk. It will feel as though we are in the same room, sitting across the desk from each other. I must know what is going on in your head, not because I want to interfere, but because we are going to create the best networked organization in the world. As a top team we will be at the hub of the global interchange of ideas and information, helping us all to make connections that put the Group one step ahead of all our competitors. Think of your brain and the electrical connections it makes every minute. Now think of all the brains in the company and the interconnections they can make. We will start this process at the top of the company. A few minutes every other day to step back, think Group, Global and Connect. I also want to know about things before our competitors or the press...so think about what I need to know. Remember I am the link to the primary sources of capital for the Group and I need to keep them informed. We will agree a form of words that clarifies the extent of the freedom that subsidiary companies have, when approval is required at Group level and when Group only requires information on a "need-to-know" basis.

To help us we will improve our financial and risk management. I trust you, but only so far! You will update the financial and risk data on a real-time basis as a priority in the format that is prescribed. There will be no exceptions.

Along with the trust that the conveyance of freedom implies there is a hard edge. One strike and you're out. I will not tolerate any breaches of trust from anyone, and nor should you. As fair employers we will develop staff to enable them to perform their roles more effectively and efficiently. But I don't believe that you can develop trust once it has been proven to have been betrayed. As senior managers we have a special responsibility to uphold the corporate values and associated behaviours. But that also includes intolerance of those we identify as having breached them.

And finally we will need to rethink our corporate management information systems to fit the new partnership culture that I envisage. Some enterprise resource systems drown their corporate clients in structural concrete. We must have flexibility and a system that enables us to achieve the partnership culture. To achieve the Group ambition we must fuse corporate culture, people and technology.

Over the next few months we will work together, have some serious fun, and hire great people to help us and put the new organization into place. This is our business challenge.'

An adapted version of this spoof speech could just as easily be delivered by

- a CEO talking to divisional heads
- a line manager talking to his staff, or
- a Minister of State talking to departmental heads about the 'New Way'.

How many chief executives do you know who would like to give this speech? Of more importance, how many divisional or subsidiary chief executives would be delighted to be on the receiving end? The commercial imperative to compete globally and maximize returns on capital employed is driving groups of companies towards adopting the partnership approach. How else can they justify their continuance as a group? The era of the industrial conglomerate that cannot prove to investors the additional value of collecting the various businesses under one banner is gone. Anglo-American, the South African mining and industrial conglomerate collected a huge array of companies during the period when it was difficult for South African companies to invest overseas because of the apartheid sanctions. It is now seeking to focus its activities more and remove the discount on its net asset value observed in its share price that comes from being a conglomerate. The company has agreed to merge with Minorco as Anglo-American plc, a UK company. Nicky Oppenheimer, the Deputy Chairman elect of the new Anglo-American plc was quoted in the *Financial Times*:

> We believe the formation of [the new Anglo] will be a major step down the road to unlocking the significant unrealised value held in the current company structure, which is reflected in the substantial discount in their market values relative to their underlying net asset values. (16 February 1998, p.29)

Before the public relations consultants altered his press release, it could have looked like this:

> The Group has been performing very poorly in the achievement of shareholder value. Our return on capital employed is below investor expectations and variable across the Group. This is reflected in our share price and we need to do better to attract international investors. In moving to London we will expose ourselves to the rigours of performing against the objective of enhancing shareholder value, and release the Group from

its historical ties that make necessary structural changes difficult to implement. We will identify those parts of the business where capital is not achieving hurdle rates of return. If they cannot be turned round or are not part of the new core businesses we will sell them. This will mean that there are some tough decisions to take, including the potential sale of our traditional commitment to South African Breweries.

The move amongst conglomerates is global as they seek to unlock value within their sprawling empires. Tomen, Japan's seventh largest trading company and the fortieth largest company in the world, is adopting a similar approach to Anglo-American. Its Managing Director stated that:

> the era in which trading companies handle everything from *ramen* [noodles] to rockets is over ... the company must now compete in an international arena in which the creation of long-term shareholder value is the only assurance of continued success. (*Financial Times*: 1998a).

For Tomen this will involve consolidating or divesting about 50 affiliated companies.

Case Study 6.1

Hoechst AG (Aventis)

Jurgen Dorman, the Group Chairman of Hoechst, started to introduce changes in the relationship between the holding company and its operating companies in 1997. At an autumn press conference the Hoechst Board of Management announced the planned realignment of the company and the formation of independent subsidiaries for its global operations. The holding company would perform the role of a 'strategic management holding company'. The Annual General Meeting of the company in May 1997 approved this strategy and the formal transformation took place on 1 July 1997. The commercial drivers for change were made explicit in the 1997 Annual Report. They were to:

- unleash shareholder value: 'Achieving an above-average return on capital employed is one of our main goals and the only way for us to safeguard our long-term independence, competitiveness and employment'
- create sustainable growth: '... this means strategically managing and actively shaping the corporate portfolio on a long-term basis'

- focus on core businesses and be amongst the global leaders in those businesses: '... we can't maintain leading positions in a number of entirely unrelated businesses. If we want to sustainably increase shareholder value, then we have to deploy our resources in a targeted way'

The Annual Report made clear the necessary requirements to move towards a Partnership relationship between the holding company and its subsidiaries:

> Hoechst AG will steer a group of affiliates but no longer directly run any operating businesses. The Hoechst Board of Management is responsible for shaping the Hoechst Group in a long-term and value-enhancing manner. It will be supported in its task by a small corporate staff. The responsibility for operating businesses will lie with the individual affiliates...After a far-reaching process of change, we believe that we have found an organizational structure that will give managers and staff more scope and strengthen our businesses in the face of global competition. The new structure also permits the clear delegation of responsibility and will increase entrepreneurial flexibility while offering our shareholders greater transparency. (Annual Report, 1996)

However, moving from a puppet to a partnership mode of operation as a group of companies is not easy and takes time. Although the formal legal transformation had taken place in July 1997, in March 1998 *The Economist* reported that,

> Jurgen Dorman now concedes that Hoechst has a corporate culture more entrenched than that of almost any other German firm ... Its sprawling Frankfurt HQ resembles an Iraqi presidential palace, rather than the nerve centre of a global corporation" (*The Economist*: 1998f).

The focus into sectors where Hoechst can be leaders is gradually taking place. Hoechst is exiting industrial chemicals through disposals, partnerships and IPOs, and concentrating on the high growth and innovative life sciences areas that have high technological and market barriers.

The structure of the Hoechst Group is moving from a Puppet to a Partnership relationship. Greater responsibility has been allocated to the operating affiliates (subsidiaries). This has given them more direct exposure to the competition. Rigid hierarchies and compensation systems imposed at group level cannot survive in this environment. Hoechst is therefore developing a performance management system that recognizes the need for flexibility and the need to evaluate by function and performance, not by career path and seniority. The new business dynamics require that a new structure be adopted. This will require a different breed of manager to the ones that operated in a Puppet environment, both at the group level and the affiliate (subsidiary) level. Some will be capable of development but others will not. The change continued to be painful for the company, but Jurgen Dorman was determined to succeed:

> Step-by-step, we are creating a new, forward-looking Hoechst. Many people shy away from the thought: a change of course o.k., but why the decentralization and cell division? Why give up size, why forfeit synergies? The answer is clear: to obtain new impetus, to grow, to remain independent. If we hadn't started in time and resolutely focused on the Hoechst metamorphosis, we would have lost considerable ground in important fields of activity. (Annual Report, 1997)

After writing the above Hoechst announced that it is to merge with its French rival Rhône Poulenc, gaining approval from its Supervisory Board in December 1998 to take the proposal to the group's annual meeting in May 1999. The new company is to be called Aventis. The merger will help the new company to achieve world leader status in a few areas rather than also-rans in many, a feature of conglomerates. It is also indicative of Jurgen Dorman's awareness that although the strategy was appropriate, time was beginning to run out as failing performance placed institutional shareholder pressures on the company. The merger buys more time.

Another German company, GEA AG has adopted a similar approach to Hoechst AG. Some 80 per cent of its sales are in areas where it is either the leader or second in its market. It specializes in thermal and energy technology, air treatment, refrigeration, liquid processing, mechanical separation, powder technology and dairy farm systems. In February 1997 the company embarked on a programme which positioned GEA AG as a strategic management holding company with a small executive board of three members who share responsibility for the management of the Group. Division presidents who have wide powers of decision-making lead nine divisions. The five process technology divisions have cooperated to produce shared customers, joint offices and production facilities. Synergies also exist between the other divisions and are taken advantage of.

> The lean management structure introduced in February 1997 with direct operational responsibility resting with the nine division presidents promotes active enterprise and the achievement of ambitious objectives Within the framework of our emphatically decentralized organization, we consciously cultivate entrepreneurial thinking, which is reflected in proximity to customers, flexibility, short chains of communication and the promotion of managers' initiative. It also finds its expression in the lean holding company with a staff of only 67 employees. (GEA AG Annual Report, 1997)

These are yet more examples of German companies moving away from the integrated conglomerate, driven by a commitment to shareholder value. As they do so these companies alter their position in the PAPA grid. The skills and attributes required of the board and its directors to make the company move also change.

The Baxi Partnership Ltd is a UK market leader in gas fired central heating systems, and a manufacturer of clean air systems and cast iron components. In order for the group to move forward it has recently altered its structure:

> We want the structure of the Group to encourage each division to achieve its full potential. With this in mind, the directors and managers of each division have been given greater responsibility and freedom of decision making, and the Group Board has been streamlined. (David Erdal, Chairman, 1997/98 Annual Report)

The board structure at Baxi now resembles a continental European dual board structure. The Group Board comprises the four non-executive directors, the Group Finance Director and the Chief Executive. An Operations Board consists of the most senior executives in the Group including the heads of the divisions.

Case Study 6.2

Sweden Match

Sweden Match is a Swedish listed company. It produces chewing tobacco, snuff, cigarettes, cigars, is the world's third largest manufacturer of disposable lighters and, of course matches, being the world's only global manufacturer. There are 6500 employees and 85 offices and factories worldwide. The company was listed only in May 1996 on the Stockholm Stock Exchange and NASDAQ. It has a highly dispersed share ownership. In February 1998 the Board of Directors introduced a 'Shareholders' Program', aimed at distributing surplus funds to shareholders, a classic method of increasing shareholder value. In order to achieve the growth that the new emphasis on market capitalization will demand, the board of directors has started to introduce a new organizational structure:

> From having been a holding company consisting of four essentially independent divisions of different geographical and historical backgrounds, the operations took

> shape within the framework of a joint corporate structure. This consists of seven global product divisions which are marketing their products through seven sales regions.
>
> The company is creating 'one global company', moving from an Autonomous relationship within the Group to a Partnership relationship:
>
> > The new global organization was developed out of four different company groups, each with its own culture. These groups are now melting together and will co-operate within one corporate entity with one joint culture.
>
> There are basic values that are intended to bring the new culture together for Sweden Match and will be reflected in the uniform performance management and reward system (see Figure 6.5). They will,
>
> > permeate the entire organization and indicates the direction and goal of the personnel policy. These basic values are addressed to all employees and establishes he guiding principles for the work performance in the company.

A clear set of values to underpin the integrity that such a partnership approach involves can assist the desire to drive decision-taking down the organization, clearing the way of internal bureaucracy and rules, thus allowing a greater focus on strategy and implementation. We have already identified this at Citizens Bank with their six 'Areas For Excellence'. Another illustration comes from a US software and telecommunications company with a UK subsidiary, ADC Telecommunications:

> Being driven by a clear set of values can provide company focus and a clear sense of what is important at ADC. Our values reduce the need for corporate policies, rules or procedures and enable people within ADC to act on their own. (*The ADC Way, A Statement of ADC's Corporate Values*)

The six values that represent 'The ADC Way' can be seen in Figure 6.6. Similarly, Intentia, a Swedish ERP provider of Movex with subsidiaries across the world, is convinced that values, '... take the place of an extensive and formal system of rules that can curb and weaken motivation' (Intentia Annual Report, 1996).

Communication
Communication across all borders is the basic theme of the new company culture.

Teamwork
The employees are to work together in teams at their own laces of work and across all geographical and cultural borders as members of Swedish Match's global team

Trust
The employees are encouraged to act on their own responsibility and without too detailed instructions. They should have confidence in Swedish Match as a company keeping its promises.

Innovation
Every Swedish Match employee should be able and willing to present his/her own creative ideas about everything concerning the company, locally or globally.

Recognition
All employees are to be recognized for their work achievements and their ideas as to how the company should be further developed.

Growth
Commercial and human growth are overriding objectives of Swedish Match. To further develop human beings is a prerequisite for achieving the company's commercial objectives.

Figure 6.5 Sweden Match Basic Values

Statements of corporate values tend to be very similar, although we saw an illustration of how they can be unique to a particular company at Tom's of Maine (Case Study 4.2, Chapter 4). Because of the similarities, they are sometimes maligned as being of no practical use within the company. In some companies this is undoubtedly the case. The CEO speech identified the approach of 'hang it on the wall and it's in place; tick that box in the management manual'. In other companies, values create a shift in perspective and are a key part of the corporate architecture that preserves the core of the company whilst allowing operational autonomy to stimulate progress (Collins and Porras: 138). Whether or not they are the same as another company's values, or pinned on the wall, is irrelevant. What is important is the extent to which the values are embedded in the behaviour of all employees, the decision-making process and are seen as a tool to enable flexibility and

---

INTEGRITY

Integrity means dealing honestly and openly with customers, fellow employees, suppliers, and other shareholders, meeting or exceeding our commitment and acting in ways consistent with other values.

RESPECT

Respecting the dignity of each individual and treating others as they would like to be treated should describe every ADC working environment.

SPIRIT

At ADC, we strive to work with energy, enthusiasm and passion, taking pride and pleasure in the work that we perform.

SERVICE

A climate of service to others is the hallmark of the ADC culture.

HIGH PERFORMANCE

Excellence in performance is what is expected of every person at ADC.

CONTINUOUS IMPROVEMENT

The ADC approach is to be always moving forward, always striving for a better way, constantly looking for new ways to serve the customer, eliminate waste and make ADC a stronger organisation

---

Figure 6.6 The ADC Way
SOURCE: *The ADC Way, A Statement of ADC's Corporate Values*

speed of decision-taking. This should be visible in the criteria that underpin the performance management system that ned to reward behaviour that reflects the values. As companies move into more global alliances and partnerships, it is these shared values that will foster an enduring relationship. The ability of boards and directors to identify this need and oversee effective implementation throughout their companies will become a key responsibility and test their dynamism.

To Resolve a Succession Problem Within a Family Company

One way of resolving succession problems in a family company is to divide the business up into separate parts for each member of the family to run. This was one of the approaches adopted in the fifth generation of Jarrold & Sons Ltd. Jarrold & Sons did not create separate subsidiary companies, but it could have, with each one managed by a different family member. This would require a non-operating holding company to develop group strategy, to receive the profits from the subsidiaries and to distribute them to the other family members in accordance with their shareholding in the holding company. One of the difficulties associated with the economic crisis in Indonesia has been the proliferation of such family companies within large family groups, supported by substantial bank loans that are unrelated to the viability of the business.

To Operate in a Different Country

There are four main reasons for establishing subsidiary companies when trading in different countries:

1. *Tax*
   Within the European Union, the lack of harmonization of tax laws encourages the conduct of business through the creation of national subsidiaries. There are even tax reasons for establishing subsidiaries within the UK, with IBM doing just this to run its leasing arm.

2. *Domestic Legal*
   Some countries require that business be conducted through national companies with a majority of shareholders from that country (e.g. China).

3. *Commercial Politics*
   In practice it is often politically astute to operate joint ventures with a national company rather than to operate a wholly owned subsidiary, particularly if part of your business comes from government contracts or is reliant on the granting of licences. In India any company holding a telecom licence has to have an Indian majority holding, although this may be relaxed in the future as the government starts to liberalize the Indian economy. BT have so far adopted this strategy in Europe with their EJVs (European Joint Ventures, for example, Telenordia in Sweden).

4. *Good Business*
   The national subsidiaries are closer to the local markets. For example, Asea Brown Boveri (ABB), formerly run by Percy Barnevik, is an electrical engineering conglomerate that consists of 1300 separate companies. He pioneered the concept of the

'multicultural multinational'. The head office function is very small (171 people from 19 different countries out of a total group workforce of in excess of 200 000). Group revenues exceed $40 billion. We have seen that Ericsson has also adopted the strategy of 'small in large' within 'one company' in order to leverage off local markets and speed up the product development cycle.

Historical Accident

Tom Hadden, a company lawyer, undertook some detective work on the composition of some groups of companies in 1983. The groups he looked at were:

- Bowater Group – the group contained 420 companies, of which 200 were overseas companies
- Rank Group – the group contained 220 companies, excluding those companies jointly held with the Xerox Corporation through Rank Xerox (now separate companies), of which 100 were overseas companies
- Reckitt and Colman Group – the group contained 170 companies, of which 120 were overseas companies
- BP – the group contained 1300 companies
- Unilever – the group contained 800 companies, of which 300 were overseas subsidiaries.

The main reason for the proliferation of subsidiaries was the pattern of expansion by these groups through the acquisition of established businesses. Like Topsy they 'just growed' and there was little evidence of planned management or control through the use of subsidiary companies.

Protection of a Trade Name

One way of protecting a trade name is to establish a company with that name. The British IBM Group had only 16 companies in its group when Hadden undertook his study. But it had one dormant company, International Business Machines, which was created just to protect the trade name. Once that company was registered the Registrar of Companies would not permit the registration of a company with the same or a similar name.

Moving the Relationship Between the Holding Company and its Subsidiary Companies

Bartlett and Ghoshal have observed executives experimenting with different ways to manage the international head office–subsidiary relationship in companies like NEC, Phillips, Ericsson, ITT, and Unilever. They concluded that:

> national companies must not be regarded as just pipelines but recognized as sources of information and expertise that can build competitive advantage. The best way to exploit this resource is not through centralized direction and control but through a cooperative effort and cooption of dispersed capabilities. In such a relationship, the entrepreneurial spark plugs in the national units can flourish. (Bartlett and Ghoshal: 94)

This cooperative effort is best illustrated in a partnership relationship between the companies in a group. The main features of the Partnership holding company/subsidiary relationship have already been detailed in Figure 6.4. As we move through each feature, it becomes clear that the senior personnel that worked for the subsidiary and the holding company in a different cell of the PAPA grid may not be the appropriate individuals to lead the group in the Partnership cell. Personnel changes will often be required. This can be achieved quickly with an understanding of the necessary pain that will be caused, taking every effort to minimize that pain. Or the process can be slow, ultimately more painful and with less chance of success.

Shared Passion for the Vision

The passion is fed by commitment, which comes from participation in the creation of the vision. Spark plugs will only spark if they share in the shaping of the vision. If the Group relationship has been located in any of the other PAPA grid cells then there has been no subsidiary input into a central vision and associated strategy. The most common complaint of the boards of the 27 subsidiaries of different Swedish multinational companies was exclusion from discussions on strategic matters. The subsidiaries apparently operated without a common goal and made decisions not really knowing what the overall group strategy was. The financial imperative was the key one (Hedlund: 25-6). To move into the Partnership cell therefore requires a dual commitment:

- A commitment from the holding company to involve the subsidiaries in the evolution of a shared vision and associated strategy for implementation; they are part of the intellectual capital of the company and their knowledge needs to be tapped
- A commitment from the subsidiary company to use their commercial freedom to make decisions that support the group vision and group strategy for implementation of the vision.

> Is there an alternative to killing the diversity of a company or beating the organization into hierarchical submission? ... It means that anyone running a large, complex institution – such as a group of subsidiary companies, a set of joint ventures or a company composed of business units – cannot simply dominate individual self-interest through the exercise of power ... Governance is a matter of assuring that the goals of the subsidiary companies and of each employee are harmonious with the goals of the larger whole – and vice versa. (de Geus: 131–2)

An empirical study of the role of 90 subsidiary boards in 36 multinational companies by Mark Kriger looked at the use of boards of directors in foreign subsidiaries of multinational companies. They had headquarters in the United States, Canada, Europe and Japan. He discovered that there was an increasing awareness of the strategic importance of the boards of nationally based subsidiaries both as a source of local economic information, and as a mechanism for coping with host country legal and political pressures. This varied according to the nationality of the holding company. Kriger concluded that subsidiary boards of Japanese multinational companies were used more proactively and more strategically than other multinationals that saw the local board as managing rather than governing the subsidiary.

It is possible for the subsidiary company to take the initiative if it sees an opportunity to manage up the group chain and influence events towards the Partnership cell. This is what happened in Case Study 1.2, when the Chief Executive of the UK subsidiary took the initiative to promote a strand of strategy that he believed in. The US holding company was receptive to this 'spark plug', encouraged the spark and the group have now moved into the Partnership cell. This is the most important business reason for the structural move to a Partnership relationship. Subsidiaries in fast moving sectors, such as tele-communications and software will need to be fast to identify the pro-active opportunities. Fast growth gives rise to rapid structural changes, and the subsidiaries need to be at the point of most influence in their holding company at the right time with the right strategic arguement.

Integrity

The holding company has to be able to trust the subsidiary management, and vice versa. This allows substantial devolution of freedom. This could involve the development of written and shared values in larger groups. For the integrity and trust to really develop you need constant communication.

Constant Communication

The group Chief Executive needs to know what is going on. Although there is trust, the Group Chief Executive's will be the first head to roll if it goes wrong. Constant communication and personal contact deepen the trust. I have yet to see trust, passion and commitment being deepened by e-mail and voice-mail. I have seen these technologies dissipate and skew the priorities of key personnel. Systems will need to be put into place and protocols developed. At the senior level there is no proxy for face-to-face contact, and we are fast approaching the time when this will be 'virtually' possible between people in different continents in a manner that will make current video-conferencing techniques as obsolete as Morse code.

Excellent Financial and Risk Management

This is one of the features that even groups with subsidiaries in the Autonomous cell normally ensured was complied with. In 1987 Good and Campbell identified these groups as financial control companies: Hanson Trust, Ferranti, BTR and GEC. They are highly decentralized structures where the group managers act as non-executive chairmen for each company. The small head office plays a surveillance role with a strong emphasis on financial monitoring. There is no partnership in respect of the encouragement of new ideas, the financial control processes creating a degree of caution in these subsidiaries (Good and Campbell: 112–16). If these companies move towards the Partnership relationship with their subsidiaries, as BTR was attempting to do, then they will have no difficulty in complying with the desire for strong financial reporting and risk analysis. The difficulty will be in encouraging the subsidiaries that climb out of Autonomous Financial Control to accept that they are part of a group. They may eventually find that they are not! Or, like BTR, they may become the junior partner in a 'merger'. This is because the other element of a Partnership that is absent in Financial Control companies is the ability to identify synergies between the different companies for their mutual advantage, perhaps because there are none. If this is the case they may find that the adoption of a Partnership approach could see them hived off, like the paints division of Hoechst or some of the subsidiaries in Metro, Europe's largest retailer. Poor financial and risk management in any company leads to the position that UBS found itself in (see Case Study 6.3).

Case Study 6.3

Union Bank of Switzerland

From 1985 the Singapore branch of the Union Bank of Switzerland was run by Lim Ho Kee as his personal fiefdom. The bank as a whole was trying to move towards more of a global partnership with its subsidiaries across the rest of the company. But risk management at the Singapore branch was non-existent and huge losses arose as a result of the positions taken in the Indonesian (SFr500m) and South Korean ($1 billion) corporate issues. UBS has now been taken over by its smaller rival the Swiss Bank Corporation (*The Economist*: 1998d).

People and Systems that Fit the Culture

The new Group Chief Executive has announced the move towards a Partnership relationship in the group. Can you imagine this discussion in the boardroom of the subsidiary that has been Autonomous when it hears the speech?

'Why don't they just let us get on with the job. We're doing O.K. All Head Office will do is interfere, but they will call it "Partnership"! We give them the figures every month on time. We know the business and the market, they don't. How can they help us? You watch, there will be reams of instructions, standard operating procedures for this and that. I don't believe there will be a small Head Office. He'll need a small army to control all of us. The videophone is an expensive gimmick. Oh well here we go, another restructuring … it will be training and development programmes next!'

Can you imagine this discussion in the Head Office of the Holding Company that has been Adrift when it hears the speech?

> 'Did he show you the speech before he wrote it? Who did he show it to? I suggest we send him all the papers on the strategy development seminar, the problem in Nigeria, and that tricky problem in Malaysia with the government. Convince him that we must have his input into these issues and it will keep him busy for months. In the meantime I will talk to the legal people to see if there are any unseen difficulties in what he is proposing. I wonder if the trade union has thought through the potential consequences for job losses yet? John [the Chief Executive of one of the largest and profitable subsidiaries] will be delighted. He has been arguing for a greater say in the development of Group strategy and an audit of all central overhead costs. I bet he got to the new Group Chief Executive when he did his tour of the company when he was appointed?'

Can you imagine the discussion in a subsidiary boardroom that has been a Puppet when it hears the speech? ... There is no discussion and no reaction other than to implement whatever comes their way ... that's the problem.

The reactions will be various. Any new Chief Executive will realize that there is a need to identify very quickly those individuals who will be able to make the transition, and those who will not. The tactics and board architecture will need to match the directions that the subsidiaries are coming from as well as the direction in which they are now headed.

Areas of Potential Conflict

In order to implement an effective global strategy companies cannot rely just on their national home-based circumstances to gain competitive advantage:

> In theory, it might appear that a multinational company could reap all the advantages of every nation through establishing foreign subsidiaries. In practice, it rarely works that way. Gaining the benefits of a home base requires insider status within the national 'diamond'. This is difficult to achieve unless another nation is truly the home base. A firm must become part of the culture, feel the local competitive pressure, and break completely into the network represented by the national cluster...[T]he more a foreign subsidiary becomes an insider in one nation, the more difficult it is for the subsidiary to influence global strategy set at another

home base. The subsidiary becomes viewed as 'captive' to its nation and loses credibility at headquarters. (Porter: 606)

The Partnership approach accepts that there is a dilemma. Features require inserting into the relationship between the holding company and the subsidiary which attempt to mitigate the tension, such as a written statement of the division of responsibilities. If the subsidiary is perceived as 'captive' then these features will have failed. Of course there will be conflicts between the boards of subsidiary and holding companies. As we saw with the family companies conflict can be resolved when there is a clear understanding of the position of each of the parties and clear values to refer to. Conflict can also be constructive if used in a way that enables constructive proposals to emerge. Conflict is more likely to arise when there is a dip in performance. This is when the urge to move away from the Partnership cell towards the Puppet cell is strongest. But, freedom once conferred is very difficult to take away. It will almost inevitably lead to a change in the board composition of the subsidiary company. The attributes of individuals and teams that are required to lead a subsidiary company operating in a Partnership framework with its holding company are fundamentally different to those required to operate in a Puppet environment. To avoid unnecessary conflict it is advisable to put in writing a set of policies regarding the relationship between the holding company and its subsidiaries covering:

- Functions of the two boards
- Roles and responsibilities of the key individuals on both boards.

An example of such a policy from an FTSE 100 company can be seen in Figure 6.7. However, it is a very dry statement focusing on the financial imperative. It doesn't help us to understand how the holding/ subsidiary relationship between the two boards will really operate. Such policy statements also need to include something on the following aspects of the holding company/ subsidiary company relationship:

- Clarification of the devolved authority of the Chief Executive of the subsidiary company and the powers and responsibilities that the Chief Executive can devolve to the board of the subsidiary (see Figure 1.2, Chapter 1).

  The board of the subsidiary company has to feel that **the board** has the freedom and the responsibility, not the Chief Executive. This will not happen if the Chief Executive keeps exercising a veto, although the board of the subsidiary also needs to respect the relationship that their Chief Executive has with the holding company. The Chief Executive is appointed by and representing the shareholder, the holding company, on the subsidiary board

- The process for resolving potential conflict, possibly through direct access for one of the subsidiary board members to the chairman of the holding company
- A commitment that the holding company will allow the subsidiary board and individual directors to play a strategic role in the development of their part of the group's operations, with guidance on how that will take place
- An express statement that subsidiary directors must consider the operation of the subsidiary not just from a financially sound perspective, but also with regard to any political, social or ethical consequences that flow from decisions.

    Where decisions could affect the image of the group as a whole they need to be indicated to the main board in advance of implementation. There could be a positive mandate from the board of the holding company for its subsidiary directors to take ethical considerations into account. This will include the special considerations that may need to be considered from operating in a particular region of the UK, or in a country with a different culture. This would also assist in situations of potentially conflicting demands of board members. In particular it should indicate that it is essential that subsidiary executives and directors in the field

---

The Parent Company is ultimately responsible for policy. It has to ensure that the Group's public and legal obligations are met and within this broad generality it delegates responsibility for executive action to individuals, Committees and Board as appropriate. In practice the Parent Board will retain exclusive decision-making power in relation to capital expenditure and disposals exceeding £2m in value, senior appointments at the level of Divisional Chief Executive and above and Officers of the Company. The Board will also review all financial information which it requires to enable it to determine dividend policy, the capital structure of the company and any financial matters having third party relevance.

The Board shall retain authority in respect of any proposed changes in the Company's statutes.

Figure 6.7 Role of the holding (parent) company and its board of directors
(Taken from a FTSE 100 company. Bain and Band: 29)

shoulder support for ethical conduct. A subsidiary board, mandated to ensure that ethical considerations are fully taken into account, can be of immeasurable help.

The process of writing a fuller statement than the one in Figure 6.7, bringing in the directors of all the companies in the group to participate, is a useful exercise in itself as it will:

- clarify the roles that are expected of the different boards of directors, and of the directors on those boards, gaining greater cost effectiveness from the structure
- develop the strategic role of the holding company and the input that the subsidiaries have in that role, leading to better informed strategic decisions
- help to assess whether or not there is really a need for all of the subsidiaries, leading to possible cost reductions
- provide an insight, through the contribution of the individual directors into the process, as to whether or not the directors on all of the boards have the necessary skills and dynamism to take the group forward; this may lead to renewal of the intellectual capital at the top of the company.

The same principles apply in any business or operation wherever you have devolved significant management functions to individuals.

Guiding Principles for Corporate Groups

The guiding principles for the group of companies are:

- Holding companies and their subsidiaries should study the options that are available for the relationship they develop, and the dilemmas that confront them in establishing the best relationship for them
- That understanding then needs to be reflected in the respective functions of each board and the appropriate qualities required of directors to fulfil those roles
- The Partnership model of operation requires that there is an identifiable common vision supported by integrity based on common values that align with the goals of the subsidiary companies in the group and indeed with the goals of each individual working in the company.

7 Policy and Business Perspectives

Perspective is worth 50 IQ points
(Anon.)

This chapter identifies key policy and business perspectives that could alter the business environment over the next decade. This is accompanied by an assessment of the extent to which the analysis of corporate variety and its impact on board architecture should influence those perspectives. The key perspectives identified in this chapter are:

- **Policy Perspectives**
  - Corporate governance – different rules for different companies
  - The impact on the corporate investor – investing in and influencing structural changes in different companies
  - The role of business support agencies – helping the wide range of companies to prosper

- **Business Perspectives: Strategy**
  - Intellectual capital – valuing and renewing intellectual capital as a function of the board
  - Innovation leadership – part of the complex leadership attributes of directors
  - Mergers and acquisitions (including intra-Group mergers) – identifying structural differences between companies to either enhance success or abandon the proposed merger

- **Business Perspectives: Operational**
  - Selling at board level – making the high level approach more effective.

There may be other perspectives that you can identify having read this far. For example, to what extent can the PAPA grid analysis be applied to government and the way that Departments of State have altered their structures. There is a plethora of Next Step Agencies and Non-Departmental Public Bodies sponsored by government Departments. The ability of the Department, the equivalent of the holding company, to hold the whole thing together and develop effective strategy will depend on the type of relationship that is adopted between the different parts of the Department's responsibilities. Government approaches have varied over time in the same way that companies go through different stages of development. There is constant reinvention. Perhaps the 'New Way' of reinventing government leads to an effective Partnership between the various agencies the Department sponsors and a new role for the head office.

Corporate Governance – Different Rules for Different Companies

Prior to the publication of the Hampel Committee's report on corporate governance, the Department of Trade and Industry responded to the European Union Consultation Paper on legislation that was necessary to complete the single market. Following a consultation exercise with various businesses and others, it concluded that British business considered that companies should have the opportunity to adopt corporate governance arrangements that best suit their individual needs:

> It is generally accepted that there is no one corporate governance structure that is ideal for all companies and all circumstances. Consequently the Department is predisposed to avoid prescriptive legislation if possible…The large number of different factors which would need to be taken into account if a regulatory system were to be introduced which did not inhibit the competitiveness of companies makes detailed legislation in this area inappropriate. (Department of Trade and Industry: 9)

The Department preferred the flexibility of non-statutory codes, although it accepted that there may be a case for legislative action so as to regulate weighted voting rights as this can be a substantial barrier to take-overs, part of the corporate governance structure in Western companies. There is also government concern about the voting behaviour of institutional investors, although the Department has decided not to intervene so far. The reliance on non-statutory Codes has a weakness. The Department stated that the principles of corporate governance are of 'universal application', but Codes are only aimed at listed companies. The monitoring, and sanctions for non-compliance, are restricted to these companies. We will look at the content of the Codes to establish whether there are provisions that require adaptation for the variety of companies we have identified. Even though there is no monitoring or official sanction for non-compliance by most companies, there may be a more powerful sanction: the company fails or performs poorly compared to its potential.

The emphasis at State level on the application of principles of corporate governance is to be expected and encouraged so as to preserve the national reputation of 'home base' companies and promote the development of a corporate infrastructure that attracts companies, as well as an economic infrastructure.

> ... with the exception of creating low inflation and greater macro-economic stability which are the province of governments, improvements in overcoming all the other main handicaps to improved economic performance either depend upon, or would be greatly benefit from, overcoming the main weaknesses in corporate governance ... it is at the heart of corporate efficiency and significantly influences both nations' international economic and hence political influence. (Sykes: 112)

This may be overstating the case for effective corporate governance, but even Porter asserts that government policy does affect national advantage, both positively and negatively. Government can be a 'pusher and challenger' of companies even though they may find the process unsettling and unpleasant (Porter: 681). This can include clear signals such as the Deming Prize created by the Japanese government to promote quality. The OECD Advisory Group on Corporate Governance supported the need for governments to shape the corporate regulatory structure,

> Because worldwide the corporation is the essential engine driving the private sector economically, and because corporate governance can be critical to competitive performance in all of a corporation's markets ... the quality of corporate governance can affect the dynamism of the private sector and ultimately the credibility of market economies in providing economic growth and promoting citizen welfare. (OECD: para.9)

Whitley also highlights the importance of national institutions in the development and effectiveness of business structures and practices in East Asia:

> ... altering well-established patterns of business behaviour which are closely interdependent with their institutional contexts is very difficult without substantial institutional changes ... attempts to change institutional structures and policies which impinge upon economic activities may fail where business systems are well entrenched and relatively effective, and where leading economic agents can elicit support from other groups...such changes do not usually come about in the absence of external pressure or large-scale internal conflict and widespread perceptions of institutional failure. (Whitley: 248–9)

There has certainly been a flourish of interest in corporate governance across the world. The OECD Advisory Group discovered 24 sets of 'Guidelines' and 'Codes of Best Practice' from 14 countries after a partial survey (OECD: 105). What has actually happened in the UK? Three reports have dominated the debate on corporate governance:

- The Cadbury Report (1993) concentrated on the financial aspects of corporate governance.
- The Greenbury Study Group (1995) focused on the remuneration and compensation of directors
- The Hampel Committee on Corporate Governance (1998), established to review the findings of Cadbury and Greenbury.

Despite the protestations in the Hampel Report that corporate governance is not a 'box ticking' exercise, the reports have led to a perception of corporate governance as only a control mechanism operating on the boards of companies. Tweaking the structure of the board, appointing a few non-executive directors and inserting a page on corporate governance in the company's Annual Report can satisfy the demands for corporate governance. Worse still is the perception that corporate governance only applies to listed companies, is only of marginal interest to the larger unlisted plc, and of no interest at all to the smaller private company. Therefore, many company directors hold negative or agnostic views about the issue of corporate governance. This involves a mixture of the following:

- I don't know what it really means
- It is all about having the right board committees and non-executive

directors, but little to do with helping us to run the company any better and increase our profitability

- It really only applies to the large listed company
- We only think about it when it comes to the preparation of the Annual Report because the Stock Exchange insists that we refer to our performance against the Cadbury Code of Best Practice and the Greenbury Code
- It only covers the financial aspects of the company and executive pay; it's nothing to do with strategy and how the company really operates.

The result is the perception of an over-worked and increasingly meaningless phrase that instead of inspiring leaves the typical director cold. Many a board of directors may have been tempted to include a statement on compliance with the Cadbury Code in their Directors' Report similar to the one inserted by the board of Arlen plc, an electrical components company, in Figure 7.1. The Arlen plc directors are disputing that there is a vacuum of accountability. Their shareholders have all the information they need about individual directors to decide 'whose performance is satisfactory'.

Arlen plc has actually done itself an injustice. The company is complying with many of the principles of good corporate governance.

Your Company does not comply with certain parts of the Code because it believes it is naïve to suppose that a set of rules can be a substitute for proper behaviour by Directors. Directors are those individuals appointed by the owners of a company to look after it and a set of rules cannot be a substitute for the owners' responsibility for the conduct of their apppointees. It is up to the shareholders to control Directors by exercising an owner's right to remover, or decline to re-elect, any Director whose performance is not satisfactory.

Like people, companies are made the same way but differ from each other. It is impossible to create a single set of rules which works for each individual company. It is up to the Directors to run the business in the best interests of the shareholders and we expect to be measured by you, the owners of the Company, in how we conduct ourselves and carry out our duties.

If your Company were to attempt to comply with the Code of Best Practice, there would be a cost. Businesses already have to labour under too great a load of expensive and oppressive regulation to wish to increase the drain on shareholders' pockets any further.

Figure 7.1   Extract from the Directors' Report of Arlen plc on non-compliance with the Cadbury Code of Best Practice on Corporate Governance
SOURCE: Arlen plc Annual Report 1996

It is not necessarily doing so in the manner that the various Codes have suggested. The reality of the contents of the Hampel Report is markedly different to the perception of an unnecessary cost and a blind set of rules for all companies. These are some extracts from Hampel which illustrate this:

On the relevance to business:

'The importance of corporate governance lies in its contribution both to business prosperity and to accountability' (para. 1.1)

On recognizing corporate variety:

'Good corporate governance is not just a matter of prescribing particular corporate structures and complying with a number of hard and fast rules. There is a need for broad principles. All concerned should then apply these flexibly and with common sense to the varying circumstances of individual companies' (para. 1.11)

'Box ticking takes no account of the diversity of circumstances and experiences among companies, and within the same company over time' (para.1.13)

On wider aspects of board structure and directors:

'... process can only ever be a means, not an end in itself: it will always be far less important for corporate success and for the avoidance of disaster than having properly informed directors of the right calibre, bringing openness, thoroughness and objectivity to bear on the carrying out of their roles' (para.1.21).

Governments can and should play a role in the development of governance structures for companies that trade within their boundaries under the privilege of limited liability. Governments also need to consider the flexibility that such structures require in order to accommodate different board architectures that reflect corporate variety. To do otherwise and impose rigid constraints on all can harm some companies. This is also supported by research undertaken by Coles and Hesterley on the US market reaction to poison pill announcements. They only looked at the combination of two governance measures: CEO and Chairman in combined roles or separated ('leadership structure'), and the presence of external non-executive directors ('board composition'). They concluded that:

... clearly there are many alternate organizational arrangements the firm may choose, which include, but are not limited to, the choice of leadership structure and board composition. The value of such different arrangements is likely to vary from firm to firm, according to variation in organizational, industrial and environmental factors. Different firms will have different optimal organizational structures. To the extent that regulation narrows the set of feasible contracts and organizational forms, regulation of leadership structure, board composition, or any other organizational arrangement can damage shareholders and other claimants'. (Coles and Hesterley: 32)

They found that the relation between the market reaction to the poison pill announcement was related to whether or not there was an independent element present on the board, either because the CEO and chairman role were separated or because there were independent directors present:

> The market perceives that outside directors can be important monitors of management when the Chairman of the Board is not independent of management. (Coles and Hesterley: 31)

Governance structures also need to accommodate different corporate cultures across the world. Sheard argues very convincingly that there is an effective corporate governance structure for Japanese companies. The nature of the development of the commercial arrangements in Japanese companies requires a deep analysis of the relationships to identify how corporate governance really works. Sheard identifies three main components of the Japanese corporate governance structure.

1. *Stable shareholder arrangements* (antei kabanushi kosaka)

Corporations hold the majority of listed shares. This share ownership is often accompanied by a stable shareholder agreement. The shares are held as if by a friendly insider, with an agreement not to sell to hostile third parties. In the event of selling there will be prior consultation with the company. This is often accompanied by the lodging of the share in custody with a securities company that is part of the group. This is why T. Boone Pickens, a US investor, failed to get a seat on the board of the Toyota supplier Koito Manufacturing despite having obtained a 26 per cent stake in the company (Sheard: 317–8). Contrary to the diffuse shareholdings in UK and US listed companies, where the dominant institutional shareholders rarely exercise a joint approach to the corporate governance of the companies they have invested in, control in these Japanese companies can come from a small number of shareholders who constitute the majority. But, the control is passive, leaving management with considerable discretion. Control has been exchanged for '... an economy of scope in transacting and engaging in stable shareholdings' (Sheard: 319–20).

The exchange includes being kept well informed about the company, having a long-term contractual relationship, and trust which flows through into other aspects of the relationship between the companies, including trading between the companies in the group. Sheard argues that in an illiquid market for shares, where the shares are not easy to sell, the commitment of shareholders to the company is enhanced. In this way the Japanese companies exhibit an approach to corporate governance that is remarkably similar to that which applies in the private company in the UK. These companies often have similar 'shareholder agreements'. In a liquid share market, which prevails on the London and US markets, shareholder commitment is low. It is easy for the shareholder to sell. This leaves a vacuum of accountability unless the company performs so poorly that it makes itself vulnerable to a take-over.

2. Interlocking shareholdings between companies

The illiquid nature of the shareholdings in Japan is enhanced through interlocking shareholdings between the companies in the *kigyo shudan*. For example, the top twenty shareholders in Daiichi Kangyo Bank (DKB) are all companies. DKB is a prominent shareholder in those companies and provides the largest share of their loan capital. The shareholding has hardly changed in the ten-year period 1981–91 (Sheard: 335). The interlocking shareholdings represent a sharing of risk between the companies. Normally shares are not traded, providing a stability that, for example, allows the creation of more permanent employment relationships.

3. Main Bank arrangements (Sheard: 331)

The main bank of the *kigyo shudan* plays a monitoring role over the companies in the group. This is similar to the role that could be played by the institutional investors in western companies. It often includes the banks having representation on the board of the companies within the *kigyo shudan*.

> An important aspect of corporate governance in Japan is the major banks frequently arrange for senior executives in late career to enter client firms as senior managerial directors. (Sheard: 337)

There has been a weakening of main bank relations as a result of the country's banking difficulties. Japanese companies have reduced their dependence upon bank loans as the means of finance, but Hoshi sees no evidence that this will lead to a breakdown of the corporate groupings (Hoshi: 306).

The practical application of corporate governance principles will vary between countries and cultures. As the Hampel Committee reported: 'Corporate structures and governance arrangements vary widely from country to country. They are a product of the local and economic social environment' (Hampel: para. 1.4).

Market forces will lead to some convergence as companies trade globally and are listed on many Exchanges. The passion behind the Directors' Report of Arlen plc conceals a respect for governance actions and processes that will lead to greater corporate prosperity. As we have seen these actions and processes will vary from company to company and are not confined to listed companies. To this extent the protestations of Arlen plc are correct.

Application of Corporate Governance to Corporate Variety

Seventeen principles of corporate governance were stated in the Hampel Report. In this section, five of the principles that have most relevance across the variety of companies are looked at further and given some practical application to all companies.

1. *The company should have an effective board that leads and controls the company (para. 2.3)*

This applies to all the companies that we have analyzed. Companies that occupy the Puppet or Adrift cell do not have effective boards. Achieving an 'effective' status for the board has been identified as one of the key requirements for entrepreneur and family companies that want to develop. To some this may appear to involve sacrificing personal or family control. These feelings can be enormous barriers to change. They need to be confronted as early as possible in the development of the company. One method is to

- write down where the company structure is now and the desired position (use the PAPA grid as a guide)

- establish and prioritize those forces that can help to reach the desired position and those that will hinder, including personal emotions
- develop a list of actions that will minimize each force that is holding the company back and enhance the forces that are driving the company forward; include the first thing that needs to be done and when it will be done by
- do it.

Any board or director or shareholder can do this on their own. It is a more powerful exercise with members of the family, friends or your current board members, or subsidiary boards. If the board considers that it is an effective board, this assumption can be tested by requesting the board members to complete the board evaluation questionnaire in the Appendix. In subsidiary companies, if the board is not effective, then this prompts the question as to why there is a subsidiary company at all? If the company has been established for technical reasons, such as the protection of a name, and not for a trading purpose then an effective board is not required. In all other cases, the creation of an effective board is being used more frequently by large companies to achieve enhanced shareholder value, innovation and speed of movement in the market.

2. There are two distinct jobs at the top of the company, Chairman and Chief Executive Officer – a decision to combine the roles needs to be explained (para. 2.4)

There is no reason why the functions of a Chairman and Chief Executive cannot be combined in the same person. As we saw from the research by Coles and Hesterley, the institutional investors were more concerned that there was an independent element on the board. It is more important that the functions of the two positions are performed well than that different individuals perform them. For example, in an entrepreneur or family company, some of the functions of a chairman that are listed below can be performed by a non-executive director who does not serve the company under the title of 'chairman':

- A respected and trusted figure for the Chief Executive to talk to, as there are some things you cannot talk about within the company, at home or socially
- Someone who the non-family or non-shareholding directors can talk to

- Someone who can mediate conflict with accepted impartiality
- A focus on the effectiveness of the board – ensuring that the board is sticking to its function
- Evaluation of the directors, including the Chief Executive, and composition of the board.

We saw in the Jarrold & Sons Ltd case study in Chapter 4 that the proposed appointment of a non-family Chief Executive would split the roles of Chairman and Chief Executive for the first time. This was an option that was being pursued to help the succession plan. There will be other instances when companies may see that the splitting of the functions is an option that helps the company to develop.

3. The board should include a balance of executive and non-executive directors (para. 2.5)

The key word is 'balance'. There isn't a single board that would not benefit from an external perspective. Finding the right person to help the company in its development is probably the most important structural change that a family or entrepreneur company can make. But it has to be the right person, and that person is not easy to find. The specification process in Chapter 4 will help in making the correct appointment. It is better not to appoint than to appoint the wrong person. Non-executives can be appointed to ease the transition during the stages of corporate development, as long as they are aware of the development cycle that is in progress. Unfortunately, many non-executive directors are appointed just for their technical or professional skill and contacts. These are important attributes, but there needs to be a corporate architect on the board somewhere if you are to get the board architecture in place to take the company forward. This highlights the importance of the specification which could be one of the actions coming out of an analysis of the most 'effective board' to take the company forward.

Subsidiary companies often have directors from other parts of the group on the board. It is rarer for them to have independent non-executive directors. As part of a 'managing-up' strategy for the subsidiary that wants to move more towards the Partnership model, an influential independent non-executive can be of great assistance. The holding company would need to approve the appointment and the business case would need to be made. Just making the case is part of the 'managing-up' strategy – it says: 'We are here and we want an input into Group strategy. This is a person who can help us to develop our strategy more effectively and therefore help the Group.' The individual could even be an existing non-executive of the holding company, an adoption strategy. The holding company seeking to achieve greater leverage between the companies in the group could implement the same approach managing downwards.

4. The board should be supplied with timely and good quality information (para. 2.6)

Timely and relevant information is part of being an effective board. When the board of directors is a Puppet, information is less important. The decisions are already made or will be made outside the boardroom. When the board is Adrift, it is either awash with detail, devoid of context, or the company is in such a hiatus that agendas are always scrapped to deal with the latest urgent matter. An approach that non-executive directors can adopt on Adrift boards is to ask the person who prepared the paper to be in attendance to answer questions. This will often reveal the real decision-takers in the company. Autonomous subsidiary companies will only have the detail and context of their part of the business with no Group context.

The challenge for all companies moving towards a Partnership relationship between the shareholders and the board of directors is to obtain the right balance between strategic and detail, context and specific. Ultimately if the board is to function effectively it is dependent upon the information it receives and the way it is presented. This is the function of the Chairman who needs to ensure that the executive information systems deliver the right information at the right time. Otherwise the Chairman's role of overseeing an effective board is impossible.

Subsidiary companies should have regular reports from the Chief Executive on the development of the relationship with the holding company, preferably with reference to some action plan as to what the desired relationship is, and vice-versa.

5. Companies and [institutional] shareholders should be ready to enter into a dialogue based on the mutual understanding of objectives (para. 2.15)

Boards need to prepare the ground for the future benefit of the company, and this includes preparing the owners of the business. Entrepreneurs ignore the shareholders, themselves, when they forget that they are mortal and not immune from human frailties. Family boards ignore their family shareholders when there are too many of them, or because it takes too much time to keep people informed. Then a conflict breaks out, a key decision needs to be taken and there is no support. In smaller companies the shareholders are the board and they can talk to themselves until they are dragged away by men in white coats to be committed to an asylum. As soon as the shareholding membership of the company is different from the board membership, communication is required. As the company goes through its stages of development, this needs to be explained. Shareholders can be brought into the decision-making. Family Councils or just family meetings can achieve this. Larger companies need to structure their contact with institutional shareholders and analysts, as well as the content of the Annual General Meeting and the information that is made available to all shareholders. Companies anticipating the shareholders' support when a hostile take-over bid comes in will prepare the ground. The information that is provided to shareholders in Annual Reports is usually pretty mundane. Does it help shareholders to evaluate the real-time prospects of increases in shareholder value? Not according to Chris Swinson, president of the Institute for Chartered Accounting in England and Wales:

> Most of the largest businesses no longer regard their full general purpose reports as a satisfactory means of communicating with all of their shareholders. They increasingly make use of the power to publish summary financial statements to provide abbreviated and limited financial data which is commonly supplemented by other information...Growth in shareholder value is increasingly seen as a prime objective of corporate management. With this emphasis comes a concern that conventional financial reporting does not provide a reliable assessment of increases in shareholder value. (Swinson)

Many companies who proclaim that they have the objective of enhancing shareholder value in the Annual Reports proceed to produce performance criteria which do not measure this objective. There are accounting constraints that companies must adhere to, but it is possible to supplement the required figures. For example, Skandia has gone to great lengths to produce company reports that interpret a company's activities to illustrate to shareholders that:

> the real value of ... companies cannot be determined by only traditional accounting measures. The worth of an Intel or Microsoft lies not in bricks

and mortar, or even in inventories, but in another, intangible kind of asset: **Intellectual Capital**. (Edvinsson and Malone: 3)

This is an example of a company attempting to develop a mutual understanding of the objectives of the company with its shareholders which are then reflected in the financial methods it uses to illustrate its performance against those objectives. Skandia's supplements to their Annual Reports since 1994 chart this process.

Subsidiary companies must appreciate that their shareholder is the holding company, and it doesn't want any surprises. The holding company will often have stated the type of information it requires, particularly the monthly financials. A strategy for a subsidiary that is seeking to move the relationship more towards the Partnership model is to start to provide information that complies with the standard format, and go further. At every opportunity the subsidiary should raise the level of the debate with the holding company to a higher strategy level that has a group as opposed to a parochial subsidiary perspective.

The governance of companies is firmly on the agenda for:

- institutional investors – encouraged by government to be more interventionist upon pain of intervention, and pushed by organizations like Pensions Investment Research Consultants (PIRC)
- Governments across the world (a Commonwealth Secretariat Conference on corporate governance in 1998 attracted delegates from 22 countries)
- the European Union (which has just concluded a consultation exercise on harmonization of corporate governance, focusing on board structures)
- the accounting profession (which has to verify in Annual Reports of listed companies that the current self-regulatory Codes are being complied with and leads the debate on corporate reporting)
- the Institute of Directors (which is seeking to establish itself as THE professional body for the establishment of standards for directors, and has even attempted to create the Chartered Director)
- companies who see corporate governance as a critical feature of the profitable operation of the company for the benefit of shareholders.

There are principles stemming from the governance debate that can help *all* companies to move more smoothly through their various stages of development. It is a matter of identifying the needs of the company at any given moment in time. This requires an appreciation of the importance of the structure and relationships at board level, the board architecture, both current and desired.

The Impact on the Corporate Investor – Investing in and Influencing Structural Changes in Different Companies

The amount invested by venture capitalists in the UK rose from £2.14 billion in 1996 to £2.8 billion in 1997. The emphasis is on bigger deals, but 20 per cent are still for sums less than £100 000. About 40 per cent of new flotations in the UK were backed by venture capitalists. Britain accounted for 44 per cent of all venture capital investment in Europe in 1997, although the balance is starting to shift to the rest of Europe. Dr John Walker, Advent International's Chief Executive has stated that venture capitalists are thinking carefully about who to appoint to management teams to ensure that their investment is protected (*Sunday Times*: 1997b). Who to appoint is just one of the issues.

> Capital providers increasingly rely on the corporate governance of the corporations they invest in, or lend to, to provide actual accountability and responsibility to investors and lenders. (OECD: para. 8)

This requires structural alterations to the way the company interacts with its substantial shareholders. Hermes manages the UK's biggest pension fund:

> As a large institutional investor we don't believe in micromanagement of companies ... We will demand certain standards, certain information and certain structures of companies and in return we will offer long-term support to companies. (Alistair Ross Goobey, CEO, Hermes UK) (OECD: para. 102)

Hermes has announced an alliance with CalPERS, the largest US pension fund with $139 billion under management (£83 billion) in 1998, of which UK investments were valued at $5.9 billion. Together they will influence effective corporate governance in their corporate investments that they have in their respective countries. CalPERS has a reputation for being very direct with the companies it invests in regarding governance standards and this type of pressure is appearing in the UK. It is fostered by political pressure on institutional investors to be less passive and fill the vacuum of accountability that many listed companies exhibit by their presence in the Autonomous cell of the PAPA grid (Clarke and Clegg: 315).

The analysis that this book provides should prompt investors, and in particular the venture capitalists, to analyze the stage of development of companies that they are supporting. There is no single boiler plate for a governance structure. By recognizing the dynamics of corporate variety, institutional investors and venture capitalists can help the companies they invest in to move forward structurally so as to improve the chances of success. For example, rather than just appointing a non-executive onto the board, the venture capitalist could ask the following questions if the company being invested in is an entrepreneur company:

- Is the structure of the board with a non-executive appointed by us going to work? What do we want the non-executive to do? Can the non-executive appointed by us achieve our objectives and help the company to achieve theirs? Are there other things that need to be done with regard to the structure at the top of the company?
- Do the venture capitalist and the entrepreneur want a Partnership relationship?
- How do the executive directors behave on the board when there is an entrepreneur dominance on a 'Puppet' board? Are they sufficiently free and competent to express their views about the actions of the entrepreneur in directing the company?
- Will the entrepreneur take any notice of the non-executive director's views?

The banks provide substantial support for companies through loans and overdraft facilities. The banks total lending to just the small business sector totalled £34.1 billion at the end of June 1997 (Bank of England, 1998: 16). To what extent can they help companies to overcome the difficulties that they encounter as they move through stages of corporate development? A survey of 261 small firms concluded that,

> the relationship between small firms and banks is sterile, uncommunicative and unimaginative and ... both must take responsibility for the situation. There seems to be scope for an all-round reappraisal of positions. (Middleton et al. 157)

This is countered by reports of higher levels of customer satisfaction following the adoption of the BBA's Statement of Principles, 'Banks and Businesses Working Together' (BBA). Some banks have informed me that they are wary of becoming too involved in the management of companies too closely for fear of being deemed 'shadow directors', thereby opening up the potential for liability for the debts of the company if the company collapses. This is a weak argument as it is fairly hard to prove 'shadow director' status. It is more important that the banks use their collective knowledge and contacts to help to make companies, particularly vulnerable SMEs (Small to Medium-Sized Enterprises) aware of their own development needs for the perspective of board architecture. NatWest, which had 26.2 per cent of the market share of the small firms sector in November 1997 (Bank of England 1997b: 24), has developed a programme for training staff dealing with SMEs. Barclays, with a 23.3 per cent market share, has a similar programme of training. Lloyds TSB, with a 19.8 per cent market share, uses a 'Developing the Business' course for its staff. The content of these programmes needs to reflect awareness of the dynamic board architecture issues that confront such companies.

The Role of Business Support Agencies – Helping the Wide Range of Companies to Prosper

There are a number of business support agencies: Training Enterprise Councils, Business Links and Chambers of Commerce comprise the largest in number. In January 1998 there were 89 Business Links in 280 offices, 79 TECs and 62 Approved British Chambers of Commerce (Bank of England, 1998: 48). A merger of the Chambers of Commerce and the TECs is gradually taking place. There needs to be a greater emphasis on the quality of the business support that is provided rather than who is providing it. In particular, the capacity for SMEs to survive the different stages of corporate development is fairly fundamental to the enhancement of employment and the growth of the regional economy. What actions can be extracted from the analysis of corporate variety and board architecture to enable the business support agencies to improve the service that they provide?

Research undertaken at the University of Paisley on the role of non-executive directors in small companies questions the value of episodic and short-term business consultancy that is the traditional publicly funded model of support. The research highlights the potential for longer-term role of the non-executive function as a more effective possibility for public support (Deakins, Mileham and O'Neill). However, the difficulty of finding the right non-executive who can make the relationship work for the business should not be underestimated.

The European Commission see SMEs as an important factor in regional regeneration (European Commission: 1996). In the UK the eight new Regional Development Agencies have a small firms remit (Department of the Environment), as does the new University for Industry which has a target of reaching 100 000 start-up businesses and 50 000 established SMEs each year, 'making high quality education and training accessible to owner-managers and employees of SME' (Department for Education and Employment).

David Blunkett, the Secretary of State, writing in the Pathfinder prospectus for the University for Industry states that,

> Every business should strive to maximise its potential to compete in today's increasingly global markets. It is no longer good enough for some businesses to expect that they can compete by doing more of the same. (Department for Education and Employment: 1)

He is right, but the same need to be innovative and progressive applies to the design and content of the training and development. Over the years there has been a great focus on the vehicles for delivering help and support to SMEs. This included the creation of Business Links that were supposed to bring together Training and Enterprise Councils (TECs), Chambers of Commerce, and Local Authorities. The politics of dealing with the phalanx of regional agencies is now to be added to with the addition of the Regional Development Agencies and the University for Industry. Policy needs to shift to the design and content of the advice, education and training that is needed to enhance business effectiveness, and away from the vehicles for delivery. Then any organization that has the ability to deliver an approved design and content effectively would be eligible for the State support that pump-primes the SME sector. The University for Industry may be the vehicle for achieving this if it can cut through the local politics and focus on content and good delivery techniques and not the nature of the provider.

The lesson from the *chaebol* is: if the State does intervene it must do so to assist companies to develop at the key stages of their corporate life-cycle, and not prevent the evolution that is necessary and inevitable. Business support agencies need to be aware of these key stages and how best they can help companies to come through them. Any training or education objectives need to include reference to the dynamics of board architecture and be aware of corporate variety.

Intellectual Capital – Valuing and Renewing Intellectual Capital

Most modern leaders of companies realize that the greatest value of the company is locked up in the knowledge of the workforce: customer and account knowledge and methods of operating outside of standard operating procedures are just two examples. Given this, the board's performance and the performance of individual directors should be evaluated against the extent to which the knowledge of the company is utilized to enhance the value of the company. I am grateful to Mary Ann Dvonch, Vice-President of Strategy and Technology of the Production Systems Group at Xerox for the following example from Xerox that illustrates this point. Xerox discovered that there was a difference between the knowledge that was being supplied in the field by its 23 000 technical representatives, and the information that was maintained in service manuals. How could this tacit experience be captured, make them more efficient and enhance the value of the company? Xerox developed the Eureka Project. Eureka captures the insights developed by the representatives in the field and shares the knowledge via a searchable knowledge base with remote access. Field technicians write tips that describe their on-the-job experiences. The tip is validated by a peer review panel, stored in the knowledge base and used to update the service manuals. The names of the contributors of the tips are displayed with the updated knowledge, recognition being the most effective incentive to share knowledge. Xerox introduced Eureka in France in 1996, extending the concept to Canada and the United States in 1997 (CIO Magazine). The intention is to operate Eureka across the world. The effect is staggering:

- each reference to the knowledge base saves 50 per cent in repair time
- there are 1.3 man years in savings
- there are savings estimated at $50–100 million from these tips
- 85 per cent of technicians access tips, with 5000 accesses per month
- 1 tip per 1000 service calls is entered into the system each month.

All of this knowledge about the real operational issues surrounding the copiers was locked up in the combined experience of the technicians. Xerox captured that knowledge to improve their service. This is an example of a company attempting to turn the latent knowledge of staff into a structural asset of the company that adds value to the company.

Case Study 7.1

Skandia

In 1994 Skandia, a Swedish insurance company, produced a supplement to its Annual Report with the title of 'Visualizing Intellectual Capital in Skandia'. The report was one of the first attempts by a company to create a value for the company that embraced a valuation of the company's intellectual capital as well as the normal book value items that are traditionally illustrated in Annual Reports.

> 'At Skandia we have always maintained that our intellectual capital is at least as important as our financial capital in providing truly sustainable earnings. That is why we have made substantial efforts in recent years to visualize and more concretely describe those assets that are difficult to distinguish in the overwhelming mass of financial information' (Bjorn Wolrath, CEO Skandia, 1994)

Skandia appointed Leif Edvinsson as the first Director of Intellectual Capital of the Skandia group. He also goes under the title of Global Knowledge Nomad. From 1991 he worked with a team to develop the Skandia Navigator, a new taxonomy for measuring the value of a company that includes intellectual capital. The first portrayal of the results of their work to shareholders came in the 1994 Supplement to the Annual Report and supplements have since appeared each year. Skandia portrays the role of intellectual capital using the metaphor of a tree as in Figure 7.2.

> ... what is described in organization charts, annual reports, quarterly statements, company brochures, and other documents is the trunk, branches, and leaves. The smart investor scrutinizes this tree in search of ripe fruit to harvest. But to assume that this is the entire tree because it represents everything immediately visible is obviously a mistake. Half the mass or more of that tree is underground in the root system. And whereas the flavour of the fruit and the colour of the leaves provides evidence of how healthy that tree is right now, understanding what is going on in the roots is a far more effective way to learn how healthy that tree will be in the years to come. The rot or parasite just now appearing thirty feet underground may well kill that tree that today looks in the prime of health. (Edvinsson and Malone: 10–11)

Dynamic Directors

Figure 7.2 The Skandia Tree
SOURCE: Leif Edvinsson, director of Intellectual Capital, Skandia

There are two aspects to intellectual capital. The company can never own people. They are free agents who have the capacity, as individuals or as collectives in teams, to think and do different things every day. This is the *human capital* of the company. The company can harness their talents and skills for innovation and service delivery. All companies do this. Processes, patents and trademarks are just some examples of the *structural capital* that companies own as a result of turning human capital into something that remains with the company when the staff go home (Edvinsson and Malone: 11). Other examples of structural capital include the customer relationships that are captured at a corporate level and do not reside with one individual or group of individuals. In many organizations, particularly service sectors such as advertising, accountancy and law, this causes a real problem. Where customer relationships focus on one or a few individuals, the human capital may not have been converted into structural capital of the company. For example, the individual may have the potential to leave the company with the account and the account information on the key influencers in the client, reducing the value of the company. Contractual attempts to prevent this happening can be put into place but they are not watertight. They are more effective the more senior the employee of the company. The Skandia approach not only provides an opportunity to provide shareholders with more information regarding the true valuation of the company; it also focuses management attention on indicators that underpin the real and future value of the company. It provides an indicator of the board and directors' achievement, or lack of achievement. We monitor what we measure. A company may be vulnerable if there is an imbalance between human and structural capital. This illustrates the value of investing in human capital and pursuing its conversion to structural capital, as illustrated in the following equation:

Human Capital + Structural Capital = Intellectual Capital

One of the reasons that Skandia decided to pursue this approach to valuing the company was that it was concerned that the market was not aware of the full value of the company. There was an information gap that affected the perception of the market of Skandia's true value. Skandia operates in the 'knowledge economy'. Its future products and services are contained in the foresight and imagination of its staff. This can be stimulated and captured by the company:

> The knowledge economy is governed by the law of increasing marginal utility ... when knowledge is shared and applied by an even greater number of users, its value increases. ('Customer Value', Supplement to Skandia's 1996 Annual Report)

When the process of conversion from human capital to structural capital leads to new goods or services, Skandia refers to the conversion as 'Knowledge Innovation':

> Knowledge Innovation is the creation, evolution, exchange and application of ideas into marketable goods and services, leading to the success of an enterprise, the vitality of a nation's economy and the advancement of society. (Debra M. Amidon, Entovation International, in Skandia's 1996 Supplement to the Interim Report).

Skandia is leveraging off its individual employees' work methods, knowledge and ideas and now describes itself as an 'innovative growth company' (CEO, Lars-Eric Petersson, 1997 Supplement to the Interim Report).

Xerox's project Eureka is converting the human capital into its standard process manual and product development. Xerox also decided to enhance the value of the human capital by providing an extra means of communication for them. This would in turn lead to an enhancement of structural capital.

There is probably not a single CEO who will not have complained at some time of the inability of the market to make accurate assessments of the true value of their company. The reporting information provided by Skandia does help to complete the information that will have an impact on the market value of the company. One of the reasons for the rise in the EVA approach within companies has been a desire from institutional shareholders to have access to information that portrays cash flow into the future. But this information is incomplete, as it takes no account of the enhancement of, or threat to, intellectual capital. The attempts to define increases and decreases in a company's intellectual capital are an important addition to the debate on measuring shareholder value. The value added to a company by its intellectual capital is a positive addition to the 'capital' of the company that the shareholders have a stake in. It will be a judgement for the shareholders as to whether it will lead to enhanced future cash flows, perhaps because the company has acquired a software genius. The market will respond as it does when a football club buys a star player. The shares go up or down dependent upon the assessment the market makes as to the likelihood of the new player enhancing the future cash flows of the club. In companies, there are only the results to look at. Measurements of intellectual capital are an attempt to provide better information flows to shareholder on a critical aspect of the company's assets. This may lead to better judgements as to how this intangible asset could lead to future cash flows and a more accurate market value based on all of the asset earning potential. But the market can only respond if it has the information about the ebbs and flows of the intellectual capital in the company. Skandia has developed a methodology for measuring Intellectual Capital (IC): the Skandia Navigator, a new value measurement that is not reflected in traditional revenue statements or profit and loss statements. This is critical information if you want to make a more informed opinion of the future value of a knowledge-based company. The shareholders can adjust their expectations of future cash flows by reference to information from Skandia that includes increases or decreases in IC. This will be reflected in the share price and Skandia's market capitalization.

This ability of the company to adopt values and structures that enable it to learn from the behaviour and thoughts of its staff is critical to the company's future success:

> An organization's ability to learn, and translate that learning into action rapidly, is the ultimate competitive business advantage. (Jack Welch, Chairman General Electric Co.)

But there have to be the right structures at board and group level for this to happen. The board needs to understand and adopt the values that are necessary to create this environment. In large global companies the 'small in large' philosophy adopted by Ericsson helps individuals to associate with the strength of the group, yet feel part of a smaller unit. But more is needed if the company is to utilize the knowledge of its staff in the knowledge economy. Clarke and Clegg conclude that:

> Understandably, in virtual organizations people feel an overpowering need to belong to something they can identify with and feel proud of. In this

relationship it is even more important that their company can offer a sense of purpose that gives meaning to work. (Clarke and Clegg: 432)

It is part of the board's function to enhance organizational capability by providing that sense of purpose.

Innovation Leadership – a Leadership Attribute of Directors and a Function of the Board

History has recorded the inability of many companies to alter their structures and processes in a timely manner so as to prevent being blown out of the water by new upstarts. There is a need to combine the thinking on intellectual capital with the reality of how companies respond to innovation. Companies can be very good at adopting innovation that sustains their dominance in a given sector, both through incremental and radical innovation. They are less prepared to accept innovation from within their organization that has the capacity to kill their existing products and processes, and ultimately the company itself as it is currently perceived. Professor Clayton Christensen of Harvard Business School has researched the reasons why successful companies ignored technologies or processes that ultimately turned in on them and hurt them badly, sometimes mortally. His book *The Innovator's Dilemma* is an outstanding piece of research. It is based on the premise that there must be a reason why companies like IBM, Seagate and Sears appeared to miss the application of technologies and processes that are staring them in the face: the PC, the 3.5-inch disk drive and discount retailing. To this list we could perhaps now add Bertelsmann, the giant German publishing group, and the destructive technology of internet bookselling. Will internet bookselling do to Bertelsmann what discount retailing did to Sears?

Christensen asks the question, is there 'something about the way decisions get made in successful organizations that sows the seeds of eventual failure' (Christensen: xii)?

This book is about the individuals and structures at the top of companies, the directors and the board of directors. It is one of their responsibilities to overcome any structural reasons that may push the company towards that eventual failure and to identify the values within the company that may accelerate impending doom. In a detailed study Christensen charts the disk drive industry and proves that, at every stage of development of different sizes of disk drives, with one exception, the incumbent main suppliers of the previous disk drive failed to take the initiative with the new size. Why? They had led the race to develop even better versions of the disks that they were producing, increasing their performance with sustaining technology. But when it came to anticipating the destructive effect of the smaller disk size, they failed. Further research showed the same pattern repeating itself in

- the mechanical excavator industry, overtaken by hydraulic diggers
- integrated steel manufacturing, overtaken by steel minimills.

Christensen gives three main reasons for their failure:

1. Listening to Customers and Driving upmarket

The first models of the new size disk drives had an inferior technical performance to the incumbent model. They couldn't store as much information. The customers of the suppliers were looking for greater capacity not less and the incumbents listened to their customers. Eventually the inferior disk drives improved to capture the incumbent's market, but not before they had found a new market for the new technology. Intel's new chip, the Pentium II Xeon is an upmarket chip that will sell for more than $1000. It is suited for high-powered server machines that use microprocessors to match the power of large mainframe systems. It expands Intel's sales outside the low-margin PC industry. Intel Vice-President, Patrick Gelsinger is quoted as saying: 'We are moving up the food chain' (*Wall Street Journal*, 1 July 1998).

Intel plans to introduce an even more powerful chip, Merced, pushing the company towards even more powerful computers. At the same time small chip manufacturers are filling the gap that is being left behind for the smaller chips which have a different application in small electronic items where cheapness and size is the prime consideration rather than power. For these smaller start-up companies the margins are still attractive, and of course they will improve the performance of their chips through sustaining technology, as did the producers of all the disk drives.

2. Margins on the new product are too low

The margins for increasing the technical performance of the existing product were far greater than the margins for investing in a new product for which there was no established large market. The finance directors applying rational resource allocation models would always opt for higher specification of the existing product:

Committing development resources to launch higher-performance products that could garner higher gross margins generally both offered greater returns and caused less pain. As their managers were making repeated decisions about which new product development proposals they should fund and which they should shelve, proposals to develop higher-performance products targeted at the larger, higher-margin markets immediately above them always got the resources. In other words, sensible resource allocation processes were at the root of companies' upward mobility and downmarket immobility across the boundaries of the value networks in the disc drive industry (Christensen: 80).

One of the advantages of running your own company is that you can decide what risks to take. Pilkingtons would never have taken the risk involved in developing the glass float technique if the investment had been judged on a net cash flow basis. The break-even period was 12 years (Utterback: 119).

3. Disruptive technologies take off when they are valued for the attributes they possess.

Disruptive technologies create an attribute that the existing technology cannot match. It is these very attributes that prevent incumbent producers from identifying their potential, as they are worthless in the markets that they currently serve. The 5.25-inch disc drive found its home in the desktop PCs where relative size was a critical issue. Of course the performance of the 5.25-inch drive then improved, increasing at 50 per cent per year from 1980 to 1990 (Christensen: 19). The incumbent's customers were not desktop PC manufacturers, so they did not anticipate the demand. Only one of the 8-inch drive manufacturers survived to produce 5.25-inch drives. The rest failed. The story continues with nearly all disk drive changes driven by disruptive technology.

How can altering corporate structures change this pattern which apparently forces companies that are at the top of their field in technological innovation to failure? There are two structural alterations that can help companies overcome this innovation dilemma. Companies may have a technostructure that can have a substantial effect on decision-making within the company. The decision is made before it gets to the boardroom. Directors need to probe the details of executive papers with the executives themselves to establish where the real power base lies within the company. Christensen recognizes the power of the technostructure:

> Typically, senior managers are asked to decide whether to fund a project only after many others at a lower level in the organization have already decided which types of project proposals they want to package and send on to senior management for approval and which they don't think are worth the effort. Senior managers typically see only a well-screened subset of the innovative ideas generated. (Christensen: 103)

There will also be destructive technologies that some individuals will deliberately avoid because they do see its latent destructive nature and its impact on them personally. They do not want to fundamentally alter the work they do and kill the company's current products or their jobs. Ironically, the failure to do so often leads to a worse fate as the opportunity for retraining when a new entrant has superseded you is much less. Therefore, companies that have a tendency to have a strong technostructure that diminishes the strategic effectiveness of the board of directors are more likely to miss the destructive technologies. Conversely, an effective board that understands the dilemma which innovation can pose for the company can see through the technocratic arguments which are put to it.

The second structural method of overcoming the natural tendency for companies to ignore destructive technologies is to create a subsidiary company that is totally Autonomous from the main company. Hewlett-Packard established a rival company to produce ink-jet printers as a direct competitor with HP's laser printers. IBM set up a separate organization in Florida, away from IBM headquarters in New York, to manufacture desktop PCs in the first five years of the personal computing industry (Christensen: 110). In this way the tension of running two different business models in the same company is mitigated.

The effect of disruptive technology is not confined to products. It also applies to services such as insurance (Skandia), and processes (word processing to voice processing?). Can wallpaper manufacturers make the leap to produce paper with electronic ink? Structural alterations on their own will not be sufficient to resolve the difficulties companies are confronted with by potentially disruptive technologies. It is a combination of:

- ensuring that the appropriate structures are in place, identifying the innovation role that the board of the company needs to play, and then

- innovation leadership at the top of the company: requiring perspective and then the bravery to 'kill the company kindly'.

Managers who confront disruptive technological change must be leaders, not followers, in commercializing disruptive technology. Doing so requires implanting the projects that are to develop such technologies in commercial organizations that match in size the market they are to address. These assertions are based on two key findings of this study: that leadership is more crucial in coping with disruptive technologies than with sustaining ones, and that small, emerging markets cannot solve the near-term growth and profit requirements of large companies. (Christensen: 125)

Part of the organizational capability function of the board is to create a board architecture that recognizes the power of innovation at a strategic level. Innovation leadership is one of the strands of the complex leadership skills that dynamic directors need and should be evaluated against, particularly in fast-moving sectors. It includes the ability to lead innovation in the way that business is conducted, such as through joint ventures, as well as technical product and process innovation.

Mergers and Acquisitions – Identifying Structural Differences between Companies to either Enhance Success or Abandon

Case Study 7.2

Pharmical plc (Fiction)

Pharmical plc is a large multinational pharmaceuticals group of companies. The head office relationship with the group's subsidiaries is based on the Partnership model. The subsidiary companies cover different sectors of the market and have substantial commercial freedom subject to

- 'one company' branding
- a centralized research and development programme, over which the subsidiary companies have a substantial influence through feedback of their sector knowledge.

The Chief Executive of the Group is well respected amongst his colleagues on the Group board, but not that visible within the group or publicly. The decisions are made as low down in the structure of the companies as possible, guided by a clear vision and strategy.

Pharmical plc is considering a merger with Drugs plc, a pharmaceutical company of similar size to Pharmical. This would make the combined company the largest in the world and lead to significant cost saving to the benefit of shareholders as infrastructures are merged. Drugs plc also has subsidiary companies on a country basis. The relationship between the Drugs plc head office and its subsidiaries is a Puppet relationship. The Chief Executive of Drugs plc is perceived as a powerful figure inside and outside the company. A lot of decisions are referred to him, as he has been known to explode if a decision has been made which he disagrees with. This means that he will get involved in even the most trivial of decisions at times. He has a reputation as a 'workaholic' and is proud of it. The subsidiary companies are trading entities only, with no strategic authority. There is a large head office function.

The merger talks are abandoned. There are rumours that this was because of disagreement as to which Chief Executive would be in charge of the merged company. The real reason is that the difficulties of merging two companies with such different cultures of operation were identified and seen as too onerous to overcome without one company being seen to be taking over the other. Neither company was prepared to contemplate the other being in the ascendancy. The two Chief Executives studied the diagram in Figure 7.3, and were advised that they had to make a decision as to which direction they wanted the merged Group to go, but could not agree.

When mergers or acquisitions are contemplated, fundamental differences in the internal structures of the companies can cause significant problems when it comes to successful implementation of the merger. In the Pharmical plc case study, one approach would have to dominate. If the Partnership approach dominated, there would be a significant development phase for the managers used to being treated as Puppets. If the Puppet approach prevailed, there would be a lot of disillusioned senior staff looking for new opportunities to be 'spark-plugs', and in the meantime a reaction could be to throw as many spanners into the bureaucratic machine as possible. The likelihood as with all mergers and acquisitions, is that the new company would spend some time Adrift until a clear vision and strategy emerged. This is an opportunity for competitors to forge ahead and to capture the best staff that fall out of the transition whilst the merging companies focus internally. The

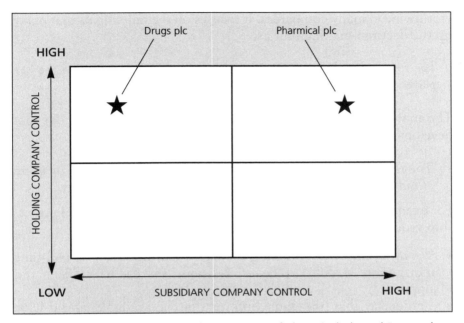

Figure 7.3 PAPA grid analysis of the merger of Pharmical plc and Drugs plc

longer the company is Adrift the further ahead the competitors will get.

The same principles apply when subsidiaries within the same group merge as part of structural reorganization. It could be divisions, departments or units that are affected. In each case it is important for the implementation of effective change management to appreciate whether the management–control relationship is being changed and whether the change is the same for all of the parties involved.

Selling at Board Level – Making the High Level Approach More Effective

The Miller and Heinman approach to effective selling and account management includes the analysis of the key decision-makers in the organization that is being sold to. These are the economic, technical and user buyers (Miller and Heinman: ch.4). A 'coach' is also identified to assist in the success of the sale. The personal benefits of the sale to each of these individuals are identified, as well as their attitude to the seller and their perception of the need for the product or service. This approach is a valuable tool for anyone who is selling and is used worldwide in many companies. It focuses on the individuals that make up the decision-making unit as,

> The foundation of every reliable sales strategy is knowing who the key players are. (Miller and Heinman: 69)

The analysis in the previous chapters adds a corporate perspective that develops the following:

1. *The features of the service or product to the company can be more closely associated with the benefits to the buying company.*

For example, in selling management information systems to a Partnership group of companies the benefits will be:

- Freeing up of decision-taking through the availability of real-time information leading to faster decisions for the customers and suppliers
- Confidence that the same information is available world-wide providing consistency of treatment for customers and all in the value chain
- The stimulation of progress across the group supported by first-class knowledge management systems that enables the sharing of intellectual capital for the benefit of customers who get better solutions from the buyer than any of the buyer's competitors
- Enhanced share value as the company realizes an untapped asset, its corporate knowledge – it is a Partnership company and the interests of the shareholders need to be included in the benefits
- Bespoke facilities following an assessment of best practice across the group of companies enabling the system in this company to match the special needs of customers and those in the value chain.

In selling management information systems to a Puppet group of companies, the benefits are put differently. They could be:

- The ability to control operations from the centre, ensuring consistency of treatment and greater value for customers through control of the value chain across the group
- Compliance across the globe with standards set by the centre, ensuring that all customers get the same high standards
- The ability to veto and approve decisions at a distance and with speed so that customers and others get fast decisions

- Bespoke facilities to be agreed by the Chairman and Chief Executive (combined roles) enabling the system in this company to match the special needs of customers and those in the value chain.

As we have seen, companies are dynamic and will move from one relationship to another. When this is happening sellers should ask: can my product or service help the prospective client to make that transition more effectively?

2. *A clearer identification of the real economic buyer*

If the seller is selling into a Puppet subsidiary company, the real economic buyer may be at head office. Are you are just talking to technical and user buyers? In an Adrift company, will there ever be a decision? In an Autonomous company, all the decision-makers are in that company. In a Partnership subsidiary company, the decision-makers may be spread around the Group. This makes identification more difficult, but it may open up other opportunities...

3. *Opportunities for selling within the Group of companies as opposed to just one of the subsidiary companies*

Leveraging off the group is a key attribute of Partnership companies. Therefore, if a product or service is received well within one of the companies within the group, the customer should be receptive to the promotion of best practice across the group. This has an implication for the definition of 'key account' status. For example, take the situation of a group of companies, the buyer, that has twenty subsidiaries across the world and a product or service that is being used in five of them. If the buyer is in Adrift or Autonomous mode in the relationship with its subsidiaries, then there may be little likelihood of the seller being able to leverage off the existing sales base to move into the other companies. This can be left to the local sales teams on an ad hoc basis. If the buyer is in Puppet or Partnership mode with its subsidiaries, then there is the opportunity of using the leverage issue to gain entry into the other subsidiaries. This then becomes a key account for which a strategy across the seller would need to be developed.

Strategic sales planning documentation can be altered to include these factors as illustrated in Figure 7.4 overleaf.

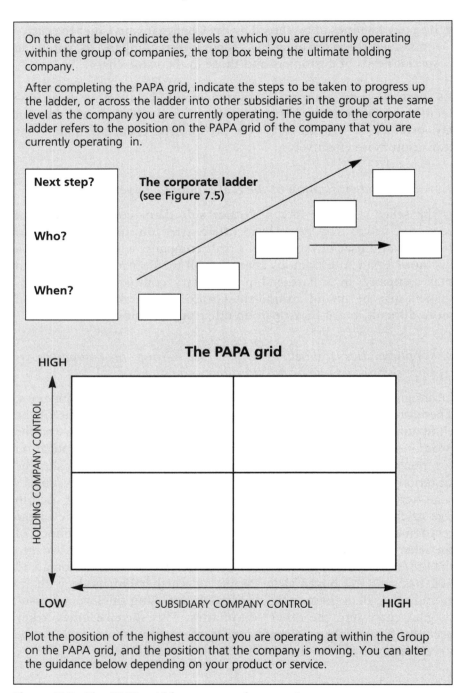

On the chart below indicate the levels at which you are currently operating within the group of companies, the top box being the ultimate holding company.

After completing the PAPA grid, indicate the steps to be taken to progress up the ladder, or across the ladder into other subsidiaries in the group at the same level as the company you are currently operating. The guide to the corporate ladder refers to the position on the PAPA grid of the company that you are currently operating in.

Next step?

The corporate ladder
(see Figure 7.5)

Who?

When?

The PAPA grid

HIGH

HOLDING COMPANY CONTROL

LOW   SUBSIDIARY COMPANY CONTROL   HIGH

Plot the position of the highest account you are operating at within the Group on the PAPA grid, and the position that the company is moving. You can alter the guidance below depending on your product or service.

Figure 7.4 The PAPA grid for a group of companies

GUIDE TO THE CORPORATE LADDER.

PUPPET: Need to get as close to the top of the corporate ladder as possible as this is where major decisions are made. 'We'll have to get Head Office approval'. Imperative to co-ordinate account activity across the various subsidiaries in the Group. The client may welcome rationalization of purchasing, but be careful it doesn't backfire.

ADRIFT: Unlikely to get a decision anywhere in the normal decision-making ranks of the company for a while, but watch very closely for movement to another position on the grid and identify how you can help the company to get there. 'Things are up in the air at the moment'. Likelihood of restructuring. Identify internal successors. Identify the real decision-makers who could be in the bowels of the company.

AUTONOMOUS: Decisions are made at the subsidiary/division level and less urgent to work up the ladder or co-ordinate the accounts from different subsidiaries of the same Group. Work on the decision-makers in the subsidiaries. 'We make the decisions here'. Look out for signs that the company is moving up the PAPA grid. The clearest sign is complaints of 'interference from the centre'. The company may actually be moving to Partnership – read the Annual Report and any statements from the Group CEO. They will probably tell you. If they are moving, how can you help?

PARTNERSHIP: You can use your current contacts to get close to the top with ideas and best practice. Shareholder Value is a key. 'I talk with the Group CEO nearly every day. I'll mention that idea to him'. Identify values of the Group and cite them/use them as part of the sale. Identify all the work that you are doing in this Group as the different parts of the company will exchange best practice and act upon it. Aim to become one of their Partners.

Figure 7.5   Guide to the Corporate Ladder in Figure 7.4

8 *Conclusion*

We have identified how the function of the board of directors and the qualities of the directors on the board need to change to reflect the dynamic relationship between the shareholders and the board. All companies need dynamic boards of directors in order to prosper and endure. This is the heart of good governance. It affects all companies, all the people who work for them and the communities in which they are based. This responsibility makes being a director on a board an onerous position to hold and the planning of the role and composition of the board of directors a key activity.

> For over a hundred years, the fate of White Furniture Company marked the fate of Mebane. In the 1990s, this is no longer the case. White Furniture is closed…The building remains but White Furniture Company is gone. For the former White workers, for anyone who has lived long in Mebane, there's no missing the silence at the center of town. (Bamberger and Davidson: 172)

Any company is susceptible to what happened to the White Furniture Company. It is a matter of choice for the shareholders and the board of directors. Understanding the relationship between these two organs of the company can at least clarify the nature of the options that are open and the consequences of those choices. Most boards that I have worked with are seeking to move towards more of a Partnership relationship between the board and the shareholders. The perceived need to enhance shareholder value is only one of the drivers, mainly to be found in listed companies where that value has a clear indicator: the share price. For other companies, the key driver is often necessity. Having looked at the other options to take the company forward, it is in the best interests for the long-term survival of the company to adopt the hard path of the Partnership relationship. It is a hard path. The other options just happen without direct intervention. The Partnership option has to be planned and worked at. We have seen that the corporate governance principles and structures that underpin the Partnership relationship need to be varied according to the category of company, but they are not confined to the listed company.

It is easy to commit to action when looking at a flip chart in a seminar room, having managed to escape from the daily business emergencies to reflect. It is much harder to go back to the office and behave and act differently. The action that seemed so sensible and even possible amidst the euphoria of the freedom to think without the mobile phone ringing or the e-mail pinging, suddenly seems very hard. The perspective of what the future can look like disappears like mist as the sun rises on the realities of the 'day job'. In these instances being a 'director' is not really the day job. The default job is the functional responsibility that the individual holds. The functional role is easier and the job that most 'directors' have been promoted from. Ultimately the director may be totally convinced that the actions that were conceived and promised are futile, even irrelevant to the business that they have to run. The job of director then ceases to exist, let alone be a dynamic one. The company will not be a dynamic one either, because 'the fish rots from the head' (Garratt).

There are the directors who do see that there has to be change in the boardroom. There are a number of great success stories told in the case studies in this book. The constant feature of their success is a successful partnership between the shareholders and the board of directors. This is the relationship that is fundamental to the dynamism of the board and of the company. Arie de Gues argues for a

> system of corporate governance that provides continuity, with all the requirements that nurture a living company and a human community, without absolute power concentrated in the hands of either shareholders or management. To develop this system of corporate governance in our age of knowledge, we need to open the debate about power and governance. As matters stand today, companies may too easily suffer the consequences of ultimate power given to one basic interest group, the shareholders, whereas the governance structure gives ample opportunity to an almost medieval exercise of absolute power by management. (de Geus: 233)

However, a company that is in a Partnership relationship deliberately creates this necessary tension between the shareholders and the management and then reflects it in the corporate governance structures and the role of individual directors. The tension generates a sense of purpose for the governance structures, a reason for their existence. This is the dialogue, conflict and structure that keeps the Partnership together. The exact scope of the appropriate governance structures and the content of the values that support them will vary according to corporate variety. There will be occasions when the company will move towards a different relationship between the board of directors and the shareholders. This may be prompted by the appointment of a new chairman or chief executive, planning for their succession, or during a financial crisis. This will test the strength of the governance structures of the company and the values they are there to uphold.

As we have moved through the chapters the key features for a successful Partnership relationship in each of the companies has been identified:

The Entrepreneur Company
- The 'chairman' function needs to be clear and not vested in the entrepreneur
- The board must operate as a professional board.

The Family Company
- The development of family values that are subsumed into corporate values
- The board must operate as a professional board
- The presence of independent directors
- A communication and participation structure for family non-board members.

The Listed Company
- A clear and shared vision which leads to the objective of enhancing shareholder value
- Delegation of responsibility to divisions, subsidiaries, and individuals who share the vision
- Excellent communication with shareholders and those who influence shareholders
- Clear financial objectives focused on shareholder value
- People and systems that match the shareholder value culture.

Corporate Groups
- A shared passion for the vision
- Integrity based on clearly understood values

- Constant communication between Group and subsidiary Chief Executives
- Excellent financial and risk management
- People and systems that match the culture.

These are just the key features. They are different for each type of company, but there are some similarities. I am reluctant to portray one theme that comes through this analysis, as I have argued that the needs of different companies need to be taken into account. However, the temptation is overwhelming, and if there is one 'golden thread' that has run through the analysis of the Partnership relationship between the board and shareholders, it is the fusing of corporate culture, people and technology.

Countries have a role to play in creating the right infrastructure for their companies to thrive in. The focus on corporate governance at the level of the listed company ignores the need to look at the great number of other companies upon whose growth and survival a large part of the economy depends. In 1996 small firms in the UK accounted for 99.6 per cent of the total business population, 44.3 per cent of total turnover and 51.2 per cent of employment (Bank of England, 1998: 11); it is important to extend governance principles to these companies. The principles are good ones; they need to be adapted to the particular needs of different types of company so as to enhance their performance and commercial life-span:

> Our industrial base will need to be strengthened by developing small businesses into a solid tier of medium-sized companies. The Government, the banking professions, and industry all have a role to play in this endeavour ... The intense competition we shall see within Europe makes it even more important that British policy making is guided towards fundamental factors and not towards thought of gimmicks or financial manipulation. Our infra-structure needs to be of the best...We need to address seriously and with an open mind, the issue of the best structure of corporate governance in the UK. (Alexander: 10–11)

Governments can provide a framework for all companies to thrive in. But, in the end it is the management of companies, particularly the senior management at board level who will determine their rate of economic performance. Whether the opportunity for change is grasped will usually be decided at the board level of companies. It will be decided by: the entrepreneur, the group of family directors of the company, the professional director who sits on a board with family or entrepreneur directors, the non-executive director or executive director of the large listed company, or any company. They may have to question their 'comfortable' status or the 'comfortable' status of others on the board. They will have to be dynamic.

Appendix: Evaluation Questionnaires for the Board, Directors, Chief Executive and Chairman

Functions of your board

This set of questions concerns the functions of your board of directors. Answer the questions from your perspective as to how the board as a whole of your company is functioning. For example, the first question asks you to assess the extent to which your board has defined its role and responsibilities. Has it been poor at doing this, fair, good or excellent?

CEO (Chief Executive Officer) is the same as Chief Executive or Managing Director for the purposes of all these questions. A non-executive director is a director of the company who does not have an executive role within that company, although they may have such a role in associated companies.

The questions are divided into five categories:

A   **Strategic Direction**
B   **Planning**
C   **Monitoring and Control of Performance**
D   **Awareness of and Compliance with Legal Responsibilities**
E   **Organizational Capability**

A. Strategic Direction

1. defined its role and responsibilities ... *Poor ... Fair ... Good ... Excellent*
2. overseen the company's strategic planning process
3. involved in the development of the company's strategic direction
4. communicated the company's strategic direction throughout the company
5. developed corporate values
6. actions reflected application of the company's values
7. considered shareholder value in the decision-making process
8. devoted time to strategic issues

B. Planning

9. identified financial risk issues that could have a significant impact on the company
10. identified non-financial risks that could have a significant impact on the company
11. received plans for the implementation of strategy from the CEO
12. analyzed plans for the implementation of strategy
13. identified the information needed to review plans
14. benchmarked the strategic plan with industry comparative data
15. planned for crises
16. reviewed parameters for allocation of resources

C. Monitoring and Control of Performance

17. developed performance objectives
18. required information showing progress against corporate objectives
19. analyzed financial information for important issues and trends
20. analyzed budget allocation against performance
21. understands the company's business well enough to provide critical oversight
22. reviewed company performance against strategic plan
23. monitored board performance
24. assessed the performance of all directors

D. Awareness of and compliance with legal responsibilities

25. approved a system of delegated authority /internal controls
26. monitored the company's system of delegated authority/internal controls
27. sought outside advice when appropriate
28. approved a process for individual directors to seek external independent advice
29. defined expectations concerning director responsibilities
30. provided ongoing development for directors on areas of director responsibility
31. trained directors in corporate governance matters
32. communicated the scope of the board's authority

E. Organizational Capability

33. considered board composition to match the needs of the company
34. developed succession plans for key personnel
35. board involved in director recruitment
36. developed a partnership with the CEO and other senior managers
37. remuneration strategy for senior executives is considered fully by the board

38. had access to corporate officers outside of board meetings
39. reviewed corporate structure required to deliver the strategic plan
40. analyzed product or service development cycles
41. analyzed approach to innovation
42. reviewed information strategy

Attributes of Directors

This set of questions assesses the attributes of you as a director of the company and your fellow directors. Answer the question for yourself and for each of your fellow directors. For example, in the first the question is whether you or your fellow director openly communicates goals, expectations, and concerns with the managing director. You are asked to answer this question based on current performance and also how often you think the behaviour should occur.

F   **Integrity**
G   **Leadership skills: Teamplayer/Communicator**
H   **Analytical: Analyze and Interpret Information**
I   **Specialist Skills and Knowledge**
J   **Thinker – Open minded/Strategic**
K   **Open Questions**

F.   Integrity

1. communicated any concerns on decisions to the CEO or Chairman ....
   Almost Always ... Usually ... Sometimes ... Rarely ... Almost Never –
   answer for both current performance and desired performance
2. disclosed personal interests in transactions and abstained from voting where appropriate
3. intervened when believed strongly about an issue
4. publicly disagreed with decision of the board when contrary to personal beliefs
5. displayed integrity beyond reproach

G.   Leadership Skills: Teamplayer/Communicator

6. demonstrated energy and commitment in dealing with issues
7. delivered on promises made
8. helped the board or committee to arrive at a decision
9. built on other's contributions to discussions
10. ignored information and opinions from others

H. Analytical: Analyze and Interpret Information

11. asked probing questions of management
12. focused on the issues in question
13. interpreted data accurately
14. brought relevant information into the discussion from unusual sources
15. made compelling arguments to support a case

I. Specialist Skills and Knowledge

16. added to board debates
17. kept current on areas of expertise
18. provided contacts for the benefit of the company
19. provided expert skills to help the company develop and achieve its goals
20. discovered specialist information from within the company for the board

J. Thinker – Open-minded/Strategic

21. offered creative and innovative ideas
22. thought through the impact of decisions
23. held predictable views
24. been susceptible to influence
25. made a strategic contribution to board decisions

K. Open Questions

26. What do you think YOU should do more of?

....

....

27. What do you think YOU should do less of?

....

....

28. What do you think YOU should continue to do?

....

....

29. What do you think [insert name of Director] should do less of?

   ....

30. What do you think [insert name of Director] should do more of?

   ....

31. What do you think [insert name of Director] should continue to do?

   ....

[Repeat 28–31 for each Director]

The Chairman and the CEO

This set of questions applies to the role of the Chairman and CEO of the company. If the roles of Chairman and CEO are combined, you will be answering this set of questions and the next set concerning the managing director with regard to the same person. This does not matter, as the questions are seeking out whether the functions that are normally associated with the two roles are being fulfilled somewhere at board level. The role of the CEO is looked at in respect of the CEO's relationship with the board only, not the general management role. You are asked to answer this question based on current performance and also how often you think the behaviour should occur.

J.   Chairman's Role

1. provided leadership to the board .... *Almost Always ... Usually ... Sometimes ... Rarely ... Almost Never* – both for current performance and desired performance
2. balanced debate required at board level with effective devolution to subcommittees of the board
3. stated Chairman's delegated authority
4. operated outside boundaries of delegated authority
5. kept the board uninformed
6. managed meetings to cover key issues for the company
7. scheduled meetings of the board
8. developed board agendas with no input from directors
9. pushed for decisions even if full information is not available
10. assigned specific tasks to members of the board/subcommittees

11. established guidelines for the conduct of the directors
12. prevented directors from contributing to discussions
13. represented the company to external groups
14. exercised a veto over board decisions
15. encouraged an open line of communication between the board and senior management
16. evaluated the performance of the CEO
17. developed plans for CEO succession
18. developed plans for chairman succession
19. glossed over CEO's proposals to the board
20. evaluated performance of all other directors
21. evaluated performance of the chairman
22. promoted healthy conflict and dialogue
23. managed interpersonal conflict between board members

K. CEO's Role

24. assisted in developing a long-term strategy and vision for the company
25. recommended to the board a long-term strategy and vision for the company
26. developed annual business plans and budgets that support the company's long-term strategy
27. recommended to the board annual business plans and budgets that support the company's long-term strategy
28. kept board uninformed on matters of high corporate risk
29. developed an effective management team below the level of the CEO
30. planned succession for management team
31. ignored succession plans for the CEO
32. listened to the board's recommendations
33. ignored board's recommendations
34. treated board as an inconvenient hurdle for decision-making
35. through actions understood the duties and responsibilities of a board of directors
36. through actions understood the different roles of chairman of the board and CEO
37. kept the board ignorant of key issues
38. stated CEO's delegated authority
39. stayed within boundaries of delegated authority
40. encouraged an open line of communication between the board and senior management
41. exercised a veto over board decisions

Bibliography

Abegglen, C. and Stalk, George, Jr. *Kaisha the Japanese Corporation* (New York: Basic Books, 1985).

Alexander, Lord, of Weedon, 'Introduction', in Dimsdale, Nicholas H. and Prevezer Martha (eds), *Capital Markets and Corporate Governance* (Oxford: Clarendon Press, 1994).

BBA, *Banks and Businesses Working Together: a Statement of Principles* (London: British Bankers Association, 1997).

Bain, Neville and Band, David, *Winning Ways through Corporate Governance* (London: Macmillan, 1996).

Bamburger, Bill and Davidson, Cathy, *Closing: the Life and Death of an American Factory* (New York: DoubleTake/W.W. Norton, 1998).

Bank of England, *Finance for Small Firms, a Fourth Report* (Bank of England, 1997a).

Bank of England, *Quarterly Report on Small Business Statistics*, December 1997 (Bank of England: 1997b).

Bank of England, *Finance for Small Firms, a Fifth Report* (Bank of England, 1998).

Bartlett, C.A. and Ghoshal S., 'Tap Your Subsidiaries for Global Reach' (1986) 64 *Harvard Business Review*, 87.

Beecroft, Adrian, 'The Role of Venture Capital', in Dimsdale, Nicholas H. and Prevezer Martha (eds), *Capital Markets and Corporate Governance* (Oxford: Clarendon Press, 1994).

Berle, A.A. and Means, G.C., *The Modern Corporation and Private Property*, 2nd edn (New York: Macmillan, 1933, 1967).

Blake, Allan and Bond, Helen J., *Company Law* 5th edn (London: Blackstone Press, 1996).

Boyers, Karla, 'Business Soul', *Association Management* 44 (1996, February).

Cadbury Committee Report, The, *The Financial Aspects of Corporate Governance* (London: Gee, 1993).

Chandler, Alfred D., Jr. *Strategy and Structure* (New York: Anchor, 1966).

Chappell, Tom, *The Soul of a Business, Managing for Profit and the Common Good* (New York: Bantam, 1993).

Christensen, Clayton, *The Innovator's Dilemma, When New Technologies Cause Great Companies to Fail* (Boston: Harvard Business Press, 1998).

CIO Magazine, *Knowledge Management – A Case Study* (1998, November 15th).

Clarke, Thomas and Clegg, Stewart, *Changing Paradigms, the Transformation of Management Knowledge for the 21st Century* (London: HarperCollins, 1998).

Coleman, Ian and Eccles, Robert, *Pursuing Value: Reporting Gaps in the United Kingdom* (London: Price Waterhouse, 1997).

Coles, Jerilyn W. and Hesterly, William S. *Leadership Structure and Board Composition: Trading Information for Independence.* Unpublished Conference Paper, Academy of Management, Cincinnati, 1997.

Collins, James C. and Porras, Jerry I. *Built to Last: Successful Habits of Visionary Companies* (London: Century, 1994).

Conger, Jay A., Finegold, David, and Lawler III, Edward E., 'Appraising Boardroom Performance' *Harvard Business Review*, 136 (1998 January–February) .

Daily, Catherine M., *The Moderating Effects of Governance Structure in Small and Entrepreneurial Firms*, Conference Paper, 23rd Annual Meeting of the Decision Sciences Institute, San Francisco (22–24 November 1992).

Deakins, David, Mileham, Patrick and O'Neill, Eileen, *The Role and Influence of Non-Executive Directors in Growing Small Companies*, an Interim Working Paper (Paisley Research Centre: 1998).

de Geus, Arie, *The Living Company* (London: Longman, 1997).

Demb, Ada and Neubauer, Fred 'Subsidiary Boards Reconsidered' (1992) 8 *European Management Journal* ,480.

Department for Education and Employment, *University for Industry, Pathfinder Prospectus* (Sudbury: DfEE Publications, 1998).

Department of the Environment, *Regions Invited to Have Their Say* (1997) Press Release 11 June.

Department of Trade and Industry, *Response to the Commission Consultation Paper on Company Law* (DTI, December 1997).

Department of Transport, *Investigation of the* Herald of the Free Enterprise, *Report of Court No. 8074* (London: HMSO, 1987).

Dimsdale, Nicholas H., 'The Need to Restore Corporate Accountability: an Agenda for Reform', in Dimsdale, Nicholas H. and Prevezer Martha (eds), *Capital Markets and Corporate Governance* (Oxford: Clarendon Press, 1994).

Directorship, Interview with Directorship (1996) vol. 22, no. 11 (Directorship Inc., Greeenwich, USA).

Drozdow, Nancy and Carroll, Vincent P., 'Tools for Strategy Development in Family Firms' (1997) *Sloan Management Review* 75 (Fall).

The Economist, 'The Mittelstand Meets the Grim Reaper' (16 December, 1995a); see also *The Economist*, 'Mittelstand or Mittelfall?' (17 October, 1998).

The Economist, 'The ABB of Management', (6 January 1996a).

The Economist, 'The Fridge Maker as Dynast' (28 September, 1996b).

The Economist, 'The *Chaebol* in Denial' (24 January 1998a).

The Economist, 'Bargains Galore' (7 February 1998b).

The Economist, 'Branson Replies' (7 March 1998c) in which Richard Branson replies to *The Economist* article, 'Behind Branson' (21 February 1998).

The Economist, 'Just a Few Loose Screws' (30 May 1998d).

The Economist, 'The Lloyds Money Machine' (17 January 1998e).

The Economist, 'Adored no More' (21 March 1998f).

The Economist, 'Internet Bookselling, Making a Mark' (10 October 1998g).

The Economist, 'When Eight Arms are Better than One' (12 September 1998h).

Edvinsson, Leif and Malone, Michael S., *Intellectual Capital* (London: Piatkus, 1997).

Eisenhardt, Kathleen M., Kahwajy, Jean L. and Bourgeois III, L.J., 'How Management Teams Can Have a Good Fight' (1997) *Harvard Business Review*, 77, July–August.

European Commission, *Consultation Paper on EU Legislation Necessary to Complete the Single Market* (March 1997. Copies available from the Department of Trade and Industry, London).

European Commission, *Maximising Europe SMEs Full Potential for Employment, Growth and Competitiveness* (1996) Com (96) 0087 CNS.

Financial Times, 'From Noodles and Rockets to Shareholder Value', 20 March 1998a, p. 24.

Financial Times, 'Toshiba soars as deep restructuring bites', 9 November 9 1998b, p.25.

Fortune, The Real Key to Creating Wealth (1993) 20 September, p.34.

Francis, Arthur, 'Improving the UK's Industrial Competitiveness: Do we Know How and Would we Know if we were Succeeding', *Royal Society of Arts Journal*, 1995, October, p.25.

Freeman, Judith, 'Small Businesses and the Corporate Form: Burden or Privilege' (1994) 57 *Modern Law Review* 555.

Garratt, Bob, *The Fish Rots From the Head* (London: Harper Collins, 1996).

Galbraith, John K., *The New Industrial State* (London: Pelican, 1967).

Gersick, Kelin E., Davis, John A., Hampton, Marion McCollom and Lansberg, Ivan, *Generation to Generation: Life Cycles of the Family Business* (Boston: Harvard Business School Press, 1997).

Gibbon Edward, *Decline and Fall of the Roman Empire* (1776).

Good, Michael and Campbell, Andrew. *Strategies and Styles, the Role of the Centre in Managing Diversified Corporations* (London: Blackwell, 1987).

Greenbury Study Report, *Report of a Study Group on Directors' Remuneration* (London: Gee, 1995).

Hampel Report, *Committee on Corporate Governance, Final Report* (London: Gee, 1998).

Handy, Charles, *Gods of Management* (London: Arrow, 1995).

Hedlund, Gunnar, 'The Role of Foreign Subsidiaries in Strategic Decision-Making in Swedish Multinational Corporations' (1980) 1 *Strategic Management Journal* 23.

Hoshi, Takeo, 'The Economic Role of Corporate Grouping and the Main Bank System', in Aoki Masahiko, Dore Ronald (eds), *The Japanese Firm* (Oxford: OUP, 1994).

Institute of Directors, *Good Practice for Directors – Standards for the Board* (London: IoD, 1995).

Kay, John, 'Corporate Strategy and Corporate Accountability, in Dimsdale', Nicholas H. and Prevezer Martha (eds), *Capital Markets and Corporate Governance* (Oxford: Clarendon Press, 1994).

Magretta, Joan, 'Governing the Family-Owned Enterprise: An Interview with Finland's Krister Ahlstrom' (1998) *Harvard Business Review*, 113.

Middleton, Miles, Cowling, Marc, Samuels, John and Sugden, Roger, 'Small Firms and Clearing Banks', in Dimsdale, Nicholas H. and Prevezer Martha (eds), *Capital Markets and Corporate Governance* (Oxford: Clarendon Press, 1994).

Miller, Robert B. and Heinman, Stephen E., with Tuleja, Tad, *Strategic Selling, Secrets of the Complex Sale* (London: Kogan Page, 1988).

Miller, Warren D., 'Siblings and Succession in Family Business' (1998) *Harvard Business Review*, January–February, 22.

Morgan, Gareth, *Images of Organization* (London: Sage, 1986).

Mueller, Robert K., *Anchoring Points for Corporate Directors, Obeying the Unenforceable* (Westport, Connecticut: Quorum, 1996).

Murphy, Thomas A., 'A Businessman's Concern For Freedom', a speech delivered at the National Honoree Lucheon of Beta Gamma Sigma, Las Vegas, Nevada, 23 April 1975; cited in Kempen, Weisen and Bagby, *Legal Aspects of the Management Process* 4th edn (St Paul: West Publishing, 1990), p.829.

NACD, National Association of Corporate Directors, *Report of the NACD Blue Ribbon Commission on Director Professionalism* (Washington: NACD, 1996).

Neubauer, Fred and Lank, Alden G., *The Family Business* (London: Macmillan, 1998).

OECD, *Corporate Governance, Improving Competitiveness and Access to Capital in Global Markets. A report to the OECD by the Business Sector Advisory Group on Corporate Governance* (OECD, April 1998).

Osborne, David and Gaebler, Ted, *Reinventing Government, How the Entrepreneurial Spirit is Transforming the Public Sector* (New York: Plume, 1993).

PA Consulting Group, *Managing for Shareholder Value* (London: PA Consulting Group, 1997).

PA Consulting Group, *The Corporate Brain, A Perspective on the Role of the Corporate Centre* (London: PA Consulting Group, 1998).

Porter, Michael E. *The Competitive Advantage of Nations* (London: Macmillan, 1990).

Rappaport, Alfred, *Creating Shareholder Value* (New York: Free Press, 1998).

Roth, K. and O'Donnell, S., *Foreign Subsidiary Compensation Strategy: an Agency Theory Perspective* (1996) 39 *Academy of Management Journal*, 678.

RSA, Royal Society for the Encouragement of Arts, Manufactures and Commerce, *Report of the RSA Inquiry, Tomorrow's Company: the Role of Business in a Changing World* (Aldershot: Gower, 1995).

Sanders, Gerard Wm and Carpenter, Mason, A., *Internationalization and Firm Governance: the Roles of CEO Compensation, Top Team Composition and Board Structure* (1998) 41 *Academy of Management Journal*, no. 2, 158.

Sandler, Martin W. and Hudson, Deborah A., *Beyond the Bottom Line* (Oxford: Oxford University Press, 1998).

Senge, Peter M, *The Fifth Discipline* (New York: Doubleday/Currency, 1990).

Shanker, M.C. and Astrachan, J.H., *Myths and Realities: Family Businesses' Contribution to the US Economy – a Framework for Assessing Family Business Statistics* (1996 Summer) 9 *Family Business Review*, no. 2, 107–124.

Sheard, Paul, 'Interlocking Shareholdings and Corporate Governance', in Aoki Masahiko, Dore Ronald (eds) *The Japanese Firm* (Oxford: OUP, 1994).

Skandia AFS, *Intelligent Enterprising, Supplement to the Six Month Interim Report of Skandia AFS* (1997).

Sölvell, Örjan, Zander, Ivo and Porter, Michael E., *Advantage Sweden*, 2nd edn (Stockholm: Norstedts Juridik, 1993).

Stiles, Philip and Taylor, Bernard, *Maxwell – The Failure of Corporate Governance* (1993) 1 *Corporate Governance* 34.

Storey D.J., *Understanding the Small Business Sector* (London: Routledge, 1994).

Sunday Times, Creating Value: the Best and the Worst (21 September 1997; 27 September 1998b).

Sunday Times, Loadsamoney for Entrepreneurs (14 September 1997b).

Sunday Times, IKEA Boss Plots British Expansion (7 June 1998).

Swinson, Chris, 'Considering the limits of Corporate Reporting' (1998) *The Times*, 22 October, p.39.

Sykes, Allen, 'Proposals for a Reformed System of Corporate Governance to Achieve International Competitive Long-Term Performance', in Dimsdale, Nicholas H. and Prevezer Martha (eds), *Capital Markets and Corporate Governance* (Oxford: Clarendon Press, 1994).

Tomasko, Robert M., *Rethinking the Corporation, the Architecture of Change* (New York: Amazon, 1993).

Tricker, Robert I., *The Independent Director: a Study of the Non-Executive Director and of the Audit Committee* (London: Tolley, 1978).

Useem, Michael, *Executive Defense: Shareholder Power and Reorganization* (Cambridge, Mass.: Harvard University Press, 1993).

Utterback, James M., *Mastering the Dynamics of Innovation* (Boston: Harvard Business School Press, 1996).

Wall Street Journal, 'Intel's New Chip May Bring Only a Small Dose of Relief' (1 July 1998).

Welch, Jack, (quoted in) *Taming the Info Monster* (1998) *Business Week*, 22 June, p.170.

Whitley, Richard, *Business Systems in East Asia* (London: Sage, 1992).

Cases

Francis v. *United Jersey Bank* (1981) 87NJ15, 432A. 2D814

Ebrahimi v. *Westbourne Galleries Ltd* [1973)] AC 360

Charterbridge Corporation Ltd v. *Lloyds Bank* [1970] Ch 62

Dairy Containers Ltd v. *NZI Bank Ltd* (1995) 7 NZCLC 96-609

Secretary of State for Trade and Industry v. *Tjolle* [1998] 1 BCLC 333

Wilton-Davies v. *Kirk* [1998] 2 BCLC 274

Re Smith & Fawcett Ltd [1942] Ch. 304

Evans v. *Brunner Mond & Co.* [1921] Ch. 359

Theodore Holding Co. v. *Henderson* (1969) 257 Atl. 2d. 398 (Del. Ch.)

Statutes and Statutory Instruments

Table A, The Companies (Tables A to F) Regulations 1985 (SI 1985/805).

Index